CODE GREEN

Rosemary Aravanis
Stuart Cochrane

B1+

Student's Book

Contents

Theme	Reading	Grammar
1 What's my line? People, relationships, work *page 6*	FCE Reading Part 3 *Career choices* • skimming text for gist • spotting key words	• present simple & continuous • *be used to* • stative verbs **Practise your English** word formation transformations
2 A place to call home City, countryside, house and home *page 16*	FCE Reading Part 1 *Wilderness survival camp* • identifying key information	• past simple & continuous • time expressions • *used to* & *would* • articles • possessive pronouns and determiners **Practise your English** multiple choice cloze open cloze
Check your knowledge 1	*page 26*	
3 Learning for life Education *page 28*	FCE Reading Part 2 *Excursions in cyberspace* • spotting reference words • finding links	• present perfect simple and continuous • present perfect and past simple • time expressions **Practise your English** transformations
4 The world of science and technology Science Technology *page 38*	FCE Reading Part 3 *The shock of the new* • scanning to spot information	• past perfect simple and continuous • comparatives and superlatives **Practise your English** transformations multiple choice cloze
Check your knowledge 2	*page 48*	
5 Holidays with a difference! Travel and transport *page 50*	B2 exam practice Reading *Walking tours of London* • skimming and scanning for information	• future forms • predictions with future perfect and continuous • *about to* • time expressions • question tags • indirect questions **Practise your English** multiple choice cloze
6 Serious fun Cinema, literature, entertainment and the arts *page 60*	B2 exam practice Reading *New titles to look out for ...* • information spotting without reading the whole text	• reported speech • reporting verbs **Practise your English** word formation transformations multiple choice cloze
Check your knowledge 3	*page 70*	

Vocabulary	Listening	Speaking	Writing
• appearance and personality • family, friends and relationships • jobs	**FCE Listening Part 1** • predicting content	**FCE Speaking Part 1** • asking for and giving personal information • Wh- / yes/no questions silent *h*	**FCE Writing Part 1** Informal transactional email • punctuation • informal register • developing points
• towns and villages • house and home (compounds and collocations) • phrasal verbs	**FCE Listening Part 2** • identifying suitable words	**FCE Speaking Part 2** • comparing pictures • describing impressions /t/, /d/ and /id/	**FCE Writing Part 2** Article (1) • organization and paragraphing • layout features • linking words
• education & learning • school collocations • phrasal verbs	**FCE Listening Part 3** • expressing ideas in different ways	**FCE Speaking Part 3** • expressing opinion • inviting others to take part falling and rising intonation in question tags	**FCE Writing Part 1** Informal transactional letter • organization • developing points • giving advice
• science • computer technology • phrasal verbs	**B2 exam practice Listening** • predicting content from pictures	**FCE Speaking Part 3** • suggesting • expressing agreement final /r/	**FCE Writing Part 2** Essay • paragraphing • signalling • getting ideas • developing points
• sights • accommodation • means of transport • travel (compound nouns)	**B2 exam practice Listening** • predicting content from multiple choice options	**B2 exam practice Speaking** • giving opinions • tentative language for suggestions words rhyming with *coach*	**FCE Writing Part 2** Formal transactional letter (asking for information) • formal register • organization • content • linking
• music and the arts • cinema and literature • phrasal verbs with *out*	**FCE Listening Part 4** • answering questions before using multiple choice options	**B2 exam practice Speaking** • polite questions • ways of saying *yes* and *no* /dz/, /tʃ/, /ʃ/ and /s/	**FCE Writing Part 2** Story (1) • narrative writing • past tenses • interesting content

Theme	Reading	Grammar
7 Turn on, tune in The media and communications page 72	FCE Reading Part 1 *A media revolution* • understanding implied information	• passive voice • causative form **Practise your English** multiple choice cloze transformations
8 The world of sport ... and leisure Sport and leisure page 82	FCE Reading Part 3 *What will they think of next?* • speed reading • information matching	• zero, first and second conditionals • conditional links • *like* and *as* **Practise your English** multiple choice cloze open cloze
Check your knowledge 4	page 92	
9 It's a weird, wonderful world The environment and the weather page 94	FCE Reading Part 1 *Secrets of the deep* • distinguishing between opinion and stated information	• modals • third conditional **Practise your English** multiple choice cloze transformations
10 Food for thought Health, food and drink page 104	FCE Reading Part 2 *Is there any truth to old wives' tales?* • checking for coherence and cohesion	• relative clauses • unreal past *wish* **Practise your English** open cloze transformations multiple choice cloze
Check your knowledge 5	page 114	
11 Vanished without a trace! Crime and mystery page 116	FCE Reading Part 1 *Kidnap ruled out ... / Farmer's discovery ...* • finding evidence to support your answers	• modal perfect • infinitives and *-ing* forms • *make, let, allow* **Practise your English** word formation transformations multiple choice cloze
12 Big Spender Shopping, money and clothes page 126	FCE Reading Part 2 *Teenage consumerism* • identifying linking words • checking for sense	• countable and uncountable nouns • *so* and *such* • *too* and *enough* • *both ... and, neither ... nor, each, every, all, none* • indeterminate pronouns **Practise your English** multiple choice cloze transformations
Check your knowledge 6	page 136	
Grammar reference	page 138	
Vocabulary file	page 154	
Speaking file	page 162	
Pairwork	pages 165 and 175	
Writing bank	page 166	

Vocabulary	Listening	Speaking	Writing
• TV and radio programmes • newspapers and magazines • communications • *see, watch, look, listen, hear*	**FCE Listening Part 1** • understanding gist	**FCE Speaking Part 2** • paraphrasing • comparing and contrasting long and short vowels /ɑː/, /æ/ and /ʌ/	**FCE Writing Part 2** Review • content • organization • language for reviews
• sports, hobbies & pastimes • expressions with *come* and *go* • phrasal verbs	**B2 exam practice Listening** • listening for key words or phrases • listening for detail	**B2 exam practice Speaking** • interrupting politely word stress	**FCE Writing Part 2** Article (2) • creating interest • developing ideas • organization
• the environment • extreme weather • weather idioms	**FCE Listening Part 3** • predicting content	**FCE Speaking Part 3** • justifying opinions • showing interest sentence stress / silent letters	**B2 exam practice Writing** Formal letter (to a newspaper) • getting ideas • linking ideas • organizing paragraphs
• injuries • health and diet • food and drink	**B2 exam practice Listening** • identifying speakers	**FCE Speaking Parts 3 and 4** • expressing preference sentence stress	**B2 exam practice Writing** Informal letter (advice) • making a good impression on the reader • giving advice • organization
• people and crime • crime and mystery • word building • dependent prepositions	**FCE Listening Part 4** • key word spotting	**FCE Speaking Part 3** • asking for clarification • expressing agreement • acknowledging an interlocutor's turn sentence stress	**FCE Writing Part 2** Story (2) • describing characters' reactions and feelings • adding drama through adjectives and direct speech
• clothes and accessories • shopping and money • money idioms	**FCE Listening Part 1** • strategies for choosing the correct answer	**B2 exam practice Speaking** • filling pauses • expressing interest vowels /iː/ and /i/	**FCE Writing Part 1** Formal letter (job application) • content • register • paragraphing

1 What's my line?

A Work in pairs. What job do these people do?

a

b

c

d

e

f

g

h

i

B Which adjectives for describing people are important for the jobs in A?

hard-working • imaginative • organized • outgoing
patient • responsible • sociable

C Choose one of the jobs for your partner. Why would it be a good job for him/her? Use the adjectives in B to help you.

Reading

D You are going to read about the jobs three teenagers would like to do. Skim the text and match a job from the photographs with each name.

zoo-keeper

Career choices

Confused about a career? You're not alone. Few young people know what they want to do when they leave school. Three teenagers wrote in and told us how they made up their minds.

A Jim

I recently completed an online careers questionnaire. According to the results, I'm not very good at science or maths (which is true, because I get terrible school reports!), but I'm imaginative and I love to create. I have lots of patience, but I'm also a bit of a perfectionist. Well, that's very accurate. My family is always complaining that I take too long to do things, but I want things to be just right. The website suggested quite a few careers. Some of them, like writer or architect, I don't really find interesting, but one suggestion was perfect: model maker. **It had never occurred to me**, but model makers work in all sorts of places – TV and film, architects' offices and museums to name only a few. Making models, you see, is my hobby. In fact, these days I'm making a model of the Parthenon with 3,000 matchsticks. Tomorrow I'm adding the last few details and it will be ready!

model maker

B Lia

I've always been good at languages. I love French and German and I go to a language school two evenings a week, but this year I'm also having lessons at home to prepare for exams in the summer. I know that people who study languages often become teachers, but I don't want to teach. You have to be very patient to be a teacher, and I'm not really patient enough. My dad is a teacher and he comes home very tired every day. A **translator** is another job for people with language skills, but that **doesn't appeal to me** either. You have to work long hours on your own translating books. It sounds **dull**! I'm quite outgoing and I like to have company, so that wouldn't suit me. I spoke to our **careers officer** at school and she came up with a great idea: **interpreter**. Interpreters meet people and travel. My mum says that interpreters can earn a lot too. It sounds great! Anyway, I'd better stop. My French lesson starts at six!

C Neil

A few weeks ago, I was watching a programme about zoos and I realized that a zoo-keeper would be a good **occupation** for me. I don't get on with people very well, but I adore animals. I own five pets and I spend most of my free time with them. In fact, while I'm writing this on my computer, Dean, my pet hamster, is walking all over my desk and Spike, my cat, is keeping my feet warm! Anyway, I've known **for ages** that I wanted to work with animals. My mum is a vet, so she's given me a love of animals. I thought about being a vet, but that needs lots of study at university. I'm not very hard-working at school (my parents are always moaning about that!), so I don't think I'd get the grades you need to become a vet. Zoo-keepers, on the other hand, don't need to study so hard. You just need to love animals!

Steps to success

To answer multiple matching questions:
- skim the text quickly to get the gist of each section.
- underline key words in the questions, and skim the text again to find those words or words with a similar meaning.

Be careful! Don't make a choice only because you see a key word. It might be a trap!

E Underline the key words in these questions.
  A Jim   **B** Lia   **C** Neil
  Which person or people …
  was influenced by something on the internet? 1 ....
  has been influenced by his or her parents? 2 .... , 3 ....
  is patient? 4 ....
  is not good at school? 5 .... , 6 ....
  can speak other languages? 7 ....
  would like to earn a good salary? 8 ....
  is sociable? 9 ....
  was influenced by something on TV? 10 ....

F Now read the text again. For questions 1-10 in E choose a teenager A-C.

G Match the words and expressions in bold in the text with a definition.
1 very boring ....
2 I had never thought about it. ....
3 job ....
4 someone who rewrites books from one language into another ....
5 for a long time ....
6 someone who gives advice about jobs ....
7 someone who helps speakers of different languages communicate ....
8 does not seem nice ....

Quick chat

What job would you like to do in the future? Why?

Grammar 1

✓ Check present simple and present continuous

See page 138 for information about present simple and present continuous.

Match these extracts with the uses of each tense.

1 My family **are always complaining** …
2 … my pet hamster, **is walking** all over my desk …
3 Interpreters **meet** people and **travel**.
4 My French lesson **starts** at six!
5 Tomorrow I**'m adding** the last few details … !

Present simple is used to talk about:
a a general truth or habit ....
b a timetabled future event ....

Present continuous is used to talk about:
c an activity taking place around or exactly at the time of speaking ....
d a plan for the future – something already decided ....
e an annoying habit ....

A Circle the correct option.

1 Careers officers **help** / **are helping** young people choose a suitable career.
2 Sally **arrives** / **is arriving** home every day at six o'clock.
3 We **stay** / **'re staying** in Paris for a few months this year.
4 My mum **tells** / **is telling** wonderful stories about her childhood.
5 Someone **climbs** / **'s climbing** that building!
6 Penguins **don't get** / **aren't getting** cold feet.

B Complete with the present simple or present continuous.

1 John! .... you .... (listen) to me?
2 This week we .... (not have) normal lessons. We .... (prepare) the school Christmas show. It's great fun.
3 Hurry up! The train .... (leave) in half an hour.
4 .... you ever .... (play) chess?
5 We .... (meet) cousins from Canada tomorrow.
6 Teachers .... (not work) during the summer holidays.

C Complete this job advertisement using the present simple or continuous form of verbs from the box.

give • look • make • play • search • speak
take place • wait • (not) work

Wanted! Summer Camp Leaders

★ (1) .... you .... great English?
★ (2) .... you .... team sports like basketball and football?
★ (3) .... you .... friends easily?
★ (4) .... you .... for some excitement this summer?

If you answered yes to all the above, then we want to hear from you.

We (5) .... for teenage group leaders for our summer camp programmes. We'll keep you busy, but it's not all hard work. You (6) .... after seven o'clock any evening, and we (7) .... you two free days each week.

Interviews (8) .... in two weeks from now, so don't delay. We (9) .... to hear from you.

✓ Check be used to

See page 138 for information about *be used to*.

D Complete the sentences with words or phrases from the box.

danger • noisy places • speaking • waking up • working

1 Doctors are used to .... long hours.
2 Postal workers are used to .... early.
3 Builders are used to ....
4 Firefighters are used to ....
5 Lawyers are used to .... in court.

E Complete these sentences using *be used to*.

1 I ....
2 My parents ....
3 Our teacher ....

Vocabulary
Describing people

A Write P next to words with a positive meaning and N next to those with a negative meaning.

1 aggressive ....
2 arrogant ....
3 big-headed ....
4 bossy ....
5 cheerful ....
6 creative ....
7 efficient ....
8 energetic ....
9 moody ....
10 reliable ....
11 selfish ....
12 well-organized ....

B Complete the texts with suitable words from A.

Nancy

My mum works in an office with another woman called Nancy, and Mum hates her! Nancy is always telling other people what to do, and Mum hates (1) .... people. Nancy is a very (2) .... person. She's always busily running around the office doing lots of things, but she's also very (3) .... She argues and shouts until she gets what she wants. The worst thing, though, is that Nancy is always complaining about my mum's desk. You see, my mum isn't (4) .... and her desk is always a terrible mess. That drives Nancy mad ... and Nancy drives my mum mad!

Aiden

Aiden is my best friend. He's a brilliant student at school, but he isn't (5) .... In fact, despite being the best in the class, he's very modest. Even better, he isn't at all (6) .... I mean, he doesn't mind helping other kids if they don't understand something. Aiden is a very (7) .... boy – he always seems to be smiling and laughing. Other boys of his age are often miserable and (8) .... , but not Aiden. He's a great friend.

C Use a prefix, *un-*, *im-*, *in-*, *ir-*, *dis-*, to make the negative form of these words.

1 ....ambitious
2 ....attractive
3 ....considerate
4 ....imaginative
5 ....polite
6 ....responsible
7 ....organized

D Complete the sentences with the words from C.

1 Alex is so .... He never thinks of anyone except himself.
2 Isn't it .... to let your dog walk around the streets on its own?
3 I think too much make-up is very ....
4 Laura's clever, but she's very .... Her room is a terrible mess.
5 My dad thinks it's .... to start eating before everyone is sitting at the table.
6 My grandpa was a great footballer, but he was .... He never wanted fame and fortune.
7 This writer is very .... There's nothing different or unusual about her books.

E Match the adjectives with the nouns. Some adjectives can match with more than one noun.

> curly • dark • fair • long • pointed • round • straight
> thick • thin • turned-up • wavy

1 hair ....
2 skin ....
3 face ....
4 lips ....
5 nose ....
6 legs / arms ....

F Work in pairs. Use the words from this page to describe a friend or a member of your family. Talk about their physical appearance and their character.

My best friend isn't very tall. She's got a very round face and dark, wavy hair. I like her because she's a very cheerful and energetic person. For example, she ...

What kind of person do you need to be to do these jobs? Tell a partner your opinion.

> nursery school teacher • police officer
> receptionist • soldier

1

Listening

A These pictures show a girl called Mina with different people in her life. Circle the word that best describes how the *other* people are feeling in each picture.

tired / annoyed / pleased
1 ....

frightened / jealous / sorry
2 ....

irritated / helpful / proud
3 ....

confused / excited / upset
4 ....

angry / embarrassed / anxious
5 ....

B 🎧 Now listen. What relationship does each person have to Mina? Write a word from the box under each picture. You do not need all the words.

aunt • brother • father • friend • mother • neighbour
sister • teacher • uncle

Steps to success
- The questions in a multiple choice activity will give you some clues about what you will hear. Always read them carefully **before** listening and try to guess what the conversation will be about.

C 🎧 Read these questions carefully. Then listen again and choose the best answer.

1 Mina is talking to a woman. What does Mina offer to help her with?
A preparing a meal
B going shopping
C tidying the house

2 Mina is talking to a boy. What has the boy done?
A broken something
B lost something
C given something to someone else

3 Mina is talking to a man. What are they talking about?
A history
B geography
C maths

4 Mina is talking to another boy. Why is the boy sad?
A His pet has died.
B He has lost something valuable.
C He has fallen out with his friends.

5 Mina is talking to another man. What does he think about Mina?
A She has hurt herself.
B She is in trouble at school.
C She has got a tattoo.

Parents sometimes get annoyed with their children. What makes your parents annoyed?

Speaking

A Sort the questions for getting to know someone into the categories below.

a Likes and dislikes ....
b Family and friends ....
c Home ....
d Free time ....
e Education ....
f Work ....
g Holidays and travel ....

1 Do you like living in a city? ☐
2 Does your family go away every summer? ☐
3 What sort of food do you like? ☐
4 Where do you usually go on holiday? ☐
5 Have you got any brothers or sisters? ☐
6 Is it difficult to find work where you live? ☐
7 Who is your best friend? ☐
8 Where do you live? ☐
9 What do you usually do at the weekend? ☐
10 Would you like to go to university? ☐
11 Do you enjoy reading? ☐
12 What is the thing you like most about school? ☐

B 🎧 Listen to Maria and Victor. Tick the questions from A that they answer.

C Complete these questions with a question word.

1 .... do you do at the weekend?
2 .... do you go to school?
3 .... is your birthday?
4 .... is your favourite singer?
5 .... do you spell your surname?
6 .... do you want to be a pilot?

D Take turns asking and answering some of the questions from A and C.

Steps to success

- When you are asked a *yes/no* question, don't simply answer with *yes* or *no*. Expand your reply with a little more information. For example:
Are you good at languages?
No, not really, but I enjoy learning them.
Have you ever flown?
Yes, I have. I flew to Italy last year with my family.

E 👥 Work in pairs. Ask and answer these *yes/no* questions. Make sure that you expand your answers a little. Use the Language chunks to help you.

Have you got any brothers?
Do you live close to school?
Do you like animals?
Is English your favourite subject?
Does your family often go to the cinema?
Have you ever tried skiing?

Language chunks

Ways to expand

Have you got ... ?
Yes, I have. In fact, I've got ... / No, I haven't, but ...

Do you ... ?
Yes, I do. I usually ... / No, I don't, because ...

Is ... ?
Yes, it is, and actually ... / No, it isn't. Although ...

Does ... ?
Yes, she does, and she's ... / No, she doesn't, and the reason is that ...

Have you ever ... ?
Yes, I have. It was ... / No, I haven't, but I'd love to because ...

Silent *h*

F Tick the words that have a silent *h*.

1 head ☐   6 have ☐
2 hour ☐   7 honour ☐
3 hear ☐   8 hourly ☐
4 horrible ☐   9 happy ☐
5 honest ☐   10 honestly ☐

G 🎧 Now listen and check.

Grammar 2

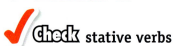 stative verbs

See pages 138 and 139 for information about stative verbs.

My dog hasn't got a nose.

Really! How does he smell?

Terrible!

Match each example of a stative verb with a category.

1 I **love** you.
2 I **hate** Monday mornings.
3 This **tastes** delicious.
4 **Does** this **contain** meat?
5 She **doesn't believe** you.
6 **Don't** you **remember** me?
7 This **belongs** to you.
8 There **appears** to be a problem.
9 You **don't seem** very well.
10 You **sound** strange.

a feelings
b senses
c mental processes
d relationships
e appearance

A Tick the sentences where the underlined verb has a stative meaning.

1 That pie <u>smells</u> delicious.
2 The room was so dark I had to <u>feel</u> my way to the light switch.
3 The chef always <u>tastes</u> the food before he sends it out to customers.
4 Do you know how much a whale <u>weighs</u>?
5 You have to <u>think</u> very carefully when you play chess.
6 That <u>looks</u> like a very interesting book.
7 This material <u>feels</u> like wool.
8 If you <u>look</u> through this window, there is a beautiful view.

B Two of the sentences are correct. Which ones? Find and correct the mistakes in the other sentences.

1 I'm not wanting any more tea, thanks.
2 Did you hear that Duffy is appearing at the Odeon theatre next week?
3 Aren't you recognizing me?
4 Your piano is sounding awful.
5 My dog's smelling your bag. What have you got in there?
6 I'm not needing this anymore. You can have it.
7 The radio is seeming to work OK now.

C Use the notes to make dialogues. Use the present simple or continuous.

1 **A:** This milk / smell bad
   B: Yes, / I / think / it's gone off

2 **A:** Why / you / taste / the soup?
   B: I / think / it / need / some more salt

3 **A:** This / material / look / like wool
   B: Yes, / but / it / not / feel / like wool

4 **A:** What / make / that strange noise?
   B: I / not / know

5 **A:** you / believe / in ghosts?
   B: No. / I / think / that's nonsense

6 **A:** Why / you / weigh / those apples?
   B: I / make / a pie

Practise your English

A Read the text quickly and answer these questions.
1. What is physiognomy?
2. Why are long heads good?
3. What do thin lips mean?
4. What is the philtrum?

B Read the text again. Use the word in brackets to form one word that fits each gap.

Steps to success
For this kind of task make sure that you:
- read the whole text so that you understand the gist.
- think about the meaning of the whole sentence with the gap.
- identify the part of speech of the missing word.
- check whether the missing word should be in the plural or singular form.
- check whether the missing word should be in the negative form.

You can judge a book by its cover

Should we form an opinion about someone's (1) .... (PERSON) only from their looks? They say that you can't judge a book by its cover. Well, apparently you can! In fact, the art of judging character from a person's (2) .... (APPEAR) has been practised for over 3,000 years. It's called physiognomy or 'face reading' and, according to the experts, it's as (3) .... (RELY) as any science.

So what can physiognomy tell us? Let's start with the shape of the head. People with wide heads are generally (4) .... (AMBITION) and want to achieve a lot. Long-headed people are careful and trustworthy, and those with short heads can be (5) .... (RESPONSE). They don't do things properly.

What about the eyes, nose or mouth? What do they reveal? Well, (6) .... (PERFECT) – people who want everything just right – tend to have eyes that are close together. (7) .... (POINT) noses can show intelligence, while (8) .... (CONSIDER) people, those who think only of themselves, sometimes have small mouths and thin lips. Even that little square below the nose, the philtrum, has a meaning. Lively, (9) .... (ENERGY) people have a strong, thick philtrum. People with a weaker philtrum are sometimes (10) .... (MOOD) or depressed.

But is this just a lot of nonsense? Well, think about the people in your life and judge for yourself.

Quick chat
Can we judge a person's character from their looks?
Are first impressions usually correct?

C Complete the second sentence so that it has a similar meaning to the first sentence. Use the word given.

1. You never remember your pencil case.
   ALWAYS
   You're .... pencil case.

2. I don't really want to be a doctor.
   APPEAL
   Being a doctor .... me.

3. I don't normally get up early and I find it difficult.
   USED
   I .... up early.

4. We've decided to spend next weekend in Paris.
   SPENDING
   We .... weekend in Paris.

5. Is this yours?
   BELONG
   .... to you?

6. Jane's been living on her own for years now. It's not a problem for her.
   USED
   Jane .... on her own.

7. My mum isn't a very organized person.
   IS
   My mum .... person.

8. Why don't you like swimming so much?
   HATE
   Why .... swimming?

9. That wasn't a very polite thing to say.
   WAS
   That .... thing to say.

10. Alison has a bad habit of leaving the bathroom light on.
    IS
    Alison .... the bathroom light on.

1

Writing: Informal transactional email

A These photos show jobs that young people sometimes do in the summer holidays. Match the words with the photos.

shop assistant
summer camp leader
tour guide
waiter / waitress

Quick chat

Would you like to do any of these jobs in your summer holiday? Why/Why not? What sort of people would be good at jobs like these?

B Imagine you received this email from an English-speaking friend. Read the message quickly and find out why they are writing to you.

Sardinia, Italy — beautiful!

local newspaper — application, letter and job interview

about five hrs/day, pay not good

good at English, sociable — yes!

To: Maria Messaggi
Cc:
Subject: Summer job

Hi,
How are things? We're all OK here in Stockholm, although it's not as warm as where you are! I'm interested in working this summer, and I just wonder if you could give me some advice?
I know you're at a summer camp, but where is it, exactly? How do your employers find people? Do they advertise? How many hours do you work each day and what sort of things do you do? Do you get paid well?
What sort of person do they want? I think you know me pretty well, don't you? Do you think that kind of job would suit me?
Questions, questions! Anyway, if you can give me some advice, that would be great.
Take care,
Sven

C Quickly Read Maria's reply to Sven's email. There are some problems with it, but don't worry about those now. Did she enjoy her summer job?

To: Sven Strindberg
Cc:
Subject: Re: Summer job

A | Dear Sven,
I am most grateful for your email. It was a great pleasure to receive your correspondence. Naturally, I am pleased to be of assistance to you should it be required. Simply make a request.

B | The camp is in Sardinia. It's a lovely island. The camp managers advertise in the local newspaper. People write in and have a short interview. It's easy!

C | I dont work more than about five hours a day. we usually finish at about one thirty, with an hours' lunch break. we do all sorts of different things We help in the kitchen? we also organize activities for the youngest children. I love it but we dont get paid very much, Im afraid.

D | You need quite good English for the job because everyone communicates in English. I think you need to be quite an outgoing and sociable person, because you work with the children all day for a whole summer. I feel sure you could do it.

Let me know what you decide to do.

Bye for now,
Maria

Skills development

Organization

D Match each paragraph in Maria's email with its function.

About the right person for the job ....
About the job ....
Introduction ....
How I got the job ....

Register

When we write to a friend, we use informal register. Register is shown through the vocabulary, grammar and punctuation that we use. For example:

	Formal register	Informal register
Punctuation	Your help **is not** required.	Your help **isn't** required.
Grammar	Your help **is not required**.	**I don't require** your help.
Vocabulary	Your help is not **required**.	I don't **need** your help.

E Read paragraph A again. What's wrong with it?

F Rewrite paragraph A of Maria's email in a more informal style. Use the phrases in the box.

It was nice to hear from you again.
Just ask!
Of course, I'm happy to help you with anything you need.
Thanks for your email.

Punctuation

All your writing must be punctuated correctly. This is true for formal and informal writing.

G Paragraph C has a number of mistakes with punctuation. Find the mistakes and rewrite the whole paragraph correctly in your notebook.

Planning and writing

Steps to success
- Use the questions and notes in the prompt email to organize your reply.
- Group similar or related questions together and answer them in the same paragraph.

H Now write your *own* reply to Sven. Write between 120 and 150 words. Use the Language chunks and the planner to help organize your work.

Paragraph 1: Thank Sven for his email.

Paragraph 2: What is your job? How do people get it?

Paragraph 3: What does the job involve? Do you enjoy it?

Paragraph 4: What sort of person could do the job?

Paragraph 5: Finish off with an offer to help more if needed.

Language chunks

Starting an informal email
Thanks for your message.
How are things?
Great to hear from you.

Finishing off an informal email
Take care,
Bye for now,
All the best,

quick check

Be sure to:
- use the questions and notes in the prompt to organize your email.
- write in an informal style.
- check your punctuation.
- make it sound natural, as though you really know this person.

2 A place to call home

A Work in pairs. Which of the following things could you *not* live without for a week?
- chocolate
- hairdryer
- TV
- mobile phone
- bathroom
- electricity

Reading

B Read the advertisement. What do you think happens on wilderness survival camps?
- hunting ☐
- sleeping in tents ☐
- staying in a hotel ☐
- learning to cook ☐
- sports ☐
- sightseeing ☐

C You are going to read about a camping experience. Read the article quickly to check your predictions in B.

Steps to success
- To answer multiple choice questions read the question, but not the options, and find the information in the text.
- *Then* look at the answer options and choose the best one.

D Underline the parts of the text that contain the answers to the following questions.
1 Why did the writer decide to go to a wilderness survival camp?
2 What did she **not** learn to do on the camp?
3 What shocked the writer on the first day of the camp?
4 What was the rest of the week like?
5 At the end of the camp, what did the writer realize?
6 How does the writer feel about her experience at the camp?

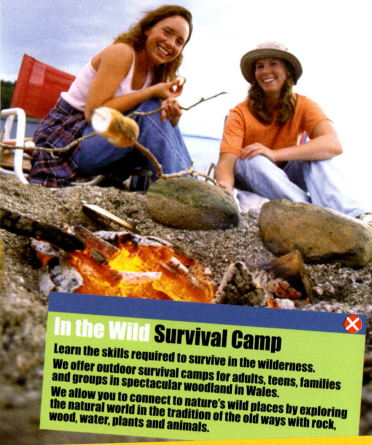

In the Wild Survival Camp
Learn the skills required to survive in the wilderness. We offer outdoor survival camps for adults, teens, families and groups in spectacular woodland in Wales. We allow you to connect to nature's wild places by exploring the natural world in the tradition of the old ways with rock, wood, water, plants and animals.

Wilderness survival camp: a home away from home?

How long can you live without everyday <u>luxuries</u>? Not for very long, as I found out on my <u>wilderness</u> survival camp experience.

I had heard about these camps from some classmates who went to one last summer. They were very excited about their experience and I was curious. So during last month's term break I decided to go to one. After everything I'd heard, I was really looking forward to it.

On the first day our instructor, James, <u>reassured</u> us that the woodland would provide us with everything we needed, well almost. James was going to show us how to find water, food and how to light a fire. We were also shown how to build a <u>shelter</u> with only branches and leaves.

The water was easy to find because the camp is in one of the wettest parts of the country, but the food was not. To my horror, I discovered that we had to find our own. This meant <u>hunting</u>, but we couldn't face it on the first day. We went out in groups and managed to find some berries and

mushrooms. One of the boys in the group was able to light a fire (without matches!) and we proceeded to prepare a meal. However, as we were cooking the mushrooms, they caught fire. I was able to save most of them, but they tasted strange!

The woodlands are very green, but they are also damp, so you can imagine how cold it gets at night. But the cold is not the only problem. On the first night, we were kept awake by strange animal noises. Owls, squirrels and who knows what else! The next morning I woke to find Sheila, one of the girls in our group, looking at me in horror. 'There is something crawling on my stomach,' she said, pointing. And indeed, unbuttoning her pyjamas, I saw a small black spider making its way across her body. The woodland is full of <u>creepy-crawlies</u>!

The rest of the week went by without any major dramas. We looked for food, lit fires, cooked and basically survived the week in the wild. We had to eat some unusual dishes, such as mushrooms with wild strawberries and barbecued fish! We also had the opportunity to take part in water sports and go rock climbing, both of which I have never done before.

But it definitely wasn't a home away from home. I realized by the second day in the camp that it is not easy to live without the things we have <u>grown accustomed to</u> in our everyday lives. It makes you <u>appreciate</u> even the smallest of luxuries – chocolate, for instance, or your own private bathroom. Would I recommend it? Yes, I probably would. It is a chance to get in touch with the natural world – even if it is only for a few days.

3
A that she had to look for water
B that it was cold at night
C that the woodland is full of spiders
D that she had to find food to eat

4
A It was full of dramas.
B They didn't work at all.
C It was not problematic.
D She enjoyed trying various interesting dishes.

5
A Living without everyday luxuries is difficult.
B It is important to connect with nature.
C She will take chocolate with her next time.
D She wants her own bathroom.

6
A She thinks it was worth it.
B She did not enjoy it.
C She thought it was dangerous.
D She can't wait to do it again.

F Match the words underlined in the text with a definition.

1 things that are nice, but not necessary ....
2 a wild place that is not inhabited by people ....
3 spiders, worms or other small scary animals ....
4 understand the importance of something ....
5 a place that gives protection from the weather, etc ....
6 be used to ....
7 looking to find ....
8 said something to make us feel better ....

E Now choose which option (A, B, C or D) best answers the questions in D.

1
A to see if she could live without everyday luxuries
B to satisfy her curiosity about such camps
C to learn to survive in the natural world
D to do some sightseeing

2
A find food
B light a fire
C build a house
D find water

Would you like to go to a wilderness survival camp? Have you ever watched TV shows like *Survivor*?

2

Grammar 1

✓ Check past simple and past continuous

See pages 139 and 140 for information about past simple and past continuous.

Match these extracts with the descriptions.

1 I **was** really **looking** forward to it.
2 ... I **was** curious.
3 ... some classmates who **went** to one last summer.
4 ... as we **were cooking** the mushrooms, they caught fire.
5 We **looked** for food, **lit** fires, **cooked** ...

Past simple is used to talk about:

a repeated actions in the past ....
b a completed action at a specific time in the past ....
c a state in the past ....

Past continuous is used to talk about:

d an action that was in progress when something else happened ....
e a temporary situation in the past ....

A Complete with the past simple or past continuous.

1 Last year, while I .... (stay) with friends on their farm, I .... (ride) a horse for the first time.
2 When I was a child, we .... (move) house at least five times.
3 Ben .... (watch) TV when he .... (hear) a strange noise coming from the flat next door.
4 John lives in New York, but he .... (grow up) in Chicago.
5 Christine .... (know) she couldn't live in that place forever.
6 I .... (not live) there, I .... (only stay) there while my house was being renovated.
7 .... (you know) that more people live in cities today than in the countryside?
8 What .... (do) when I .... (call) you earlier?

✓ Check time expressions in the past

See page 140 for information about time expressions in the past.

B Complete with a time expression.

1 .... I was living in Paris, I ate croissants every day.
2 Sarah was able to relax .... her visit to the countryside.
3 I went horseback riding .... I was there.
4 .... Tom was a child, his family moved to London.
5 Twenty years .... there were more people living in the country than there are now.
6 I haven't been back to my village .... many years.

✓ Check used to and would

See page 140 for information about used to and would.

Circle the correct option.

1 Did you **used to** / **use to** walk everywhere before you got a car?
2 We **used to** / **use to** enjoy walking in the countryside.
3 Jason **would** / **used to** prefer living in the city.
4 My friends didn't **used to** / **use to** go out a lot.
5 Mum **use to** / **would** take us on picnics when we were younger.

C Four of these sentences contain mistakes. Find them and correct them.

1 Jane used to living with her parents, but now she lives alone.
2 I would live in that house.
3 Paul used to came over a lot, but he doesn't anymore.
4 I would play with the children next door every day after school.
5 Didn't you used to live in my street?
6 Most big cities used to be less polluted than they are today.

D Work in pairs. List five ways life used to be different 100 years ago.

Vocabulary
Town and village

A Where would you find these places – in urban areas, in rural areas or both?

> block of flats • multiplex cinema
> multi-storey car park • shopping centre/mall
> skyscraper • country house • farmhouse
> public garden/park • garden • gym/sports centre
> field • industrial area

B Decide if these adjectives are positive, negative or both. Then work with a partner to describe your area.

> busy • dangerous • depressing • dull • exciting • green
> historic • interesting • lively • lovely • modern • noisy
> peaceful • pleasant • polluted • quiet • safe

> My town is a very lively place. There are lots of shopping centres and multiplex cinemas. Unfortunately, it's polluted and noisy.

House and home

C Complete with *house* or *home*.
1 Most people don't leave .... until they're at least 18.
2 The .... with the red shutters is for sale.
3 Our football team always wins when we play at ....
4 Please deliver it on Friday. There'll be nobody .... tomorrow.

D Make compounds with *house* and *home*. Which word can take both?
1 ....hold
2 ....less
3 ....made
4 ....sick
5 ....town
6 ....warming
7 ....wife
8 ....work

E Complete with a compound from D.
1 We had a .... party when we moved into our new flat.
2 New York is not my .... I moved here when I was 18.
3 .... ice cream is delicious.
4 I always get .... when I'm away from home for more than a week.
5 Does every .... have a computer?

F Complete the collocations. Then answer the questionnaire. Compare your answers with a partner.

> do (x 5) • clear / lay • load • make
> take • tidy • walk • water

Do you ever ...
1 .... your bed? ....
2 .... the cooking? ....
3 .... the dishwasher? ....
4 .... the household shopping? ....
5 .... the rubbish out? ....
6 .... the ironing? ....
7 .... your room? ....
8 .... the washing-up? ....
9 .... the table? ....
10 .... the plants/garden? ....
11 .... the laundry? ....
12 .... the dog? ....

Phrasal verbs

G Circle the correct option. In one sentence both options are correct. Then match the phrasal verbs with their definitions.

1 Our house was run down so we did it **up** / **down**.
2 I don't want to go out. I'll just stay **in** / **on** and watch TV.
3 I need to throw **out** / **up** some of the old clothes in my wardrobe.
4 Come **over** / **on** to my house tonight!
5 If you're in the neighbourhood, drop **by** / **in** and see us.

a to remain at home
b fixed
c visit without an appointment
d visit
e get rid of

2 Listening

Casa Batlló

Casa Vicenç

A Look at these pictures of two buildings. What makes them unusual? Use these words and phrases to help you describe them.

Parts of a building	Talking about a building
the outside	colourful
the roof	impressive design
the walls	a lot of detail
the ceiling	rich design
the staircase	decorative features
a room	amazing

The roof of the first building has got a lot of detail.

B 🎧 Listen to a radio programme about the two buildings. Which parts of the buildings are mentioned?

Steps to success
- Make sure you read the text in front of the gaps, **and** the text which follows the gaps, as these may affect your answer.

C Read through these sentences. What type of word(s) or information is missing from each gap?

ANTONI GAUDÍ
ARCHITECT

Many of Gaudí's buildings can be found in the city of (**1**) ....
The rich (**2**) .... of the buildings is what makes them special.
Gaudí designed the Casa Vicenç when he was only (**3**) ....
The outside of the building is decorated with (**4**) .... tiles.
The (**5**) .... are not flat like in most buildings.
It took Gaudí (**6**) .... to complete the Casa Vicenç.
Parts of Casa Batlló look like different parts of an (**7**) ....
The roof of the Casa Batlló looks like the backbone of a (**8**) ....
The Gaudí walking tour starts at (**9**) .... every Friday.
The tour is (**10**) .... of charge.

D 🎧 Now listen to the interview again and complete the sentences.

Do you like Gaudí's buildings? Why/Why not?
Do you know of an extraordinary building in your town or area? What makes it special?

Speaking

A 🎧 **Listen to someone comparing two pictures and answer these questions.**
1 What do the pictures show?
2 What similarities are there between the pictures?
3 Which of the places would the speaker prefer to visit?

B Look at the pictures described on page 175. Did the speaker do well?

C 🎧 Listen again and match the comments in the Language chunks.

Language chunks

Impressions

It looks like …	that the first place is in a wet country …
It's a very …	it could be a farm …
I get the impression …	a dangerous place to visit.
It makes me think of …	peaceful place.
I think it's probably …	the Amazon rainforest.

Steps to success
- When describing pictures, use phrases that make it clear you're talking about your opinions and impressions.

D 👥 **Work in pairs. Speak for one minute each. Listen to your partner and complete the checklist. Then give feedback.**

Student A: Compare pictures A and B. Which place would you like to live in?
Student B: Compare pictures C and D. Which place would you like to live in?
Which place would you like to live in?

Checklist:	Yes	No
1 Talks about the similarities.		
2 Talks about the differences.		
3 Answers the question about their preference.		

E 👥 **Work in pairs. Which of these things are important when choosing where to live?**
- a garden
- space for parking
- parks or public gardens nearby
- a good school nearby
- shops within walking distance
- good public transport
- a variety of entertainment facilities

Sounds /t/, /d/ and /id/

F 🎧 **Listen and put the verbs in the correct column.**

/t/ wished	/d/ discovered	/id/ decided

2

Grammar 2

✓ **Check** *a/an*, *the*, the zero article

See page 140 for information about articles.

Find and correct the mistakes in these sentences.
1 Nile is the longest river in the world.
2 A lot of the European cities are built on a major river.
3 What is capital of Austria?
4 I live in beautiful village.
5 I've lived in a same house my whole life.
6 The George is my next-door neighbour.

A Complete the text with *a*, *an*, *the* or *-*.

Tatami rooms

A Tatami room is (1) _____ room in (2) _____ Japanese house which has one or more tatami mats. These mats, which are (3) _____ traditional type of Japanese flooring, are associated with (4) _____ Japanese tea ceremony. Made of straw, they measure 90 cm by 180 cm. In Japan, (5) _____ size of a room is typically measured by the number of tatami mats it can fit. There are certain rules that must be followed with regard to (6) _____ number and layout of (7) _____ tatami mats. (8) _____ mats must not be laid where (9) _____ corners of three or four mats touch. If you do not follow these rules, it is believed you will have (10) _____ bad luck.

B Read this sequence and answer the questions.

> There's a boy sitting on a chair. The chair is in a room. The room is in a house. The house is in a street. The street is in a city. The city is in Ireland.

1 Where's the boy?
2 Where's the room?
3 Where's the city?

C Work in pairs. Write similar sequences beginning with these sentences. When you've finished, compare your sequences with another pair.

There's a bee on a flower.
There's a fly on the wall.

✓ **Check** possessive pronouns and determiners

See page 140 for information about possessive pronouns and determiners.

Circle the correct option and then complete the rules.
1 This is **my** / **mine** house.
2 This house is **my** / **mine**.

Possessive pronouns or determiners?
a _____ (my, your, his, her, its, our, their) are followed by nouns.
b _____ (mine, yours, his, hers, ours, theirs) are not followed by nouns.

D Choose the best answer.
1 A friend of _____ spent a week in a wilderness survival camp.
   a my   b mine
2 _____ grandmother lived in five different countries before settling here.
   a My   b Mine
3 Is that _____ car over there?
   a your   b yours
4 No, that's Frank's. This is _____ .
   a my   b mine
5 This is _____ and this is Sam's.
   a your   b yours
6 _____ chemistry teacher moved here from Sri Lanka.
   a Our   b Ours

22

Practise your English

A Choose the best answer.

1. I was doing my homework when the phone ....
   - A was ringing   C ringed
   - B rang   D did ring

2. What .... between the time you got home and the time you went to bed?
   - A you did   C you doing
   - B did you   D were you doing

3. I .... live in a very small house by the sea.
   - A did   C used to
   - B used   D would

4. Every night my father .... home from work and sit in that chair.
   - A used come   C was coming
   - B would come   D comes

5. I .... her many times.
   - A visited   C was visiting
   - B visit   D am visiting

6. The only .... I don't mind doing is the ironing.
   - A homework   C household
   - B housework   D home life

7. Who .... your bed every morning?
   - A made   C did
   - B makes   D does

8. Which is the tallest .... in the world?
   - A field   C house
   - B apartment   D skyscraper

9. Can you please tell John to .... the rubbish out?
   - A get   C take
   - B do   D make

10. This place is so .... There's nothing to do in the evenings.
    - A polluted   C modern
    - B exciting   D dull

B Discuss these questions in pairs.

Can the colours in your bedroom affect your sleep?

Can the position of your bed in your bedroom affect your sleep?

C Read the text quickly to find answers to the questions in B.

The power of Feng shui

Is there a room in (1) .... home that everyone likes to spend a lot of time in? What about (2) .... space that no one seems to use very much? Are you finding it difficult to sleep at night? These questions can easily be answered using (3) .... art and science of ancient Chinese Feng shui (pronounced fung shway). Feng shui, which literally means the wind and the water, teaches us how to create harmony and balance around us by making changes in our work and living spaces. By arranging our furniture and decor in a way that aligns with nature, we draw harmony and good health into (4) .... lives. According to this ancient philosophy, the placement of everything from (5) .... front door to the toilet can affect our overall well-being. (6) .... Chinese believe in this philosophy so strongly that they employ a Feng shui master before building or buying a home.

Here is (7) .... story to illustrate its power. A few years (8) .... Ken Taylor bought a luxurious apartment that had a large light-filled bedroom. After living in (9) .... apartment for a few months, he noticed that despite its beauty he was not comfortable in the bedroom and as a result he (10) .... not sleeping well. A few weeks later, after learning about Feng shui, he understood why. He needed to rearrange the furniture, including his bed. In Feng shui, it is believed that in order to get (11) .... restful sleep, you need to place (12) .... bed where you can see the entrance. That's what Ken did. He also changed the colour of the walls and curtains from dark to light shades. After making these necessary changes, he began sleeping soundly, started feeling happy and comfortable at home, and began to experience more happiness in his life.

D Read the text again and write one word in each gap.

Quick chat

Have you ever heard of Feng shui? If you were a Feng shui master, what advice would you give the person who sleeps in this bedroom?

2

Writing: Article (1)

A Match the pictures with the descriptions. Which words helped you decide?

1. This historic building used to be used as a temple in ancient times. It was dedicated to the goddess Athena, which is how Athens got its name.

2. This impressive building, or tower, was built for the International Exhibition of Paris in 1889. At the time it was the tallest building in the world.

3. This 102-storey skyscraper is a New York landmark. When it was built, in 1931, and for 40 years after that, it was the tallest building in the world.

The Sydney Opera House

B Read this article about the Sydney Opera House. Why is it the writer's favourite building?

A The Sydney Opera House is considered the most important landmark in Sydney. As soon as people see it, they think of the city. It is on Bennelong Point on the harbour close to another important landmark, the Sydney Harbour bridge.

B It was designed to look like the sails of a boat, which is appropriate (**1**) **as / because of** it is situated right on the water's edge. It's covered in white, shiny tiles that glimmer in the sunlight. (**2**) **Whether / Either** you are looking at it close-up or from a distance, it's very impressive.

C (**3**) **Since / For** it was completed, in 1973, it has been used mainly as an opera house.
(**4**) **But / However**, it's also used for other shows, like theatre productions and concerts.

D What I like most about the building is its original design and the fact that it can be seen from many parts of the city. (**5**) **And / Moreover**, its history is also fascinating. (**6**) **Because of / Because** an argument between the architect, Jørn Utzon, and the government, Utzon, who lived in Denmark, never saw it completed!

Quick chat

Have you visited any of the places above?
Which of the places would you like to visit?
Why/Why not?

Skills development
Organization

C Each paragraph in the article focuses on one topic. Match the topics to the paragraphs.

What it looks like ....
Why it's my favourite ....
Where it is ....
What it is/was used for ....

Linking ideas

D Read the article again and circle the correct linking word or phrase.

E Complete the sentences with a linking word or phrase from the box. Do not use a word or phrase more than once.

> as • because • because of • however
> moreover • since • whether

1 .... you like modern buildings or not, you will find this one impressive.
2 I like this building .... the fact that it's so old.
3 .... it is so unusual, most people know about the Sydney Opera House.
4 The Parthenon has been standing .... the fifth century BC.
5 I find it impressive, ... it is one of the tallest buildings in the world.
6 It is not considered to be a beautiful building. .... , most people find it interesting to look at.
7 The Palace of Versailles is probably the most famous palace in the world. .... , it is one of the biggest palaces ever built.

Language chunks

Talking about a building
It is situated in ...
It was built by ...
It was completed in ...
It was designed by ...

Planning and writing

F Read this writing task. Choose a building from A or one that you know something about and complete the planner.

> Do you have a favourite building either in your country or anywhere else in the world? We want to hear about it!
> Write an article of between 120 and 180 words.

Planner

Title: ....

Paragraph 1: Where is it? ....

Paragraph 2: What does it look like? ....

Paragraph 3: What is/was it used for? ....

Paragraph 4: Why is it your favourite building? ....

G Write your article. Use the Language chunks to help you.

Steps to success
- To make your piece of writing look more like an article, give it a title.

quick check

Be sure to:
- write four paragraphs.
- talk about one topic only in each paragraph.
- use linking words or phrases to link your ideas.
- use an informal or neutral style.
- make it interesting.

Check your knowledge 1

A Circle the correct option.

1 I get really **tired / annoyed** when people are late!
2 My sister is so **selfish / aggressive**. She only thinks of herself.
3 We had a **housewarming / homewarming** party to celebrate moving in to our new place.
4 After the fire, they were left **houseless / homeless**.
5 Our **house / home** is bigger than yours.
6 Heather is really **bossy / moody**. She has to control everybody.
7 When I fell over I was so **embarrassed / anxious** that my face went bright red!
8 **Come over / Come on** to my house at about six o'clock.
9 Let's **stay in / stay on** tonight. There's a good film on TV.
10 Is there anyone **house / home**? I've been knocking for ages.

B Complete with the correct form of the verb in brackets.

1 .... this hot chocolate .... (contain) any sugar? I can't have sugar.
2 You .... (look) tired. What have you been doing?
3 My grandparents .... (come) from Spain.
4 At the moment, I .... (learn) a new language.
5 Hurry! The bus .... (leave) at five o'clock.
6 This weekend the whole family .... (get) together.
7 I .... (do) the washing-up, when she called.
8 At ten o'clock, I .... (hear) a strange noise coming from next door.
9 We .... (have) dinner, then we .... (go) to the cinema and then we .... (come) home.
10 When I .... (be) a child, we .... (live) in the country.

C Complete with the correct adjectives. Use the words in capitals.

Louise: a case study

Louise Little is a clever girl, but she is (1) .... When she left school she didn't go to university, she got a full-time job as a sales assistant at a clothes store.   **AMBITION**

Her parents aren't happy about her choice. They think she is (2) .... Neither do they want her to move out and live on her own. They say that if she is too (3) .... to tidy her room, how can she look after a place of her own.   **RESPONSIBLE**   **ORGANIZE**

Louise is popular, though. She is a very (4) .... girl and she is always (5) .... with others. Her family don't understand that she is just a simple girl who wants a simple life. 'I do my job well and I'm very (6) .... Honestly, I can't see what all the fuss is about.'   **ATTRACT**   **CONSIDER**   **RELY**

D Complete with *a/an*, *the* or –.

Guggenheim – Bilbao

One of **(1)** .... most interesting buildings in **(2)** .... world is undoubtedly **(3)** .... Guggenheim Museum in Bilbao. It has **(4)** .... very characteristic design, which is easily recognizable. **(5)** .... building itself is made of **(6)** .... glass, limestone and **(7)** .... metal known as titanium. **(8)** .... titanium panels reflect **(9)** .... light and make **(10)** .... building look as if it is covered in fish scales, which is fitting as it is situated right on **(11)** .... waterfront. If you are ever in **(12)** .... Spain, **(13)** .... Guggenheim Bilbao is well worth **(14)** .... visit.

E Choose the best answer.

1 Kelly and I were best friends .... years.
A during   C while
B for   D as

2 Louis and I sat next to each other .... we were in primary school.
A during   C while
B for   D as

3 My dad .... staying up so late. He gets really sleepy.
A isn't used to   C used to
B is used to   D didn't used to

4 My family .... live in that house.
A would   C use to
B am used to D used to

5 A cousin of .... is getting married this weekend.
A my   C me
B mine   D I

6 .... sister is taller than my brother.
A You're   C You
B Yours   D Your

7 Denise has got the most fabulous .... red curly hair.
A thin   C fair
B thick   D straight

8 Tom is such a(n) .... person. He's never without a smile on his face.
A energetic   C cheerful
B creative   D efficient

F Complete each gap with one word.

Should children help out around the home? Of course they should. **(1)** .... I was growing up, I **(2)** .... to have to help with **(3)** .... housework. I would have to **(4)** .... the supermarket shopping, **(5)** .... my bed and **(6)** .... my room. I must admit I hated doing these things, but I had no choice in **(7)** .... matter. Now that I am **(8)** .... grown-up, I understand that this was a good way to teach responsibility. Now I'm used **(9)** .... doing my fair share of household chores. I'm even thinking of doing **(10)** .... the house.

G Complete the second sentence so that it has the same meaning as the first sentence. Use the word given.

1 Sally doesn't usually get up so early.
USED
Sally .... up so early.

2 I never thought she would get so upset.
OCCURRED
It had .... that she would get so upset.

3 Jasmine came round every day after school.
COME
Jasmine .... every day after school.

4 Didn't you live in Smith Street?
TO
Didn't you .... in Smith Street?

5 Sam usually forgets his mobile phone. It's annoying.
ALWAYS
Sam .... mobile phone.

6 What is your occupation?
JOB
What .... do?

7 You keep mixing up their names!
ALWAYS
You .... mixing up their names!

8 The flight is at four o'clock.
LEAVES
The .... at four o'clock.

9 Do you have any plans for this weekend?
YOU
What .... this weekend?

3 Learning for life

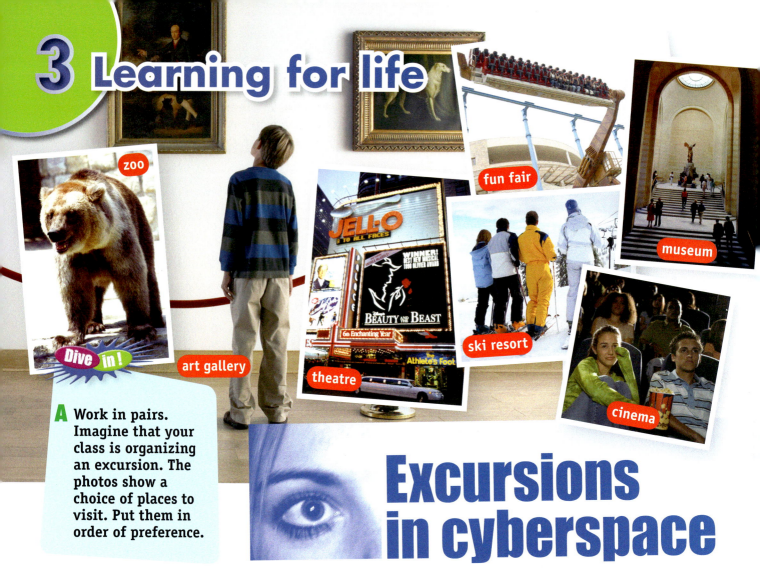

A Work in pairs. Imagine that your class is organizing an excursion. The photos show a choice of places to visit. Put them in order of preference.

Reading

B You are going to read about a new sort of school trip. Skim the article and match paragraphs a-g with the headings 1-7.

1 What are other schools doing? ....
2 Traditional trips ....
3 The future of the traditional trip ....
4 What's happening in Lemmington? ....
5 The equipment you need ....
6 The benefits it brings ....
7 What is videoconferencing? ....

School trips have never been so exciting!

Excursions in cyberspace

a Where did you go on *your* last school excursion? Maybe you went to a nearby museum, or did you go for a stroll to the local art gallery? If you were really lucky, perhaps you were all taken to the theatre! (**1**) .... Most schools don't have the money or time to take their students to more exciting places. However, for children at Lemmington High, school trips have changed forever.

b This year alone, lucky Lemmingtonians have seen Pisa in Italy; they've taken a tour of the Louvre in Paris; they've even visited a school in Ulan Bator. And the school year hasn't finished yet! They have plans to meet children in the Outback of Australia and to interview a famous footballer in his own home! But how? (**2**) ....

c These, you see, are virtual excursions and they take place in 'cyberspace'. The children haven't been to Italy and they haven't flown to Mongolia. They've seen these places on a large computer screen in their own classroom. (**3**) .... 'With videoconferencing, learners experience these far-flung places for real,' says Bowen, who leads the videoconferencing project at Lemmington High. 'A videoconference is a live video link over the internet. During a conference, our students can see and speak to real people almost anywhere else in the world.' Indeed, the only requirement is that the other school, museum or footballer's house, also has videoconferencing equipment.

Steps to success

To find the right place for a sentence in a text:
1. read the whole text to get the gist.
2. look for reference words in the sentence choices; *this, these, she, it, one, such,* etc. What do they refer to?
3. read the sentences before and after each gap in the text.
4. look for any question and answer pairs — sometimes the question is missing, sometimes the answer is missing.

d But are these virtual excursions as useful as real ones? 'Certainly,' says Bowen. 'Pupils learn about other cultures by communicating with people who live there. It's an amazing experience for everyone involved.' (**4**) .... The school has been using the system for a year now, and the pupils have become quite addicted. 'We've been doing it about once a month, but we'd do it every day if we could,' says 14-year-old Shelly Brookes. 'We've learnt a lot, but I also feel like we've made friends around the world.' Another advantage, of course, is that virtual excursions are not affected by the weather. If it's been raining non-stop for the last week, that's not a problem!

e Not surprisingly, other schools have been trying videoconferencing too. (**5**) .... Another has spoken to a group of native American children from their school in California. The possibilities are endless.

f How can your school start videoconferencing? Well, first of all you need the right equipment. (**6**) .... However, you don't need to buy state-of-the-art equipment, as Leonard Bowen explains. 'Our screen is quite big, but it's connected to a cheap computer. Our internet connection isn't the fastest available. The whole system has cost under 600 pounds. Cheap, but effective.'

g The wonders of technology have truly brought the world into the classroom. (**7**) .... Leonard Bowen, who has worked with children for over 20 years, doesn't think they're history quite yet. 'We've been doing them for years,' he says, 'and kids still enjoy them.' After all, you can't buy a souvenir through a video screen!

C These sentences have been removed from the article. There is also one extra sentence. Look through the sentences and follow steps 2 to 4 from the Steps to success box.

A However, as teacher Leonard Bowen explains, this isn't the same as watching a documentary on TV.
B Excursions have always been part of the school year, but they seldom get more adventurous than this.
C Perhaps you've been wondering if the traditional school trip will disappear forever.
D And it's not just the teachers who are enthusiastic.
E Sometimes it can be difficult to get a good connection.
F Some systems cost almost 5,000 pounds, but these are the very best cameras and screens available.
G One, for example, has interviewed researchers in a camp in Antarctica.
H The answer is videoconferencing.

D Now choose from the sentences (A-H) the one which fits each gap (1-7). Remember that there is one extra sentence that you do not need to use.

E Match the words and expressions underlined in the text with a definition.

1 a relaxed walk
2 all you need
3 distant
4 not real
5 the most modern available
6 can be used in many different ways
7 gone forever
8 very keen on

Quick chat

Should school excursions be educational or fun? Can they be both?

3

Grammar 1

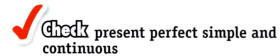 present perfect simple and continuous

See page 141 for information about present perfect simple and continuous.

Match these extracts with the uses of each tense.

1 ... who **has worked** with children for over 20 years ...
2 ... we**'ve made** friends around the world.
3 We**'ve been doing** it about once a month ...
4 ... they**'ve taken** a tour of the Louvre in Paris, ...
5 ... it**'s been raining** non-stop for the last week ...

Present perfect simple is used to talk about:

a an action in the recent past that has a result in the present ....
b an experience ....
c a situation or state that was true in the past and is still true today ....

Present perfect continuous is used to talk about:

d an action that started in the past and continues up to the present ....
e an action that first occurred in the past and has occurred repeatedly up to the present ....

A Complete with the present perfect simple or continuous.

1 Where have you been? I .... (wait) for you all morning.
2 I can't go out tonight. I .... (not finish) my homework.
3 We've got PE today and I .... (not bring) my PE kit.
4 John .... (revise) hard all week for his chemistry test.
5 .... (you / meet) my sister before?
6 Isabelle .... (not learn) German very long, but she already speaks well.

B Circle the correct option.

1 Jane's not here at the moment. She's **been** / **gone** to drama club.
2 I've never **been** / **gone** to Africa, but I'd love to go.
3 Is Marcus here? No, he's just **been** / **gone** to the staff room.
4 Has anyone here **been** / **gone** to that new sports club in town?
5 How many times have you **been** / **gone** to the Head's office?
6 Mum and Dad have **been** / **gone** to the theatre tonight. They're seeing a Shakespeare play.

C Complete the email with the present perfect simple or continuous.

Hi Kevin,

I'm in Greece, but I bet you can't guess what I (1) .... (do) the last few days. Skiing! That's right. My class (2) .... (come) to Greece for ten days and for the last two days we (3) .... (stay) in the mountains. It's great. I (4) .... (never go) skiing before. Have you? A Greek ski instructor (5) .... (teach) us to ski since we arrived. She's very nice and I think I (6) .... (become) quite good already. My friend Kelly (7) .... (not be) so lucky, though. She (8) .... (have) an accident and so she can't ski. She (9) .... (not watch) TV all day, though. She (10) .... (be) busy with her camera. She'll put her photos on the school website when we get back.

Bye for now,
Stella

Vocabulary

School and education

A Match a word from box A with a word from box B to make collocations about school.

A: do, follow, get, get into, work, lose, pass, pay, play, show

B: attention, exams, hard, interest, interest, rules, suspended, trouble, truant, well

B Complete the story with a collocation from A in the correct form.

Jim Yelland (1) .... interest in school when he was about 11 or 12. At primary school he was a good student. He (2) .... attention in class and always did his homework. He was (3) .... well and getting good marks, but his parents never (4) .... interest in his efforts and eventually he stopped trying. In secondary school he gave up altogether. He didn't (5) .... the rules, and he (6) .... trouble again and again. He (7) .... truant from school for two or three days at a time. Eventually, he (8) .... suspended from school for a month. But one person really seemed to care. Mr Goodall, the English teacher, went to visit Jim at home. They talked and Mr Goodall persuaded Jim to try again. This year Jim has (9) .... hard and he has (10) .... his end-of-year exams. Sometimes all you need is someone who believes in you!

C Circle the correct option.
1 Most children go to **state** / **public** schools run by the government.
2 **Private** / **Individual** schools are often very expensive.
3 **Vocational** / **Occupational** courses teach learners useful skills that they can use at work.
4 Some schools have an **open** / **public** day when parents can visit.
5 The school year is divided into three **seasons** / **terms**. Each one lasts about three months.
6 Most schoolchildren in England wear a **costume** / **uniform**.
7 Hand your homework in by the **deadline** / **finish line**.
8 Some adults attend evening **classes** / **lessons** to learn new skills.

Phrasal verbs

D Replace the words in bold in each sentence with a phrasal verb from the box in the correct form.

> break up • get marked down • give back • hand in
> hand out • take up

1 I **submitted** my homework a few days late. ....
2 Mr De Lay took ages to **return** our tests. ....
3 Jane **distributed** the photocopies. ....
4 Dad **started to learn** Chinese two years ago, but he didn't study hard. ....
5 Our school **closed** for Easter very early last year. ....
6 I **lost points** in the test for my poor spelling. ....

E Make pairs of words with similar meanings.

adolescents   age group   head   peers   teenagers   siblings
brothers and sisters   helper   principal   assistant

F Circle the best word to complete each of these opinions.

1 Children are most influenced by their **peers** / **adolescents**.
2 The **head** / **assistant** of the school should always be a woman.
3 **Siblings** / **Age groups** should do their homework together.
4 Teachers ought to have **assistants** / **adolescents** to help them in class.

Do you agree or disagree with any of the opinions above? Why? Why do you think some children play truant?

3

Listening

A What problems at school do these pictures show? Do you have these problems at your school?

B Look at these opinions about school. Which ones are illustrated in the pictures? Do you agree with these opinions?

A Homework should have a purpose.

B Teachers and pupils need to respect each other.

C Teachers shouldn't judge students all the time.

D Pupils should keep classrooms clean.

E Teachers shouldn't give so much homework.

F Pupils should wait to be asked by the teacher.

Steps to success

- The sentences in multiple matching exercises express what the speakers say, but with other words. Read the sentences, and try to think of other ways to express the same ideas.

C Choose the sentence which is closest in meaning to the opinions from B.

Opinion A
1 Homework is useless.
2 Homework should be worthwhile.

Opinion B
1 Pupils should be polite to teachers.
2 Teachers should be polite to pupils and pupils should be polite to teachers.

Opinion C
1 Pupils shouldn't be compared for everything they do.
2 All pupils' work should get a grade.

Opinion D
1 Pupils should look after their classrooms.
2 Classrooms should be cleaned more often.

Opinion E
1 Homework is a bad idea.
2 There should be a limit on homework.

Opinion F
1 Children shouldn't speak in class.
2 There should be rules about when to speak in class.

D  You will hear five different people talking about life at school. Match each speaker to one of the opinions listed in B. There is one option you do not need to use.

Speaker 1 ....
Speaker 2 ....
Speaker 3 ....
Speaker 4 ....
Speaker 5 ....

Quick chat

Do schools need rules? Why/Why not?

Speaking

A Look at the bad things pupils sometimes do at school. Put the list in order of seriousness. Share your ideas with the class.
- being late for class
- dropping litter within the school grounds
- eating in class
- writing on desks
- shouting in class
- not doing homework
- writing graffiti on walls
- being rude to teachers and other pupils

B How can teachers encourage pupils to behave better? These pictures show some ideas. Match the phrases in the box with the pictures.

> be in detention • be sent to the Head • clean the school
> get marked down • get suspended • speak to parents

C 🎧 Listen to Anna and Peter. Circle the ideas from B that they mention.

D 🎧 Look through the phrases in the Language chunks box. Listen again and tick the expressions you hear.

Language chunks

Expressing opinions
- I think …
- I believe …
- In my opinion, …
- I don't know if …
- If you ask me, …

Agreeing and disagreeing
- I think you're right.
- I'm not so sure.
- Well, yes and no.
- I wouldn't say so, no.

Inviting others to speak
- What do you think?
- What do you reckon about … ?
- Wouldn't you agree?
- Don't you think?
- What's your opinion on … ?
- Question tags: *isn't it?* / *don't you?*, etc

Steps to success
- A discussion is not a speech! Give your partner chances to speak, too. Invite them to speak using the Language chunks.

E 👥 Work in pairs. You have been asked to think of ways to improve your school. Here are some suggestions. Discuss the ideas with a partner and choose the best two.
- longer school day, with more breaks
- more varied lessons, for example more languages or learning music
- fewer students per class
- better equipment for science classes
- more school trips

F 🎧 Are these questions 'real' or 'checking'? Listen and tick, then repeat.

	real	checking
1 You haven't read this before, have you?	☐	☐
2 This is our classroom, isn't it?	☐	☐
3 I'm not disturbing you, am I?	☐	☐
4 Katie's writing a test tomorrow, isn't she?	☐	☐

3

Grammar 2

✓ Check present perfect and past simple

See page 141 for information about present perfect and past simple.

Read the sentences and answer the questions which follow.

A: I forgot my homework yesterday. Mrs Bruce went bananas!

B: I've forgotten my homework. I'm terrified. Mrs Bruce is going to go bananas!

Which sentence ...
1 talks about a finished moment in the past? ....
2 connects a moment in the recent past with the present time? ....
3 describes an event and result in the past? ....
4 describes an event in the past with a result in the present or future? ....
5 mentions the exact time that an event happened? ....

A Two of the sentences are correct. Which ones? Find and correct the mistakes in the other sentences.

1 James has gone to a different school before this one, but he didn't like it.
2 Last year my class has visited Berlin and Munich.
3 I haven't been at school the day before yesterday because I was ill.
4 At last I've finished my homework!
5 'Have you ever changed schools?' 'Only when I started secondary school.'
6 Alice was in the exam room for three hours. I don't know when she'll come out.

B Complete with the present perfect or past simple.

1 Colin Long .... (be) in detention three times this year.
2 .... you .... (enjoy) primary school when you were small?
3 Our exam results still .... (arrive). I wonder how I did?
4 I'm really enjoying history this year. We .... (learn) a lot.
5 Mr Dawson is the best teacher we .... (have).
6 Oh dear! I don't know what I .... (do) with my German books.
7 We .... (have) a great chemistry lesson earlier today.
8 What time .... you .... (arrive) at school this morning?

✓ Check time expressions with perfect tenses

See page 142 for information about time expressions with perfect tenses.

C Complete the email with words from the box.

already • ever • for • just • never • since • still • yet

Hi Owen,
How are you? I haven't heard from you (1) .... ages! I wrote to you two weeks ago, but you (2) .... haven't replied. Is everything alright? I'm fine. I haven't quite got used to being at boarding school (3) ...., but it's getting better. I can't believe that I've (4) .... been living here for three months. I haven't made many friends, but there's one girl that I've been speaking to a lot. She's been here (5) .... she was only eight years old. Imagine!
Anyway, I'm going to the cinema with my class tonight. There's a film with an actor called Bernard Butch. I've (6) .... heard of him, but all the girls here are mad about him. Oh, and have you (7) .... heard of a band called the Bogus Brothers? Everyone here's nuts about them. I have to go now because the bell has (8) .... rung for bedtime.
Write soon.
Love,
Ellie

Practise your English

A Read the text quickly. What is 'spaced learning'?

Eight-minute mini-lessons boost learning

Just imagine: it's about twelve o'clock on a typical morning at school. The school day hasn't finished (1) **still / yet**, and you probably can't wait for the next break, can you? But how many breaks have you (2) **yet / already** had today? One? Two? How about 15?

That may sound ridiculous, but for pupils of Wythenden High School in England, it's quite normal to have 15 breaks in a morning. That's because they've (3) **used / been using** a new educational method called 'spaced learning'. The children have not (4) **followed / been following** normal lessons of 50 minutes. Instead, they've (5) **had / been having** short bursts of learning that last only eight minutes. After every eight minutes, the children take a break for ten minutes. They play sport or word games and then start again on their next eight-minute lesson.

'Spaced learning' is based on scientific research that (6) **was / has been** carried out a few years ago in the USA. The research has (7) **shown / been showing** that memory develops best with short bursts of learning. But has the new method (8) **been a help / helped** Wythenden pupils? 'Certainly it has,' says Ron Mackinly, the school's headmaster. 'We've been using "spaced learning" (9) **for / since** two years, and the children have (10) **ever / never** done better in maths and science. It's an amazing improvement.'

So there you have it! And now ... I think it's time for a break, don't you?

B Read the text again and circle the correct option.

Quick chat
What do you think of 'spaced learning'?
Do you get enough breaks at school?

C Complete the second sentence so that it has a similar meaning to the first sentence. Use the word given.

1 My dad often travels to distant parts of the world.
FLUNG
My dad often travels .... places.

2 Are you still doing your homework?
YET
Haven't you .... ?

3 Hasn't Gareth got out of bed yet?
IN
Is Gareth .... bed?

4 Mike went a few minutes ago.
HAS
Mike .... gone.

5 That's the best photo I've ever seen.
NEVER
I've .... better photo.

6 I don't like pop music anymore.
LOST
I've .... pop music.

7 Colin Smith hasn't been going to school.
TRUANT
Colin Smith has ....

8 You haven't been listening, have you?
PAYING
You haven't .... , have you?

9 Sally has never been in detention before.
TIME
This is the first .... in detention.

10 Jane wasn't allowed to go to school for two weeks because of bad behaviour.
GOT
Jane .... two weeks, for bad behaviour.

3 Writing: Informal transactional letter

Amateur dramatics
Information Technology
Debating

A Does your school offer any of these extra activities? Which activities would you like to do?
- amateur dramatics
- arts and crafts
- debating
- information technology
- photography
- sports
- traditional dancing

B Imagine this is part of a letter you received from an English-speaking friend, Thomas. Read the letter quickly and find out why he is writing to you.

> ... We haven't written to each other for ages! I'm fine, but I've had a lot of exams recently. I've got plans for other things, now that they've finished. Actually, that's why I'm writing to you.
>
> When I visited your school last year, I was really impressed with the amateur dramatics club you run. I've been thinking about doing something similar here in my school. Could you give me some advice?
>
> **(1)** How could we get other students interested in the club? **(2)** How often should we put on plays, do you think? I was very impressed with the show. **(3)** Do you rehearse a lot? How many rehearsals are needed to put on a good show? **(4)** Have the teachers been helping you at all?
>
> I've been thinking of ...

- posters around the school / word of mouth
- two or three a year
- about one or two hours a week
- Yes — our English teacher

C Read this reply to Thomas' letter. How many people are in the drama club altogether?

> Hi Thomas,
>
> Yes, it has been a long time since we've written, hasn't it? I've been busy, as well.
>
> I'm really glad you've decided to start your own drama club. I'm happy to give you any advice you need.
>
> **(A)** I suggest you do two or three plays a year. That's not very many, but you can't do more because every play takes a lot of time. **(B)** If I were you, I'd rehearse about one or two hours a week. You can't really rehearse more often because everyone is busy with school things. Apart from me there are about 15 other children in the club now. **(C)** You should try putting up posters to tell people about your club. People will hear about you through word of mouth too. **(D)** The only teacher who's in the club is Mr Mason, our English teacher. You've met him, I think. He's great fun!
>
> If you need any more help, just drop me a line.
>
> Kathy

Skills development
Organization

Steps to success
- You don't have to answer the questions in the same order that they appear in the prompt letter.
- Make sure you answer all the questions in the prompt letter.

D Thomas asks questions in his letter. Read Kathy's reply to the letter again and match the questions (1-4) with the answers (A-D) given in the reply.

Question 1 ....   Question 3 ....
Question 2 ....   Question 4 ....

Planning and writing

E Imagine this is part of a letter you received from an English-speaking friend, Tony. Read it quickly to find out why he is writing.

no – some friends write, too

every two weeks

about ten days

we sell copies (very cheaply!)

Thanks for sending a copy of your latest school magazine with your letter. It's great! Have you been writing all the articles yourself or are other people involved?

Actually, I'd really like to start a school magazine. Can you give me some advice? How often should we bring out the magazine? Is once a month a good idea? How long does it take to make each issue? I'm sure that it must cost some money to make. Where could we get the money from? Have you been selling the magazine or giving it away?

Sorry to ask you so many questions, but I'd really like to …

F Now write your reply to Tony's letter. Write between 120 and 150 words. Use the planner to help organize your letter, and try to use some of the Language chunks for giving advice.

Planner

Paragraph 1: Thank Tony for writing – briefly give your news. ....

Paragraph 2: Write about the articles. ....

Paragraph 3: Write about getting money for the magazine. ....

Paragraph 4: Write about making the magazine and how long it takes. ....

Language chunks

Why don't you … ?
What we did was to …
I suggest you …
You should try …
You might like to …
If I were you, I'd …

quick check

Be sure to:
- begin with a natural opening paragraph, thanking your friend for his / her letter.
- think about organization **before** you write.
- answer all the questions in your reply.
- check punctuation and spelling.

4 The world of science and technology

Dive in!

A Work in pairs. How much do you know about science and technology? Do this quiz and find out.

1 If you drop two balls of different weight from a high place, which will fall first?
a the heavier item
b They will both fall at the same time.

2 When was the telephone invented?
a in 1918   b in 1876

3 Which scientist lived in the 20th century?
a Einstein   b Newton

4 When did dinosaurs live?
a more than 65 million years ago
b about 10 million years ago

5 When was the first email sent?
a in 1971   b in 1991

 Check your answers on page 175.

Reading

B Read the title and subtitles in the article. Match each subtitle to a photo. What do you think the article is about?

Steps to success
- Scan the text quickly until you find the information you need.
- Don't read the whole text in detail.

C Now read the text quickly. What can you find out about the names, dates and places in the article?

The shock of the new

Years later, scientists who make great discoveries are admired for their cleverness and originality. But some of the great discoveries were not praised at the time they were made.

1 First dinosaur fossils identified

In 1822, the geologist William Buckland had been doing research when he came across some really big teeth. Big-sized bones and teeth had been found earlier by other people, but they were not considered important. Why not? Because they thought they had belonged to giants, which, at the time, were not interesting to scientists. In fact, these teeth belonged to an extinct species of animal that had lived more than 160 million years ago! Buckland knew they were important. He did not come up with the name dinosaur to describe these creatures, Sir Richard Owen did that years later in 1842. But he did publish the first ever scientific paper describing fossil dinosaurs. The name Buckland gave to the dinosaur he discovered was Megalosaurus, which, in Greek, means 'great lizard'.

2 Theory of natural selection

Charles Darwin published his book *On the Origin of Species* in 1859. He had developed a theory, which he called natural selection. It was a theory of evolution, stating that the 'stronger' characteristics of a species become more common in later generations. These are the ones that help an animal or plant survive in their own environment.

At the time, Darwin's theory shocked the world because it didn't agree with what the church had been teaching. Even today, in some parts of the world, Darwin's theory is not taught in schools. Darwin came up with his theory while he was on a five-year scientific expedition to the Pacific coast of South America. He got many of his ideas from the data he collected on the Galapagos Islands.

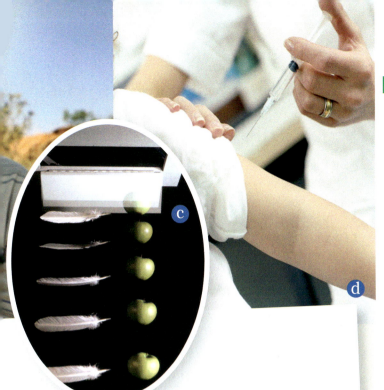

3 The law of falling bodies

In 1604, astronomer and physicist, Galileo Galilei, proposed his theory of falling bodies. For nearly 2,000 years, people had accepted Aristotle's theory that heavier bodies fall faster than lighter ones. Galileo proved that this was false. He showed that all bodies fall at the same rate no matter how much they weigh.

In a book written by one of Galileo's pupils, an experiment which proved this theory was described. Galileo is said to have dropped two balls of the same material, but different weights, from the Leaning Tower of Pisa. He wanted everyone to see that the balls would reach the ground at the same time. And they did!

People have questioned whether this experiment really ever happened, however Galileo's theory is now regarded as a scientific fact.

4 First vaccination

In 1796, Edward Jenner, an English country doctor, gave someone the world's first vaccination. In the 18th century, people were terrified of getting a common disease called smallpox. One in three people who caught the disease died. If you did survive, you were left with terrible scars all over your body.

Jenner noticed that after people had come into contact with cowpox, they didn't catch smallpox. Cowpox was similar to smallpox, but it only affected cows. He decided to inject the cowpox disease into healthy people. It was a risk, and other doctors were sceptical. But Jenner had made a major scientific breakthrough. He had come up with a smallpox vaccine. Thanks to his discovery, the threat of smallpox no longer exists and people today are protected from many other dangerous diseases.

D For questions 1-10, choose a scientist A-D.

A William Buckland   C Galileo Galilei
B Charles Darwin   D Edward Jenner

Which scientist(s) …

experimented on people?	1 ....
may not have conducted an experiment he is well known for?	2 ....
proved that a previous theory was wrong?	3 ....
invented a name for a new discovery?	4 .... 5 ....
wrote a book about his discovery?	6 ....
discovered that something was more important than people had previously thought?	7 ....
discovered that characteristics are passed on to next generations?	8 ....
came up with his theory after watching people?	9 ....
developed his ideas while travelling?	10 ....

E Find words in the texts that mean the following.

Paragraph 1
1 animals ....
2 the remains of an animal ....

Paragraph 2
3 a group of animals or plants with similar characteristics ....
4 the development of plants or animals over time ....

Paragraph 3
5 speed ....
6 doubted ....

Paragraph 4
7 marks left on the skin or body ....
8 not easily convinced ....

Which discoveries do you think were the most important? In pairs, come up with two more important scientific discoveries.

Grammar 1

✓ **Check** past perfect simple and continuous

See pages 142 and 143 for information about past perfect simple and continuous.

Look at these extracts. Which event happened first, A or B?

1 ... Buckland (A) **had been doing** research when he (B) **came across** some ... teeth.
2 ... it (A) **didn't agree** with what the church (B) **had been teaching**.
3 ... after people (A) **had come** into contact with cowpox, they (B) **didn't catch smallpox**.

A Circle the correct option.

1 The internet **had not been / had not been being** around for very long before it became popular.
2 I realized my mistake only after I **had sent / had been sending** the message.
3 I **sent / had sent** the email a week ago and I still haven't received a reply.
4 Darwin began writing a book when he **had developed / developed** his theory.
5 Kate **had been planning / had planned** to buy a new computer for months.
6 Mr Benn **had been doing / had done** a chemistry experiment when the phone rang.

C Complete the sentences with words from the box.

after • already • before • for • just • since • soon • when

1 By the time I asked, she had .... given her mobile away.
2 Rachel had .... arrived home when she realized she had left her laptop on the bus.
3 I had been sleeping .... an hour when she called.
4 I had finished all my work .... I went out.
5 I hadn't seen her .... we were in primary school.
6 James and I watched TV .... we had finished dinner.
7 Sally had been working on her computer for ten minutes .... the screen went blank.
8 As .... as he had got home, Colin checked his email.

D Work in pairs. Imagine you saw your partner doing something strange yesterday. Ask and answer questions to find out more. Use the ideas in the box to help you.

covered in paint • crying • laughing • limping
running in your bathing suit • sleeping in the park

I saw you yesterday. Why were you laughing so loudly?

I had just heard a funny joke.

B Complete with the past simple, past perfect simple or continuous form of the word in brackets.

How wrong can you be?

Today more than one billion people have a computer in their home. But in 1977, Ken Olsen, an engineer and co-founder of the Digital Equipment Corporation, (**1**) .... (predict) that there would be no market for the home computer. Engineers at the company (**2**) .... (work) on a project to make computers smaller, faster and cheaper when he famously said, 'There is no reason for any individual to have a computer at his home.' In fact, Ken Olsen (**3**) .... (refer) to the dangerous home computer of science fiction films – quite a different thing.

In the 1930s, before TV became popular, film producer Darryl Zanuck, (**4**) .... (say) that television would never succeed. To a certain extent Zanuck (**5**) .... (be) right, as television (**6**) .... (not take) off) until the 1950s. But by the 70s and 80s, it (**7**) .... (become) a huge part of our lives. In most households today you can find two or even three TV sets!

4

Vocabulary
Science

A Complete the spidergram with words from the box.

astronomy • physics • biology • chemistry
mathematics • geology

1. solar system, stars, planets
2. chemicals, gases, liquids
3. height, length, volume
4. numbers, space, amounts
5. animals, plants, cells
6. earthquakes, rocks, stones

B Choose the best answer.

1 The litre is the unit we use to measure ....
 A volume C height
 B weight D length

2 Ice is the solid form of water. When it melts it becomes a ....
 A gas C solid
 B liquid D powder

3 The .... of this paper is 20 centimetres and the length is 28 centimetres.
 A height C weight
 B width D length

4 The telephone was the best .... ever.
 A discover C discovery
 B invent D invention

5 We conduct experiments in a ....
 A theories C laboratory
 B research D scientific

6 Einstein's theory of relativity was a very important scientific ....
 A breakthrough C experiment
 B research D scientist

Computer technology

C Circle the correct option.

My desk

Last year I bought myself a laptop. For years I had had a (1) **desktop / table top** computer, but I decided I needed something smaller and more (2) **portable / moveable**. I love it. At home, I use it with a wireless (3) **mouse / key** as moving the arrow around the (4) **keyboard / screen** with the touch pad is tricky. It took a while to get used to the position of the (5) **keyboard / scanner** because it is so close to the screen, but I managed. I log on to the internet every day to check and send (6) **documents / emails** and spend about an hour a day (7) **online / internet**, surfing the Web. On my desk, I also have a (8) **scanner / printer**, which I use to copy pictures and documents. And of course a colour (9) **printer / scanner** which I use when I need to see documents and pictures on paper.

Phrasal verbs

D Match the phrasal verbs with their definitions.

1 hack into   a enter
2 set up   b illegally access
3 log into   c make a copy of
4 click on   d press
5 plug (sth) into e create
6 back up   f insert

E Complete with a phrasal verb from D in the correct form.

1 You need to type in your username and password to .... this website.
2 An outsider .... the company's private files last night.
3 My computer died this morning! Luckily I had .... all my files.
4 If you want to see another website, put the arrow here and .... this link.
5 Let me show you the website we .... at school.
6 To connect the mouse to the computer, ... it .... here.

4

Listening

A Look at the first set of pictures in E. What do you think the conversation will be about?

B Which words or phrases will you hear in this extract? Why?
- mobile phone
- GPS tracking device
- gadget
- email
- radio
- MP3 player
- expensive

C 🎧 Listen to the first extract. Were you right?

Steps to success
When you have to choose a picture to answer a question:
- look at each picture carefully before you listen.
- try to guess from the pictures what you will hear.

D Work in pairs. For the remaining sets of pictures:
- guess the topic of conversation.
- come up with three words or phrases you expect to hear.

E 🎧 You are going to hear six conversations. After each conversation, there is a question. For each question choose the correct picture, A, B or C.

What do you think the best and the worst inventions of all time are?

Speaking

A 🎧 Listen to two people having a discussion. What are they talking about?

B 🎧 Listen again and tick the expressions you hear.

Language chunks

Making suggestions
- How about … ? ☐
- What about … ? ☐
- We should … ☐
- We could … ☐
- Can I suggest … ? ☐
- Why don't we … ? ☐

Expressing agreement
- I agree. ☐
- Alright. ☐
- Yeah, OK. ☐
- Perfect! ☐
- Exactly! ☐
- Absolutely! ☐
- You're right. ☐
- That sounds like a good idea. ☐

Steps to success
- When you have a conversation, be polite. Show you are listening to your partner. Always **look** at your partner. Also **nod**, **agree** or **disagree**. Say things like *aha, right, yes*.

C 👥 Work in pairs. Suggest four things you could do together this weekend. Use expressions from the Language chunks box.

How about going to the cinema?

That sounds like a good idea.

D 👥 Work in pairs. Your school is organizing an exhibition of important inventions and scientific discoveries. There will also be a talk on the two most important inventions and/or discoveries. Look at the pictures and discuss these questions:
- What have the benefits of each discovery or invention been?
- Which two do you think the talk should be on?

microscope

electricity

mobile phone

TV

aeroplane

computer

Say it right!

final /r/

E 🎧 Listen to the way these sentences are read out. Pay special attention to the sound between the words in bold.
1. Technology makes life **far easier** than it used to be.
2. Modern cars are **more attractive** than old ones.
3. In the 20th century there **were a** number of important discoveries.
4. We have **better aeroplanes** today than we've ever had.

F Practise saying the sentences.

Grammar 2

 comparatives and superlatives

See page 143 for information about comparatives and superlatives.

Look at these sentences. Which ones compare two things? Which ones compare more than two things?

1 The aeroplane is *faster than* the car.
2 But the car is *more useful than* the aeroplane.
3 House alarms are not *as bad as* car alarms.
4 Car alarms are *the worst* invention ever.

Circle the correct option to complete these rules.

1 We use the words *more*, *less* or the ending –*er* to make **comparative / superlative** sentences.
2 We use *the most*, *the least* or the ending –*est* to make **comparative / superlative** sentences.
3 We use *than* after **comparative / superlative** adjectives or adverbs.
4 *Not as bad as* means **worse than / better than**.

A Find and correct the mistakes in these sentences.

1 Physics is more harder than maths.
2 A mobile phone is most convenient than a landline.
3 The washing machine is more easy to use than the dishwasher.
4 Old planes aren't as fast than new ones.
5 What is the farest you've ever ridden?
6 The best computers get the faster they get.
7 The least you know about this the better.
8 Of all the maths problems we had to solve, this one took the less amount of time.

B Complete these scientific facts. Use the correct form of the words in brackets.

1 Dinosaurs were by far .... (big) animals on Earth.
2 .... (fast) speed a falling raindrop can hit you is 29 km per hour.
3 The temperature at the centre of the Earth is much .... (high) the temperature on the surface.
4 No rock on Earth is .... (hard) as a diamond.
5 The more you know .... (strong) you grow.
6 A dog's sense of smell is 1,000 times .... (sensitive) than a human's.
7 To avoid catching someone else's cold, it is .... (safe) to kiss them than to shake their hand.
8 If you want to be safe, the plane is .... (good) way to travel.
9 The .... (mountainous) a region the more earthquakes it has.
10 The squid has by far .... (large) eyes of any animal on the planet.

C Complete these sentences. When you've finished, compare your answers with a partner.

1 My country is warmer ....
2 The best machine ever invented ....
3 The most amazing thing ....
4 The strangest experience ....
5 The older I get ....

Practise your English

A Read the text quickly. What does the writer think about the devices in the photographs?

Technology:
A blessing or a menace?

In the 20th century we saw many revolutionary (1) **inventions / events** that promised to improve our lives and to reduce the amount of work we do. The belief was that the more technology we allowed into our lives the (2) **better / best** our lives would be.

But many technological (3) **device / discoveries** have caused more problems than they have solved. It is an accepted fact that some (4) **household / homemade** appliances have increased rather than reduced the amount of work we do around the home. For example, the more kitchen appliances you have, the more work you do in the kitchen.

But this is not the only problem modern technology (5) **had / has** had. Some technology has turned out to be more of a nuisance (6) **than / as** a good thing. Look at the mobile phone. There is no doubt that when it was invented, the regular phone or landline (7) **is / was** an invention that made communication (8) **more easy / easier** and more effective. However, the mobile phone has crossed that line. In many situations it is an invasion of privacy and in others just plain rude. How many times have you (9) **been / being** sitting chatting with someone over coffee or dinner, when the person you're with receives a call? Instead of turning it off or just ignoring the call, they answer it. Clearly, you are not as important (10) **as / than** the caller. Let's stop fooling ourselves. Life has not improved in the way the technological revolution of the 20th century (11) **had promised / had been promising** it would. It has simply got (12) **worse / bad**.

B Read the text again and circle the correct option.

Have technical devices and applications made our lives better? Do they ever create problems?

C Complete the second sentence so that it has a similar meaning to the first sentence. Use the word given.

1 This device is not as good as that one.
THAN
That device .... this one.

2 Travelling by plane is expensive compared to travelling by train.
CHEAP
Travelling by plane is not .... travelling by train.

3 As I get older, I enjoy life more.
THE
The older I get .... life gets.

4 I started watching TV at nine and she came over at ten.
FOR
I had .... an hour when she came over.

5 I was born after the DVD player had been invented.
ALREADY
By the time I was born, ... been invented.

6 How wide is that door?
THE
What is .... that door?

D Choose the best answer.

1 You need to .... some internet sites before using them.
A hack into   C log into
B click on   D plug into

2 Laptops are more .... than desktop computers.
A portable   C moveable
B bigger   D mobile

3 There is a sun and eight planets in the Earth's ....
A solar system   C stars
B space   D planet

4 All living organisms are made up of tiny ....
A animals   C plants
B cells   D stones

5 The .... of these two phones is different. The one on the left is heavier.
A weight   C volume
B height   D length

Writing: Essay

A Which of the following do you do in your free time? Why?
- play sports
- watch TV
- play computer games
- read a book
- see friends

B Read this essay topic.

> Your school magazine has asked students for their opinion on computer games. Write an essay giving your opinion about the advantages and disadvantages of playing computer games. Write 120-180 words.

C Work in pairs. Brainstorm the advantages and disadvantages of playing computer games and make notes. Then discuss your ideas.

Advantages	Disadvantages

D Read the essay below and answer these questions.
- Were any of your ideas mentioned?
- What is the writer's opinion of playing computer games?

The internet has become widely available and computer games have become more popular than ever before. But is this a good thing? In my opinion it isn't, but others might disagree. On the one hand, playing computer games is fun. Young people work hard at school and need to take time off their studies to enjoy themselves. Furthermore, computer games can improve your thinking skills because you need to think and react quickly to situations in a game. On the other hand, many young people spend more time online playing games than doing sport or exercising. What is more, computer games can be addictive. This means that people are not in control of their habit and spend hours in front of a computer screen. As a result, they don't study or spend time with family and friends. In conclusion, because of the negative effects computer games can have, I think there is a real danger they can do more harm than good. Young people should avoid computer games, or control how much time they spend on them.

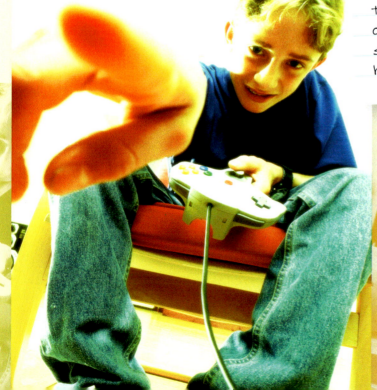

Skills development
Paragraphing

E Work in pairs. Decide how you would divide the essay into four paragraphs and complete the plan.

Paragraph topic	Ideas
1 Introduction	1 introduce topic 2 my opinion
2	1 .... 2 ....
3	1 .... 2 ....
4	1 sum up 2 ....

F Find expressions in the essay that signal:
1 the writer's opinion. *I think*
2 one side of the argument.
3 the other side of the argument.
4 the conclusion.
5 additional points.

Getting ideas

G Read this essay topic and look at the spidergram a student has begun. In pairs:
- discuss which points you agree with.
- add more ideas to the spidergram.
- decide what your opinion is on the use of mobile phones.

> Your school magazine has asked students for their opinion on mobile phones. Write an essay giving your opinion about the advantages and disadvantages of mobile phones.
> Write 120–180 words.

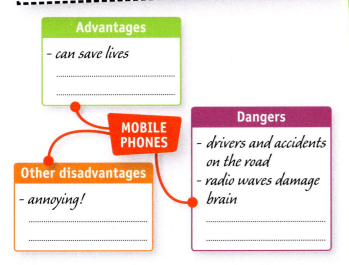

Advantages
- can save lives

MOBILE PHONES

Dangers
- drivers and accidents on the road
- radio waves damage brain

Other disadvantages
- annoying!

Planning and writing

H Complete the planner.

Steps to success
- When writing an essay, it is important to have a few good ideas.
- Develop your ideas with an explanation or an example.
- Don't include a lot of undeveloped ideas.

Paragraph 1: How will you introduce the topic?

Paragraph 2: What advantages will you include?

Paragraph 3: What disadvantages will you include?

Paragraph 4: What is your opinion?

I Write your essay. Use the Language chunks to help you.

Language chunks

Presenting ideas

In my opinion …
Most people agree that …
Some believe that …
… can often be …
I think …

quick check

Be sure to:
- follow your plan.
- use a few good ideas.
- develop your ideas with explanations or examples.
- organize your essay into four paragraphs.
- make your opinion clear.
- use a formal or neutral style.

Check your knowledge 2

A Choose the best answer.

1 .... is the study of the Earth, mountains, rocks and events such as earthquakes.
A Chemistry   B Geology   C Astronomy

2 Each school year is divided into three ....
A seasons   B months   C terms

3 Our local college offers .... courses such as car mechanics and hairdressing.
A vocational   B occupational   C academic

4 The air we breathe is a mixture of ....
A liquids   B gases   C solids

5 Do children have to wear .... at your school?
A uniforms   B costumes   C suits

6 Who was the first person to .... a dinosaur?
A discover   B invent   C conduct

7 A .... is a useful thing for copying documents and photos.
A printer   B screen   C scanner

8 My cousin goes to a very expensive .... school.
A individual   B state   C private

B Complete each sentence with a preposition.

1 Mrs Daunting still hasn't given us .... our history tests.

2 The earphones plug .... this socket just here.

3 I'd like to take .... a musical instrument, but I don't have the time.

4 If you click .... this link, you'll be taken to another page.

5 If you don't know the password, you won't be able to log .... the site.

6 When do schools break .... for the summer?

7 Can you hand .... these photocopies to the class please, Simone?

8 You need to set .... an account before you can buy anything from the website.

C Complete the sentences with words from the box.

already • as • just • more • most • still • than • yet

1 I think the internet has been more important .... the telephone for changing our lives.

2 Helen's only been coming to this class for a month, but she's .... made lots of friends.

3 I've .... made a pot of tea. Would you like some?

4 Learning online isn't as much fun .... learning in a classroom with others.

5 What do you think has been the .... important discovery ever?

6 Mike hasn't got his exam results .... , but he'll have them soon.

7 Alan is much .... determined to succeed this time.

8 You .... haven't met my new girlfriend, have you?

D Circle the correct option.

1 We don't usually go on holiday abroad, but last year we **have gone / went** to Poland.

2 I **have bought / bought** some cakes earlier. Do you want one?

3 Miles **hadn't met / hadn't been meeting** me for a long time.

4 I'm really exhausted. How many of these boxes **have we moved / have we been moving**?

5 I **haven't seen / didn't see** Mandy all day. I don't know where she could be.

6 We've **tidied / been tidying** the house all morning, but it still seems a mess.

7 When I was a very small child we didn't have much money, but we **had been / were** happy.

8 By the age of 15, Maurice Hobbs **had passed / passed** the exams for university.

E Complete the second sentence so that it has the same meaning as the first sentence. Use the word given.

1 Learning German is easier than I'd thought.
   AS
   Learning German .... I'd thought.

2 Ben always loses marks for his bad spelling.
   DOWN
   Ben .... for his bad spelling.

3 I've never had a computer as bad as this one.
   EVER
   This is the .... had.

4 Karen Young isn't allowed to come to school for two weeks.
   BEEN
   Karen Young .... for two weeks.

5 He wasn't listening to me.
   PAYING
   He .... to me.

6 Haven't you finished your homework yet?
   STILL
   Are you .... homework?

7 You should make a copy of those files.
   UP
   You .... files.

8 Do you know how long the Channel Tunnel is?
   THE
   Do you .... the Channel Tunnel?

9 Tom began guitar lessons when he was six and he's still taking them.
   SINCE
   Tom's been .... he was six.

10 The blue whale is the biggest animal that has ever lived.
   BEEN
   There .... animal than the blue whale.

F Choose the best answer to complete the text.

Hi Jed,
How are things? It's only Tuesday and I've (1) .... been having a difficult week. This morning I (2) .... a maths test and I don't think I've done very well. I (3) .... enough for it. What's (4) .... is that on Monday Mr Cole handed back our history essays and I hadn't done nearly as well (5) .... I had expected. I'll certainly have to work (6) .... next year if I want to pass my exams. Talking of work, I (7) .... to finish my chemistry homework for the last half an hour, but I'm finding it difficult to (8) .... attention. So I've (9) .... this message to you instead.
What's your news? When you last wrote you (10) .... hard on a science project about the (11) .... system. Have you finished it? I came across a website that might be useful for you. Click (12) .... this link: www.exploreastronomy.com. What do you think?
Speak soon,
Mandy

1
A already
B yet
C since
D still

2
A have done
B have been doing
C did
D had done

3
A haven't studied
B haven't been studying
C don't study
D hadn't studied

4
A bad
B worse
C good
D better

5
A than
B that
C of
D as

6
A tough
B tougher
C hard
D harder

7
A 've tried
B 've been trying
C 'd tried
D had been trying

8
A pay
B show
C give
D make

9
A been writing
B written
C wrote
D writing

10
A have worked
B have been working
C had worked
D had been working

11
A planet
B sun
C start
D solar

12
A in
B on
C at
D over

5 Holidays with a difference!

A Work in pairs. How much do you know about travel and transport? Do this quiz and find out.

1 Which word best completes this sentence? The plane is the safest way to ....
   a journey   c trip
   b travel   d voyage
2 Which is the odd one out?
   a bed and breakfast   c five-star hotel
   b guesthouse   d resort
3 Which form of transport cannot be used on roads?
   a a yacht   c a rickshaw
   b a lorry   d a semi-trailer
4 During peak hour traffic, you are likely to get stuck in a traffic ....
   a jam   c queue
   b line   d block
5 Which word or phrase is not connected with plane travel?
   a boarding pass   c jet lag
   b checking in   d driver

 Check your answers on page 165.

Reading

Steps to success
When a text has many sections, read it very quickly.
- **Scan** it to find out what type of text it is.
- **Skim** the different sections to locate the specific information you need.

B Scan the text. What type of text is it?
1 an advertisement   2 a brochure   3 an article

C Skim the text. Where do you find information about:
1 tour guides?
2 cost?
3 what you will see and hear on each tour?
4 comments from customers?

Walking tours of London

About us

Are you visiting London any time soon? Don't miss one of our walks. Samuel Pepys and Charles Dickens both liked nothing better than strolling around London to take in the sights and smells of the city. On our guided walks, we give you the chance to see as much of London as possible. Our walks will take you <u>off-the-beaten-track</u> and show you places that are not on the tourist trail. Our guides are all knowledgeable professionals, who will astonish and entertain you with interesting facts about the city and its history. Our tours are an experience you will never forget.

Our tours

1 Harry's London

5.00pm Fridays and Sundays
Harry Potter isn't just for kids. There are very real places behind the stories. On this walk you will visit many of them.
What is an Invisibility Cloak or a Philosopher's Stone? Where is the entrance door to The Ministry of Magic? By the end of this fantastic walk, Angela will have answered these questions and lots more. She will also <u>enlighten</u> you about all the legends, superstitions, and <u>tales</u> of ghosts and giants found in the series and take you to the locations where the movies were shot.
Guide: *Angela Peterson*

2 Ghosts of London

7.00pm Wednesdays and Saturdays

On this tour you are going to experience one of the most frightening nights of your life. The stories, the drama and the scenery will transport you to another time. You will visit dark backstreets and narrow alleyways and hear terrifying ghost stories. But be warned: stick close to the group, as you never know what could be <u>lurking</u> in the streets after dark. Bring a friend. After this tour, you will be too scared to <u>make your way back</u> to your hotel alone!

Guide: *Greg Jones*

3 Spies of London

3.30pm Tuesdays and Saturdays

Ever wondered what <u>inspired</u> Ian Fleming's James Bond books? On this walk you will find out about the world of secret agents and double agents. You will explore the secret world of MI5 and MI6. You will also hear real stories of Cold War London, visit places where spy world exchanges took place and where many mysterious meetings were held. By the end of this walk, you will have experienced for yourself what went on in London during the Cold War.

Guide: *Tom Sims*

4 London Murders

4.00pm Thursdays and Sundays

Enjoy being scared? If so, you're going to love the London Murders tour. On this <u>spine-chilling</u> walk, our guide will take you to all the <u>grim</u> places in London where horrific crimes took place. You will see where murderers like Jack the Ripper and the notorious Dr Crippen hung out and searched for their unsuspecting victims. Hear their stories, but beware. These crimes may have taken place in the past, but the terrifying atmosphere is still very much alive!

Guide: *George Macdonald*

'The Ghost tour of London was truly magnificent. The next time I'm in London I will be doing it again!' Sam Peters

'Anyone who does the Spies of London tour is going to learn about a side of London they never knew existed.' Annie Duncan

Price of our tours
Adults: £5
Children (under 16)**:** £3
Senior citizens: £3
Groups of four or more: £3.50 for adults and £2 for children

Walking Tours of London
Email: WTL@tours.com
Phone: 020 7767 8790
Fax: 020 7767 8791
www.walkingtourslondon.com

D Read the text and choose the best answer (A, B, C or D).

1 What is not true about the guides?
A They are all from London and know the city well.
B Their tours are full of surprises.
C They know a lot about the history of London.
D They will take you on unusual routes.

2 How much will it cost for two adults and two children to go on a tour?
A £11   B £12   C £16   D £20

3 Which tours have been influenced by novels?
A 1 and 2   B 1 and 4   C 1 and 3   D 2 and 4

4 Why should you go on the Ghost tour with someone else?
A It is more enjoyable with company.
B There is a special offer for two people.
C so that you have someone to go home with
D to have someone to talk to

5 Which places will you not see on the London Murders tour?
A where the murderers spent their time
B where the murderers lived
C where the murderers found their victims
D where the police found the victims

6 What did Charles Dickens like to do?
A go for walks with Samuel Pepys
B visit London when he could
C go sightseeing around London
D walk around London in a relaxed way

7 What does the Harry's London tour offer?
A a tour of the studio where the film was shot
B an opportunity to ask lots of questions
C stories for kids
D a visit to the places mentioned in the books

8 Who is Annie Duncan?
A a tour guide   C a tour organizer
B a character from history   D a satisfied customer

E Match the words and expressions underlined in the text with a definition.

1 extremely frightening ....
2 stories ....
3 hiding in a suspicious way ....
4 return ....
5 gave the idea ....
6 dark and depressing ....
7 not much visited by tourists ....
8 inform ....

Which of these tours would you like to go on? Why?

Grammar 1

✓ Check future forms

See page 144 for future forms.

A Complete with the correct form of the verb in brackets.

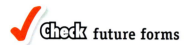

1 'How am I going to get home?' 'I .... (call) you a cab.'
2 Can I go on the school trip? I promise I .... (be) good.
3 When Tom gets a job, he .... (save) money to travel around the world.
4 The train .... (leave) at ten o'clock. You'll need to leave soon if you're going to make it.
5 The passengers are all disembarking. I think the ship .... (leave).
6 .... (you fly) to Germany from France or taking the train?

✓ Check future tenses for predictions

See page 144 for information about future tenses for making predictions.

Match these extracts with the use of each tense.

1 After this tour, you **will be too scared** to make your way back …
2 Enjoy being scared? … you're **going to love** the London Murders tour.
3 The next time I'm in London I **will be doing** it again!
4 By the end of this … walk, Angela **will have answered** these questions …

Which sentence talks about:
a a prediction we are sure about? ....
b a prediction based on what we know, believe, hear or see? ....
c a completed future action? ....
d an activity in progress at a certain time in the future? ....

B Circle the correct option.

1 If you want a different sort of holiday, you**'ll be loving** / **'ll love** India.
2 This time next month, we will **be lying** / **have lain** on a beach.
3 I didn't enjoy the long flight, but you **might** / **will** like it. But then again you **might** / **will** not.
4 I think going on more than one tour **will be** / **will have been** too tiring for us.
5 By the end of our trip we will **be visiting** / **have visited** five countries.
6 For the long weekend we**'re going** / **'ll go** on a skiing trip.

C Complete the second sentence so that it has the same meaning as the first sentence. Use the word given.

1 They've predicted rain for this weekend.
TO
It .... this weekend.
2 There's a chance we'll go camping this summer.
MAY
We .... this summer.
3 This year I plan to walk to school.
AM
This year .... to school.
4 I promise to be good on the school trip.
WILL
I .... on the school trip.
5 We're leaving any minute now.
ABOUT
We .... leave.
6 Next week I'm flying to the Bahamas.
WILL
This time next week .... to the Bahamas.
7 Would you like me to carry your suitcase?
SHALL
.... your suitcase?
8 My brother is going to travel around South America before starting university.
INTENDS
My brother .... South America before starting university.

Quick chat

What are you going to do on your next school holiday?
What will you be doing in five years' time?
Where will you have travelled to by the time you're 30?

Vocabulary

Sights

A Think of an example of each of these sights in any country around the world.

1 ancient ruins/archaeological site ....
2 castle ....
3 church/cathedral ....
4 monument ....
5 museum ....
6 palace ....

Accommodation

B Complete with words or phrases from the boxes.

a Hotels

> double • en suite • guests • luxury • room • stay

Deciding where to (**1**) .... when on holiday is not always easy. It depends on personal preference and of course on what you can afford. By far the most expensive accommodation is a(n) (**2**) .... hotel or a five-star hotel. The price of a hotel (**3**) .... will also depend on whether it is a(n) (**4**) .... room or single room, whether it has a(n) (**5**) .... or whether you will need to share the bathroom with other (**6**) ....

b Apartments

> alone • in • out • self-catering

You will find that (**1**) .... apartments are a good option if you're not travelling (**2**) .... They come equipped with kitchens, which means you can save money by cooking and eating (**3**) .... rather than eating (**4**) .... in restaurants.

c Other alternatives

> bed • book • campsite • rates • tent • visiting • youth hostel

If you don't mind roughing it, then staying in a (**1**) .... on a (**2**) .... is a good option. Of course, this is not an option if you're (**3**) .... a city. The cheapest accommodation in a city is usually a (**4**) .... , but they offer very few services. You will also need to take a sleeping bag. It may be better to pay a little extra and (**5**) .... a room in a guesthouse. They are more personal and offer (**6**) .... and breakfast at lower (**7**) .... than hotels.

Travel and transport

C Which means of transport are private ☺ and which are public ☹? Add some more to the list.

bike/bicycle .... coach ....
motorbike .... sailing boat ....
taxi/cab .... ferry/ship ....
the Underground .... yacht ....

D Which means of transport can you:

drive? ....
ride? ....
catch? ....
get on/off? ....
get in/out of? ....
sail? ....

E Match a word from each list to make as many compound nouns as you can.

bike	bike
bus	country
camp	helmet
foreign	hostel
guided	ride
hotel	room
motor	site
private	station
public	stop
railway	ticket
train	tour
walking	transport
youth	

F Circle the correct option.

1 This year we're going **abroad** / **foreign country**.
2 You've just **lost** / **missed** the bus.
3 Paris has a lot of **sights** / **sightseeing** to see. You'll spend your whole trip **sights** / **sightseeing**.
4 Last year, we went **to** / **on** holiday abroad. We went **to** / **on** Morocco. This year we're **spending** / **going** our holiday at home.
5 Did you come here **on** / **by** foot or **on** / **by** bus?
6 Yesterday my sister **set off** / **started off** on her trip around the world.

Quick chat

- How do you usually get around?
- What's your favourite/least favourite means of transport? Why?

5

Listening

A What do you know about Australia? Answer these questions.
1 What is the capital city?
2 What sights is it famous for?
3 What is the climate like?
4 What animals do you associate with Australia?

Steps to success
- If the questions are not on the page with the options, read carefully through the options and try to predict what the questions will be about.
- Each extract from the interview is short so listen carefully.

B You are going to hear an interview about a trip to the Australian Outback. Before you listen, read the options for each question and answer.
- What information about the trip do you expect to hear in each section?
- What questions do you think you might hear after each section?
- Write possible questions for each group of options.

1 ....?
A the busiest parts of Australia
B the greenest parts of Australia
C the driest parts of Australia

2 ....?
A Perth
B Kakadu National Park
C Darwin

3 ....?
A the waterfalls
B the varied landscapes
C the desert

4 ....?
A in Darwin
B in Kakadu National Park
C in Kimberley

5 ....?
A The rivers were named after an English explorer.
B There are many alligators in the rivers.
C An English explorer thought the crocodiles were alligators.

6 ....?
A The camels were brought there by early explorers.
B The camels have always been there.
C The camels find it too hot.

C 🎧 Now listen to the interview. Choose the correct answer for each question.

Have you ever been on an exciting holiday? What would make a holiday exciting for you?

54

Speaking

A 🎧 Listen to three students talking. Which of the following are they talking about?

a Where they're going on their next holiday.
b How they're going to entertain students from another country.

B 🎧 Listen again and tick the ways of expressing uncertainty they use.

Language chunks

Expressing uncertainty:

Giving opinions
- Yes, I suppose you're right. ☐
- I'm not sure … ☐
- They might like that … ☐
- They may not … ☐
- I don't know, I think … ☐
- Maybe … ☐
- Perhaps … ☐

Making tentative suggestions
- I suppose we could … ☐
- We could …, couldn't we? ☐
- They can … ☐
- (Perhaps) we could … ☐
- It might be better to … ☐

Steps to success
- Use expressions like the ones in Language chunks to show others that you are not sure about something.
- Modals like **might**, **may**, **can** and **could** make opinions and suggestions sound less 'strong'. As a result, you are easier to agree with and more persuasive.

C 👥 Read the task below. Then work in pairs to come up with a solution to the problem.

Your school will be hosting four students from another country for three days (Friday, Saturday and Sunday). They have never been to your country before. They will be staying in a hotel. Your teacher has asked you to come up with ideas to entertain them. Use the information below to create a programme that will satisfy everyone for the three days. Make notes in the table below.

Christina 15
Loves: shopping, the beach, dancing, sightseeing, trying new food
Hates: museums

George 15
Loves: watching sport, skateboarding, swimming, fast food, amusement parks
Hates: shopping and sightseeing

Anna 14
Loves: amusement parks, meeting people, shopping, dancing
Hates: lying in the sun

Tony 15
Loves: sports, sightseeing, fast food, dancing, meeting people
Hates: shopping and museums

IDEAS
- ✓ Walks
- ✓ Museum visits
- ✓ Sightseeing (monuments, churches, castles, archaeological sites)
- ✓ Shopping
- ✓ Eating
- ✓ Visits to the seaside
- ✓ Sporting events

	Friday	Saturday	Sunday
Morning			
Afternoon			
Evening			

Say it right!

D Which of these words rhyme with *coach*?

1 coat
2 boat
3 rope
4 abroad
5 go
6 goat
7 hot
8 road
9 broad
10 board

E 🎧 Now listen and check.

F Practise saying the words. Think up two more words that rhyme with *coach*.

Grammar 2

✓ Check time expressions with future forms

See page 145 for information about time expressions: *as soon as*, *when*, *until* and *before*.

Circle the correct option.
1 I'll phone Heather *as soon as* I **get** / **will get** home.
2 I'll let you know what happens *when* **I've spoken** / **'ll speak** to him.
3 I won't stop using my car *until* the public transport system **improves** / **will improve**.
4 Pick up your rubbish *before* you **leave** / **will leave** the park.

Do the sentences refer to the past, present or future?

A Complete the email with the correct form of a verb from the box.

call • email • get • leave • see

Dear Mum and Dad,
Hope you're well. Venice was gorgeous! Today we're leaving for Florence. As soon as we (1) .... there, we'll be having a long hot shower – we haven't had a proper shower for a week!! We're exhausted, but we won't stop until we (2) .... all the places we can visit with our InterRail passes! Before we (3) .... for Rome, we're thinking of popping over to Pisa for a day – it's only an hour from Florence by train!
We (4) .... you when we get to Rome.
We (5) .... you again before then.
Love,
Gill and Fran

✓ Check question tags

See page 145 for information about question tags.

B Complete the question tag.
1 You couldn't give us a lift, ... ?
2 You're not flying, ... ?
3 You told him how to get here, ... ?
4 Tamsin's afraid of flying, ... ?
5 Rob's been to the States, ... ?

C Rewrite the second sentence with a question tag.
1 I don't think you agree with me.
You .... ?
2 Surely you're not going to walk all the way!
You're .... ?
3 Could you open the door for me?
You .... ?
4 Don't you think Mike drives too fast?
Mike .... ?
5 Don't you agree that the walking tour was great?
The walking tour .... ?

✓ Check indirect questions

See page 145 for information about indirect questions.

Which question in each pair is an indirect question?
1 a Could you please tell me how much the holiday package costs?
  b How much does the holiday package cost?
2 a Do you know what time the plane is expected to land?
  b When is the plane expected to land?

D Complete each sentence so that it means the same as the sentence before it.
1 What kind of room would you like?
Can you tell me .... ?
2 Where are you going on your next holiday?
Do you know .... ?
3 Is an en suite important?
Can I ask you .... ?
4 What time does the tour begin?
I wonder if ....
5 How much will it cost?
Could you tell me .... ?

Practise your English

A Read the text quickly. Which means of transport does Nick Hunter think we will use in the future?

Getting around in the future

The different means of transport we use in our day-to-day lives have come a long way. Just think, a little over 100 years ago many forms of (**1**) **private / public** transport – the motorbike, the car, the bicycle – would have been inconceivable. But today most households have at least one car and many have a motorbike or a bicycle. But what's in store for us in the future? What will we (**2**) **have driven or ridden / be driving or riding** 50 years from now? We asked Nick Hunter, a futurist, whose job it is to predict future technological innovations to tell us his views.

'If we take into consideration the problem with fossil fuels, the next big change (**3**) **is going to be / is about to be** the use of more environmentally friendly cars. In fact, within the next 20 years, most people (**4**) **will have replaced / are replacing** the petrol powered cars we're driving today with a car that (**5**) **will have / will** run on alternative energy sources such as electricity or even solar power.

Another type of car we (**6**) **might be driving / are**

driving very soon, is a "smart" car. When our streets (**7**) **are / will be** fully automated, which I'm sure they will be soon, drivers with "smart" cars (**8**) **will be able to relax / will be relaxing** while their cars detect magnets placed along specialized highways. The cars (**9**) **will / are about to** run automatically as the highway computer system calculates the flow of traffic, resulting in steady, safe transportation.

Looking further into the future, it's hard to know for sure. We (**10**) **could / are** very well be (**11**) **driving / riding** cars that can also fly in 100 years' time or perhaps (**12**) **driving / riding** hover bikes with jet engines and propellant tanks in place of wheels!'

Quick chat
How realistic do you think Nick Hunter's predictions are? Why/Why not?

B Read the text again and circle the correct option.

C Choose the best answer.

1 I wonder .... let me know how much the tickets are.
A if could you C what you could
B you could D if you could

2 I'll call you as soon as I .... at the airport.
A arrive C arrived
B will arrive D will be arriving

3 What time .... the next coach leave?
A do C will
B does D did

4 In the future, will we be driving as much as we do now or will we be getting around .... foot?
A in C on
B by D with

5 I .... the tram at eight o'clock this morning.
A drove C got
B sailed D caught

6 You live right opposite the railway, ... ?
A don't you C aren't you
B doesn't it D are you

7 I'm .... holiday at the moment.
A at C in
B to D on

8 Next year, they'll be going to Italy, ... ?
A will it C aren't they
B are they D won't they

9 Will you spend your holidays .... again this year?
A board C foreign country
B abroad D another country

10 In Paris, ... is called the metro.
A the underground C the bus stop
B the train D public transport

5

Writing: Formal letter/email asking for information

A What kind of information would you need to know before you booked a cruise holiday?

B Now read this advertisement and the notes made on it. What information does this person want to know about the cruise?

- Which?
- Ask for more details.
- Ask about dates.
- What are they?

Skills development

Content, organization, linking and style

C Read the email and underline the parts that contain the information from the four notes. Are they all in the same paragraph?

D Complete the email with the missing linking words.

> also • finally • first • regarding dates

E Underline all the indirect questions the Contis use. Why have they used them?

Dear Ms Papadaki,

We are writing to enquire about the four-day Greek Island cruise your company is offering. My family and I are interested in going on this cruise, but we were wondering if you could answer a few of our queries first.

(1) ...., your advertisement states that we will visit four Greek islands. Could you please let us know which ones? We are particularly interested in visiting Santorini and were wondering if this is one of the islands we will be visiting. Could you (2) .... let us know which archaeological sites we will visit and if you offer free guided tours?

(3) ...., my family and I are interested in travelling in the first week of July. Could we ask if you have a cruise that week? If so, please let us know the exact dates.

(4) ...., in your advertisement you mention that you have special discount rates. Would you mind telling us what these rates are exactly?

Thank you in advance for your help.

Yours sincerely,

Emily and Giuseppe Conti

F This email was written by someone else. What's wrong with it? Use these ideas to help you.
- style of language
- content
- organization
- linking
- beginning and ending

Dear Helen,
My friend and I want to go on one of your cruises, but we have some questions. Which islands will we visit? Santorini will be one of them, won't it? What about the archaeological sites? Which ones will we visit? We want to go on a cruise in June. What dates will it leave on?
Please get back to me ASAP.
Bye for now,
Rhona

Planning and writing

G Now read this task and complete the planner below. Use indirect questions when asking your questions.

For example?
Ask for details.
Ask how much.
How early?

Youth Camp – Wilderness Survival

Come on a three-day wilderness survival camp for 14-18 year olds. We specialize in wilderness survival education. On our camps, we will teach you the skills you need to survive in the natural world.

You will also enjoy a range of sport and activities. We have choices for all tastes.

We have special rates for those who book early!

For enquiries, contact: Tom Maynard • Youth Camp – Wilderness Survival
PO Box 367 • Godalming, Surrey, GU7 1JF • United Kingdom
TEL and FAX: (+44) 01483 429379 • email: YCWSC@btconnect.com

Steps to success

Paragraphs make letters or emails easier for the reader to follow.
- Organize your letter or email into four paragraphs based on the four 'notes' and link them with simple linking words.
- Use indirect questions to ask for information in a polite way.

H Write your email or letter in 120-150 words. Use the Language chunks to help you.

Language chunks

Formal letters/emails
I am / We are writing to enquire about …
Your advertisement states …
In your advertisement you mention …
Thank you in advance for your help.
Dear Mr/Ms …
Yours sincerely,

Planner

Start your email / letter: Dear .... ,

Paragraph 1: reason for writing ....

Paragraph 2: first question and anything else you'd like to say regarding this note ....

Paragraph 3: second question and anything else you'd like to say regarding this note ....

Paragraph 4: remaining questions ....
express thanks ....

Sign off: Yours sincerely, / Yours faithfully, …

quick check

Be sure to:
- include all four notes.
- write at least four paragraphs.
- talk about one topic/note only in each paragraph.
- use linking words to link your paragraphs.
- use a formal style.
- use indirect questions to be polite.
- begin and end the letter/email appropriately.

6 Serious fun

Pokemon
Johnny Depp
Pablo Picasso
J K Rowling
Coldplay
Dive in!

A Work in pairs. What do/did these people do? Can you name any of their films, books, songs, paintings or games?

New titles to look out for ...

The Dragon's Cage

Kip promised he would never go into the forest alone. Ever since he was a small child, his parents had warned him not to. But when Viceroy, his beloved bird, escapes its cage and disappears into the forest, Kip goes in search. So begins an incredible voyage and Kip discovers that Viceroy is no ordinary bird.

'An amazing **debut** novel. This is going to become a classic.'
Rob Burlington, The Times

'A truly **gripping** story. I read through it in two nights!'
Jack Robinson, The Daily Scandal

Brave New Worlds Publishing
Ages 7-12
RRP £10.99

Winner of the **2009** Guardian prize for Best First Novel

Tales of Utter Terror

Thirteen terrifying stories of terror for teenagers by the world's greatest **authors**. This new edition of *Tales of Utter Terror* includes classics such as Edgar Allan Poe's *The Black Cat*, plus stories from new writers like Kelly Drew and Mike Smith. There are also two newly translated works by the popular Scandinavian horror writer Karen Christensen.

'I was reading this book alone one night and had to stop. If you're easily scared this is definitely not a book for you!' Vincent Rice, Choice Magazine.

Albatross Books
RRP £12.00

Reading

B You are going to read some book blurbs. Quickly read them. What kind of books are they? Choose from the list.

- children's literature
- children's picture book
- fairy tale
- fantasy
- horror
- mystery
- romance
- science
- science fiction

I Won't Fly

③

The Robinsons are all set for a fantastic holiday in the sun. Robbie and Rose just can't wait. Their tickets are bought, their bags are packed, their plane is waiting ... , but oh dear! All of a sudden Rose realizes she's afraid of flying. She refuses to get on the plane. Her family try to persuade her that flying is safe, but nothing will change her mind. Then Captain Johns suggests doing something very special!

The latest in the Smarties Prize winning Robbie and Rose books sees the twins in a summer holiday adventure. As ever, the book teaches young readers about the world around them through a **delightful** story. With line drawings by Jane Moston.

'I haven't read a better children's book in years!' Ken Graham, The Guardian.

'My kids are reading their 12th Robbie and Rose book and they're enjoying it as much as their first.' Helen Murray, Good Housekeeping Magazine

Walton Young Scholars: Range (ages 6-8)
Confident Readers

RRP £4.99

DARE TO DISCOVER:
Electricity

Another voyage of discovery with Professor Dick Dynamo and his companion, Fritz. This time, Dynamo and Fritz are your guides into the world of amazing amps, crazy currents and vicious volts. Along the way you'll get to know why a conductor is more than a mad man at the front of an orchestra. You'll also learn the shocking truth about electric eels and the incredible, but true, story of a man struck seven (!) times by lightning. Read on if you dare.

Ages 10-14
Ballistic Publications

'A fantastic dose of real learning that kids will swallow whole thanks to Francis' witty prose and Monroe's hilarious colour **illustrations**.' Julia Jones, Goodbye Magazine

RRP £9.99

④

The Call

A week ago Harriet received a strange and disturbing call from her boyfriend, Alex. But the next day Alex denied making any calls. He seemed cool and distant ... not the Alex that Harriet knows and loves. Things **take a sinister turn** when the police visit Harriet as part of a murder investigation. Their main suspect is ... Alex. Why have they accused Alex? Harriet is sure there has been a mistake. What has happened to Alex and what was the meaning of that call?

Ages 14+
Hobber & Hobber
RRP £14.99

'500 pages of pure excitement!' Ken Bodd, Liverpool Echo

'Such vivid characters! You will not forget them for a long time after reading.' Dan Lewis, The Observer

⑤

Steps to success
- Skim the texts very quickly to find specific information.
- Read each question and think carefully about the type of information you need to find.
- Does the question ask you to compare prices, ages or other numbers? Go straight to the information you need.

C Now choose the best answer (A, B, C or D).

1 You want to buy a book for your teenage sister for Christmas. She often reads writers from around the world. She doesn't like long novels. Which book is best for her?
A 2   B 3   C 4   D 5

2 Which books include pictures?
A 1 and 2   B 2 and 3   C 3 and 4   D 4 and 5

3 Which books are part of a series of similar books?
A 1 and 2   B 2 and 3   C 3 and 4   D 4 and 5

4 Which books cost over £9.00, but under £12.00?
A 1 and 4   B 1 and 5   C 2 and 4   D 2 and 5

5 You want to buy a book for your best friend's 14th birthday. She loves fantasy books and mystery books. Which book will you buy?
A 1   B 2   C 4   D 5

6 Which books are about a journey?
A 1 and 3   B 1 and 4   C 2 and 3   D 2 and 5

7 A teenage friend of yours doesn't read very much, but has a good sense of humour. He's not so interested in fiction. Which book would you buy for his birthday?
A 2   B 3   C 4   D 5

8 Which books have won an award?
A 1 and 2   B 1 and 3   C 3 and 4   D 4 and 5

D Match the words and expressions in bold in the text with a definition.

1 become serious and frightening ....
2 exciting ....
3 first ....
4 lovely ....
5 pictures ....
6 writers ....

Which of these books would you like to read? Why? What's your favourite form of entertainment? Why?

6

Grammar 1

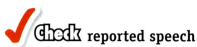 reported speech

See page 146 for information about reported speech.

Complete the table. How do the tenses change?

Direct speech	Reported speech
'............................ their 12th Robbie and Rose book.'	She said <u>her kids were reading</u> their 12th Robbie and Rose book.
'I <u>haven't read</u> a better children's book in years.'	He said .... a better children's book in years.

A Circle the correct option.

'My mum is writing a novel.'
1 Angie told me that her mum **wrote / was writing** a novel.

'We were playing *Tomb Raider*.'
2 Paul admitted that they **have been / had been** playing *Tomb Raider*.

'Have you ever been to an art gallery?'
3 Our teacher asked us if **we had / had we** ever been to an art gallery.

'This will be my last film.'
4 He warned us that this **had been / would be** his last film.

'Does James like classical music?'
5 Olga wondered **if James liked / does James like** classical music.

B What did they actually say? Write the direct speech in the speech bubbles.

1 ....

John claimed that I had broken his CD.

2 ....

Anne told me she had seen that movie two years ago.

3 ....

She asked me if I liked her new book.

4 ....

Mum asked me what we'd seen at the theatre the night before.

C 🎧 Anne and Tim are singers in a band. Listen to an interview with a journalist and report what they say.

1 Tim said ....
2 Tim said ....
3 Tim said ....
4 Anne said ....
5 Anne said ....

D Yesterday the celebrity actress Mavis Stilton met the press. What did the reporters ask her? Report the questions.

What do you do in your free time?

1 They asked her what ....

Do you ever watch your own movies?

2 ....

Who's your favourite actor?

3 ....

Is Mavis your real name?

4 ....

Where did you go on holiday last summer?

5 ....

Do you like London?

6 ....

Vocabulary

Entertainment

A Organize these words into two groups. Use a dictionary to help you.

audience • choir • composer • conductor • exhibition
keyboards • landscape • portrait • sculptor • sculpture

At the concert hall

At the art gallery

B Find the odd word out. Use a dictionary to help you.

1 actors	cast	credits
2 outfit	costume	make-up
3 rehearse	practise	practice
4 author	writer	composer
5 rehearsal	practise	practice
6 plot	set	story
7 role	stage	part
8 location	setting	cast

C Complete the sentences with words from B.

1 The .... includes Brad Pitt and Johnny Depp.
2 The actress in the lead .... wore a beautiful ....
3 His last movie was filmed on .... in Antarctica.
4 I found the .... hard to follow.
5 J K Rowling is my brother's favourite .... He's read all her books.
6 Our final .... was great. We were ready for the show.

D Complete the text with words from the box.

actor • actress • awards • comedies • criticized
director • dramatic • performances

Everyone has heard of the Oscars, the (**1**) .... for the year's best films, but have you heard about the Razzies? These are awarded to the worst movies of the year.
Razzie record-holders include Sylvester Stallone. Stallone's (**2**) .... have won many prizes for Worst (**3**) .... Funny man Eddie Murphy has made millions laugh with his (**4**) .... , but he's a Razzie record-holder too. In 2007 the comic received a record three awards for his unimpressive acting in *Norbit*.
But Razzies aren't only for actors. In 2007 Chris Siverston won the Worst (**5**) .... award for making the film *I Know Who Killed Me*. Since most stars don't like to be (**6**) .... , only a few winners have ever collected their Razzie awards. However, in 2004 Halle Berry accepted the Worst (**7**) .... award for her role as Catwoman. She gave a very (**8**) .... acceptance speech!

Phrasal verbs with *out*

E Match the phrasal verbs with the definitions.

1	bring out	a	be careful
2	carry out	b	become in the end
3	go out	c	have a relationship
4	look out	d	do
5	sell out	e	express your opinion
6	sort out	f	have no tickets available
7	speak out	g	organize
8	turn out	h	publish

F Complete with a phrasal verb from E in the correct form.

1 Has J K Rowling .... a new novel?
2 This book .... to be quite good after all.
3 Some film stars .... about poverty.
4 Stunt men .... dangerous tricks.
5 The newspapers are full of stories about who celebrities are .... with.
6 The Robbie Smith concert has totally .... !
7 .... the CDs! They are in a mess.
8 .... ! You're going to fall over.

Who would you award these Razzies to?
Worst Actor\Actress \ Movie

6

Listening

A Work in pairs. Look at the pictures. What could the connection be between them?

B 🎧 You are going to hear a radio interview about a famous art award called the Turner Prize. You will hear the speakers mention the following artists. Listen and match the names with the pictures from A.

Cathy Wilkes ....
Tracey Emin ....
Martin Creed .... , ...
Simon Starling ....
Mark Wallinger ....

Steps to success

- For multiple choice questions, first try to think of your own answer for each question.
- Then, compare your own answer with the options you are given. Which option is closest to your own answer?

C Work in pairs. Read these questions about the interview and discuss possible answers.

1 Why do people argue about the Turner Prize?
2 What does Dave think about Cathy Wilkes' art?
3 How does Dave feel about the fact that *My Bed* did not win the prize?
4 How much money did Martin Creed win?
5 How did Simon Starling sail down the River Rhine?
6 Why hasn't Mike got a favourite winner?
7 What was special about Mark Wallinger's winning entry for the 2006 prize?

D 🎧 Now listen again and choose the best answer for each question.

1
A because it costs so much money
B because the entries are controversial
C because the competition is unfair

2
A He likes it.
B He thinks it's boring.
C He thinks it isn't art.

3
A He is surprised.
B He is disappointed.
C He is glad.

4
A £19,000   B £20,000   C £25,000

5
A in a boat   B in a shed   C in a bed

6
A He thinks they were all bad.
B He thinks they were all good.
C He likes too many of them.

7
A Using video was a new idea.
B It was funny.
C It used animals.

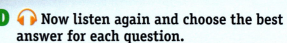

What do you think about the Turner Prize? Is it nonsense?
Do you like modern art or do you prefer more traditional art?

Speaking

A These cards show information needed for two students to take part in a roleplay activity. Look at the cards. What is the roleplay about?

Student A:

You are a journalist working in London for the magazine *Celebrity World*. Your editor has asked you to interview one of these stars for the next edition. Both stars have the same manager.

First
Speak to the stars' manager and find out this information:
- the amount of time they can give
- will they travel to London
- their interview fee
- any special news they want to talk about

Then
Choose the best star to interview. Explain why you made your choice.

Chuck Warren   Whitney Tears

Student B:

You are the manager of the celebrities below. A journalist wants to arrange an interview with one of them. Answer the journalist's questions with the information you have about each celebrity. Then ask who he/she would like to speak to and why.

Chuck Warren
- has time for a ten-minute interview
- will only speak over the phone
- charges $1,000 per interview
- recent news: will star in a new thriller next year

Whitney Tears
- has time for a half-hour interview
- will be in London next week
- charges $1,500 per interview
- recent news: is getting married to a famous film star

B If you were the journalist, which star would you choose to interview and why? Work in pairs. Tell each other what you think.

C Now listen to two students acting out this roleplay activity. Which star does Student A choose to interview?

D The Language chunks box includes some ways of politely asking questions and saying yes or no to a request. Listen again and tick the expressions you hear.

Language chunks

Polite questions
- I was wondering if …
- I'd like to know if …
- Could you tell me … ?
- Would you mind telling me … ?
- Do you happen to know … ?

Polite ways to say yes
- Of course.
- Absolutely.
- Certainly.

Polite ways to say no
- I'm afraid not.
- Unfortunately, …
- I'm sorry, but …

Steps to success
- Remember that in formal situations you need to ask and answer questions politely. One way to ask politely is to use indirect questions. However, you don't need to make every question an indirect one!

E Work in pairs. Now it's your turn to do a roleplay. Student A, your role card is on page 165. Student B, your role card is on page 175. When you've finished swap roles.

F How do we say the underlined sounds in these words? Put the words in the correct column.

ba<u>dge</u>   ma<u>tch</u>   bu<u>s</u>   bu<u>sh</u>   <u>J</u>une   <u>t</u>une   <u>sh</u>e   <u>s</u>ee

1 /dʒ/ ca<u>ge</u>	2 /tʃ/ chur<u>ch</u>	3 /ʃ/ <u>s</u>tation	4 /s/ fa<u>ce</u>

G Listen, check and repeat.

Grammar 2

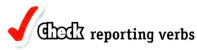 reporting verbs

See page 147 for information about reporting verbs.

A Circle the correct option.
1 Jane **told** / **said** / **asked** me she had spent £5,000 on a painting!
2 We **told** / **said** / **asked** if we could see the film again.
3 Mike **told** / **said** / **asked** that he enjoyed your book a lot.
4 Jessica **told** / **said** / **asked** Jim that she loved reading romantic novels.
5 I **told** / **said** / **asked** that I didn't want to go to the cinema tonight.
6 Nelly **told** / **said** / **asked** me if I'd seen the last episode of *Lost 5*.

B Read the news story quickly ignoring the gaps. Why was the artist sent to prison?

C Now read the news story below again and complete with reporting verbs from the box.

added • admitted • asked • claimed • denied
said • told • warned

D Listen and choose a reporting verb for what the people say.

a admit .... e deny ....
b advise .... f promise ....
c beg .... g refuse ....
d complain .... h threaten ....

E Report what the people say using reporting verbs from the box.

admit • invite • promise • complain
suggest • warn

1 'I've never read a book in my life,' said Alex.
....

2 'There's nothing good on TV tonight,' said Karen.
....

3 'Why don't we go to the theatre for a change?' Mike said.
....

4 'Don't worry. I'll get you tickets for the show,' George said.
....

5 'Don't go to see the new James Bond film. It's terrible,' said Mandy.
....

6 'Would you like to come to the exhibition with me?' Angela said.
....

Five years for fooling the art world

A 47-year-old Bolton artist has been jailed for five years. In court, Bob Harris (1) .... that he was guilty. However, Judge Sir Toby Knuckles (2) .... that Harris must be punished. He (3) .... that Harris had wasted his great skills to deceive instead of making an honest living. Harris' skills certainly were impressive. His forgeries ranged from fake ancient Roman sculptures to copies of modern landscape masterpieces. Bolton Council, for example, agreed to pay Harris £400,000 for a fake Egyptian statue. Today, Ned Bungle, who bought the statue for the Council, (4) .... that he should have been more careful. However, lawyers (5) .... the court that Bungle was not the only one deceived by the fakes.
The Bolton-born artist (6) .... he had inherited the 'masterpieces' from his grandparents. He had hoped to sell a fake portrait to London's Tate Gallery, but an expert realized it was not authentic. When police (7) .... him if he knew the works were forgeries, Harris refused to admit anything. Judge Knuckles (8) .... galleries not to be fooled by artists like Harris in the future.

Quick chat
Was Bob Harris an artist or a criminal? What do you think? Would you buy a fake work of art if it looked good?

Practise your English

A Read the text quickly and answer these questions.
- What is being reviewed?
- Who are these people: Graham Swanky, Neil Dibble, Miriam Figg?
- What is the critic's opinion?

When I spoke last week to the (**1**) .... (ACT) Graham Swanky about his new show, *Wolf*, he didn't seem very happy. 'It's a great play,' said Swanky, 'but our (**2**) .... (REHEARSE) aren't going well.' His words surprised me, so I decided to go to the Garrick Theatre, where the show is currently playing. The play is a (**3**) .... (COMIC) based on the comic novel by J J Keller. I was (**4**) .... (IMPRESS) by the novel when I read it. I didn't laugh once. I found the (**5**) .... (ILLUSTRATE) on the cover the only funny thing about the book. The play, however, is (**6**) .... (DELIGHT). The cast is generally very strong, and Swanky's (**7**) .... (PERFORM) was excellent. The only weak member was Neil Dibble. I saw him singing last year in the (**8**) .... (MUSIC) *Bananas*. He may have a good voice, but his acting is hopeless. Nevertheless, *Wolf* turned out to be a great success. The music, by world-class (**9**) .... (COMPOSE) Morris Batt, is perfect. The (**10**) .... (DIRECT) Miriam Figg has done a fantastic job. Graham Swanky needn't have worried!

B Read the text again. Use the word in brackets to form one word that fits each gap.

What was the last play or film you saw? Did you like it? Why/Why not?

C Complete the second sentence so that it has a similar meaning to the first sentence. Use the word given.

1 Philip Pullman has published a new novel.
OUT
Philip Pullman .... a new novel.

2 'Have you ever seen a James Bond movie,' Greg asked me.
HAD
Greg asked .... ever seen a James Bond movie.

3 Could you organize these books for me?
OUT
Could .... for me?

4 Do you know what happened in the last episode?
MIND
Would .... what happened in the last episode?

5 This story is full of drama and excitement.
AND
This is a very .... exciting story.

6 'I was reading my book all morning,' said Ann.
SHE
Ann said .... her book all morning.

7 I rehearse twice a day.
TWO
I have .... a day.

8 'Don't touch my book!' said Jessica.
WARNED
Jessica .... her book.

D Choose the best answer.

1 All the papers .... Angelina's new film.
A critic   C critical
B criticize   D critically

2 She asked me .... be at the cinema.
A if Sarah would C would Sarah
B will Sarah   D shall Sarah

3 I asked her .... she liked art galleries.
A does   C what
B whether   D would

4 I wanted to go to the 50 Cent concert, but all the tickets are .... out.
A bought   C found
B given   D sold

5 James .... that he had lost my CDs.
A admitted   C refused
B promised   D ordered

6 Mary .... me that she loved the film.
A told   C asked
B said   D invited

6

Writing: A story (1)

A Work in pairs. Look at these pictures and think of a story that connects them. Then tell the class your story.

B Quickly read the story. Is it the same as yours?

A
This story happened (1) .... when I was only ten months old.

B
It was my first ever Christmas day. My brothers had opened their presents (2) .... that morning and now they were playing with them. My mum was getting the Christmas dinner ready. Unfortunately, nobody noticed what I was doing!

C
What was I doing? Well, I was sitting by the Christmas tree playing on my own. I was holding a tiny light bulb that had fallen from the Christmas tree lights. My brother Neil turned round. He noticed the bulb in my hand. (3) .... , he noticed something else. Two bulbs were missing from the tree. Not one ... two!

D
'Mum, Fiona's eaten a light bulb!' shouted Neil. At that age, you see, I used to put everything in my mouth. Mum rushed in. She looked at me. She turned white. She ran and got my coat.

E
(4) .... , my mum and I were leaving for the hospital. (5) .... , my brothers rushed up. They were smiling and holding two tiny light bulbs. Not one ... two!

C Find examples of these verb forms in the story.

1 past simple for a state or situation in the past
2 past continuous for a temporary situation in the past
3 past perfect for an event that happened before another event in the past
4 *used to* + infinitive for habitual actions in the past

Skills development

Organization

D Read the five stages of a good story. Match them with a paragraph from the story to put them in order.
1 Bring the story to a close. ....
2 Attract the readers' attention. ....
3 Develop the story with further events. ....
4 Introduce the first 'event'. ....
5 Set the scene. ....

Language chunks

Time phrases

just then
earlier
a moment later
a long time ago
in an instant

E Use the time phrases in the Language chunks box to complete the gaps in the story. There may be more than one correct answer for each gap.

F The techniques below make stories more enjoyable to read. Find an example of each technique in the story.
1 using direct speech
2 speaking directly to the reader
3 using short sentences after long ones
4 repeating a phrase for effect
5 adding suspense at the end of a paragraph

Steps to success
When writing stories:
- keep the story simple – don't have too many events or too many places.
- include two or three characters only.
- make sure the story has a beginning, a middle and an ending.
- use some descriptions of people and places to bring your story to life.

Planning and writing

G Take a look at these pictures. In pairs, think of a story that could include all the objects and people.

H Now write your story. Use the planner and write between 120 and 180 words.

Paragraph 1: Attract the readers' attention.

Paragraph 2: Set the scene.

Paragraph 3: Introduce the first 'event'.

Paragraph 4: Develop the story with further events.

Paragraph 5: Bring the story to a close.

quick check
Be sure to:
- plan first, giving each paragraph a purpose.
- keep your story simple.
- include some of the writing techniques discussed in this unit.
- read through your finished story and check for spelling errors.

Check your knowledge 3

A Use the clues to complete the crossword puzzle.

Down

1 Can you believe they sailed around the world on a .... ?
2 This painting won a major ....
4 Could you tell me how much the bus .... costs?
6 The .... of the artist's son was life-size.
8 The Queen of England lives in Buckingham ....
10 We took the .... across to the island.

Across

3 We went from London to Edinburgh by ....
5 Greece and Italy are full of ancient ....
7 His .... of the queen was extremely lifelike.
9 The painting showed a beautiful green ....
11 The .... on top of the hill is a war memorial.
12 When we went camping, we stayed in ....

B Complete each gap with one word.

Our trip to St Petersburg

On our next (1) .... abroad, we've decided to go (2) .... St Petersburg. Apparently it's a magnificent city, so we're really looking forward to it. We'll be (3) .... in a five-star hotel, which I'm sure (4) .... make the holiday even more special. We've booked a room with a huge en suite and Jacuzzi and the view from the hotel window is supposed to be breathtaking. While we're there, we'll (5) .... sightseeing on our own – we plan to take in a huge number of sites (6) .... foot. We've decided to have a guided (7) .... of the Hermitage Museum, however, as it's supposed to be the best way to see it. (8) .... the end of the trip, we'll (9) .... taken in most of the city's sites by which time I'm sure we'll (10) .... exhausted!

C Complete the sentences with the correct form of the verb in brackets.

1 I .... (call) you when I .... (get) home.
2 We .... (not start) until everyone .... (get) here.
3 What .... (do) this weekend? Do you want to see a film?
4 Just think. This time next month we .... (fly) to Europe.
5 By the end of the day I .... (finish) all my work.
6 When Jamie leaves school, he .... (travel) around the world.
7 I'm sorry. I .... (not do) it again.
8 I don't want to walk. I think I .... (take) the bus.

D Choose the best answer.

1 It's quick and easy to travel to .... if you live in Europe.
   A abroad   C a country
   B a foreign country   D a holiday

2 Oh, you've just .... the last tour.
   A been   C missed
   B had   D lost

3 When we .... on our trip we were very excited, but by the end of it we were exhausted!
   A set off   C got off
   B started off   D went off

4 There was a huge traffic .... on the way here.
   A line   C queue
   B block   D jam

5 .... There's a car coming!
   A Look out!   C Go out!
   B Speak out!   D Get out!

6 The play we went to see .... to be fabulous.
   A found out   C turned out
   B went out   D carried out

7 The whole .... of the film were magnificent.
   A credits   C actors
   B performance   D cast

8 The production has been such a success that every performance has .... !
   A sold out   C found out
   B carried out   D turned out

9 You're not coming on the camping trip, ... ?
   A aren't   C do you
   B are you   D don't you

10 You couldn't help me with this, ... ?
   A could you   C do you
   B couldn't you   D don't you

11 Could you .... me how much a double room costs?
   A tell   C say to
   B told   D said to

12 Can .... breakfast is included in the price?
   A tell us if   C you tell us if
   B you told us if D you tell us

E Put the following statements and questions into reported speech.

1 'I really enjoyed the exhibition.'
   She said ....

2 'I wonder if we'll see any stars here tonight.'
   She wondered ....

3 'It was the scariest film I've ever seen!'
   She claimed ....

4 'What films do you like?'
   I asked him ....

5 'Did you enjoy the book?'
   She asked me ....

6 'Have you ever been to Budapest?'
   He asked me ....

F Complete the second sentence so that it has the same meaning as the first sentence. Use the word given.

1 This year I plan to get my driver's licence.
   AM
   This year .... get my driver's licence.

2 The coach is leaving in the next few minutes.
   ABOUT
   The coach .... leave.

3 Where are you going this summer?
   KNOW
   Do you .... going this summer?

4 'Have you ever read a book?' he asked.
   HAD
   He asked me .... read a book.

5 'Don't drive so fast!' my mother said to my brother.
   WARNED
   My mother .... to drive so fast.

6 'I'll show you my photos,' she said.
   TOLD
   She .... show me her photos.

7 'Why don't we take the train?' asked Tina.
   SUGGESTED
   Tina .... the train.

8 'I didn't steal her car I tell you,' said Pete Smith.
   DENIED
   Pete Smith .... car.

9 'Would you like to come with us next Saturday?' asked Nicole.
   INVITED
   Nicole .... them the following Saturday.

10 'OK. I'm the one who took the bike,' said Fran.
   ADMITTED
   Fran .... the bike.

7 Turn on, tune in

A Work in pairs. Do you recognize any of these letters and words? Which would you use for:
- connecting to the internet?
- contacting friends?
- finding information?
- following the news?
- listening to music?
- sharing photos?
- watching a film?
- watching a music video?

Reading

B You are going to read about a popular website called You Tube. Skim the article. Which five paragraphs match these headings?

Facts and Figures ....
Finding fame ....
What is You Tube? ....
What's there? .... , ...

Steps to success
- Multiple choice questions often test your understanding of *implied* opinions or facts, so you need to 'read between the lines'. When you find an example of the writer's opinion, try to rephrase it in your own words.

C Now choose the best answer (A, B, C or D).

1 What does the writer imply about You Tube in paragraph A?
A Many people waste their time on it.
B It has changed the internet a lot in recent years.
C Most people who use the internet know about it.
D It's the most popular site on the internet.

2 According to the writer, what is special about You Tube?
A It hosts millions of videos.
B Its videos are not made by professionals.
C Its movies are very short.
D It's like a television station.

A media revolution

A
What do a sneezing panda and a mobile phone being blended have in common? If you've spent any time on the internet in the past few years, you probably already know the answer. These, and a million even weirder things, can be found on You Tube.

B
For those of you who don't know already, You Tube is the biggest video-sharing website on the net. Videos are uploaded to the site by <u>subscribers</u>, and they can be viewed by anyone in the world with internet access. The video <u>clips</u> are short, but there are millions of them. Imagine having a TV that receives homemade programmes which are broadcast by thousands of homemade 'channels' – that's You Tube. And that's what makes it special. It's all done by amateurs.

C
Nevertheless, their creativity is amazing! Whole soap opera series have been written, performed and filmed by just a few friends. There are beautiful animations. There are professional-looking documentaries from <u>amateur</u> journalists. There are <u>any number of</u> 'How to ...' videos that teach you everything from 'How to build your own aeroplane' to 'How to be emo'. It's all there on You Tube.

D
So who's watching? Well, according to the figures, nearly everybody. Around one hundred million videos are <u>downloaded</u> from You Tube daily; about five billion clips are viewed annually; each minute 13 hours of new video are uploaded and sixty-five thousand new movies are added every day. The numbers speak for themselves, and they are rising all the time. It's no surprise that You Tube is the third most visited website on the internet.

3 What does the writer want to emphasize about You Tube in paragraph C?
A It's unprofessional.
B It's varied.
C It's funny.
D It's free.

4 How many clips are watched every day?
A sixty-five thousand
B one hundred million
C five billion
D a million

5 What does the writer mean by 'The numbers speak for themselves' in paragraph D?
A Large numbers of people subscribe to the service.
B The video clips play automatically.
C The statistics prove that You Tube videos are good quality.
D The figures show that You Tube is very popular.

6 Which type of video is not mentioned in paragraph E?
A educational material
B comedies
C news and current affairs
D music

7 Why does the writer think You Tube is a 'media revolution'?
A because of who makes the material
B because of how people access it
C because of the material it contains
D because of how much it costs

8 What do Lucas, Jessica, Lisa and Savannah have in common?
A They are all actors or actresses.
B They have all been discovered by agents.
C They have all created their own fame.
D They all have their own You Tube channels.

E
The site also has some of the funniest content on the net. <u>Hilarious</u> clips of dancing hamsters and unfortunate accidents are viewed by millions. However, You Tube isn't just for laughs. If you're a music lover, almost every pop video that has ever been made is there. If you're a teacher, there are a host of school channels for your learners. If you have a hobby, however strange, there will be a channel for you on You Tube. In short, people are offered an enormous range of choices.

F
But You Tube shouldn't be thought of as just an entertaining, informative website; it's a media <u>revolution</u>. Until now, audiences have had their entertainment made for them by TV and radio professionals. The traditional media have been given a huge shake-up by You Tube. Why? Because the audience make the programmes for themselves!

G
What's more, fame and <u>stardom</u> are being changed by You Tube forever. Until recently, if you wanted to be famous, you had to get your act seen by a show business agent. Not anymore! You want fame? Put yourself on You Tube. That's what teenage internet celebrity Lucas Cruikshank did. Cruikshank made his own show, called *Fred*. It is now one of the most popular shows on the net. New Zealand actress Jessica Rose, comic Lisa Donovan and singer Savannah Outen have all found fame the same way.

H
Could all our media look like You Tube in the future? Unlikely. Nevertheless, over the next few years more videos will be uploaded, more internet stars will be made and more people will fall about laughing at the sneezing panda.

D Match the words and expressions underlined in the text with a definition.
1 a sudden, huge change ....
2 being a celebrity ....
3 lots of ....
4 not professional ....
5 people who sign up to a service ....
6 short movies ....
7 got from the internet ....
8 very funny ....

E Skim the text once more to find words connected with the media and communications.

How often do you surf the internet?
What are your favourite websites?
Have you ever watched anything on You Tube? What?

Grammar 1

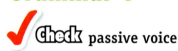 passive voice

See page 147 for information about passive voice.

Find examples in the article of the passive forms below.

1 with present simple
2 with present continuous
3 with present perfect
4 with future *will*
5 with modal

Can this extract from the article go into passive voice?

... they are rising all the time. **yes / no**

A Tick the sentences with passive voice. How did you identify the sentences with passive voice in each case?

1
a All through the summer newspaper articles had been written about the fires.
b The newspapers had been writing articles about the fires all through the summer.

2
a He was sent a mysterious letter.
b A mysterious letter was sent.

3
a These photos have been downloaded from the Web.
b I downloaded these photos from the Web.

4
a We have been broadcasting regular reports since last summer.
b Our regular reports have been broadcast since last summer.

5
a The BBC websites have been improved.
b The BBC have improved their websites.

6
a It's believed that several thieves took part in the robbery.
b People believe that several thieves took part in the robbery.

B Rewrite these sentences in the passive. One sentence cannot change. Why not?

1 Robert told me this very strange story.

2 The virus may infect millions of computers.

3 They are going to send new subscribers an email.

4 Our TV hasn't been working properly for days.

5 They had offered me a job as a foreign correspondent.

6 Many people think that mobile phones are bad for your health.

C Look at the diagram and rewrite the description in your notebooks using passive voice. As you do this exercise, think about:
- what tense to use
- sentences that may not go into passive
- whether or not to mention the agent (*by* ...)

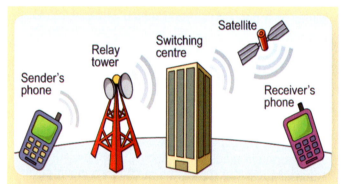

Someone sent my friend a text message a few minutes ago. How did she receive it so quickly? The service works like this: The mobile phone company divides the country into areas called cells. A relay tower serves each cell. These towers are constantly receiving and sending our messages. Once we have pressed the 'send' button, our mobile phone sends the message to the nearest relay tower. The relay tower transmits the message to the nearest switching centre. The switching centre checks where it will send the message. Up in space, a satellite is waiting to relay messages. Switching centres are sending it messages all the time. When the switching centre has sent my friend's message to the satellite, the satellite beams it to her.

My friend was sent a text message a few minutes ago ...

Vocabulary

Media and communications

A Find the odd word out. Can you explain your choice?

1 documentary | report | article
2 audience | viewers | subscribers
3 watch | browse | surf
4 headlines | titles | articles
5 image | text | picture
6 editor | reporter | correspondent

B Now complete the sentences with words from A.

1 Did you see that fascinating .... about the life of Einstein last night?
2 I like to .... the net to find interesting new websites.
3 Your .... about judo for the local newspaper were excellent.
4 Images on a web page take longer to download than ....
5 Over 10,000 .... to our magazine receive it each week.
6 The .... is responsible for choosing the stories to include each week.
7 This morning's .... are all about the forest fires.
8 This show has a huge .... each week.

C 🎧 Listen to the extracts. What kind of programme is it? Write the number.

chat show ....
documentary ....
game show ....
reality show ....
sitcom ....
soap opera ....

D Work in pairs. Match the words to make jobs in the media. Then describe a job and ask your partner to guess.

1 chat show   a artist
2 disc   b critic
3 film   c designer
4 make-up   d engineer
5 sound   e host
6 web   f jockey

> This person works on television and presents a programme where celebrities are interviewed.

> It's a chat show host.

E Can you explain the difference between ...

1 *keeping in touch* and *losing touch*
2 *making a call* and *taking a call*
3 *downloading files* and *uploading files*
4 *surfing the net* and *searching the net*
5 *a search engine* and *a social networking site*
6 *glancing at the headlines* and *hitting the headlines*

F Find and correct the mistakes in these sentences. One sentence does not have a mistake. Which one?

1 I think email is a fantastic way to lose touch with friends.
2 I'm trying to upload a music file from this website, but it's taking a long time.
3 Could I borrow your phone for a moment to take a call?
4 You've been ages on that computer. Are you searching for something in particular?
5 All my friends have created their own pages on search engines like Facebook or MySpace.
6 It didn't take long for such a shocking story to glance at the headlines.

see, watch, look, listen, hear

G Circle the correct option.

1 Could you turn the radio up a little? I can't **listen to** / **hear** it very well.
2 **See** / **Look** at this amazing photo in this morning's paper!
3 Have you ever **seen** / **looked at** a Shakespeare play?
4 Did you **see** / **watch** that funny photo of the president in all the papers yesterday?
5 My mum always **listens to** / **hears** the radio in the car.
6 I was **seeing** / **watching** a great film last night when you rang.
7 Have you ever **seen** / **watched** the film *Titanic*?
8 I don't usually **watch** / **look at** television during the week.

What's your favourite kind of TV programme? Is TV in your country good quality? Why/Why not?

7

Listening

A These photos show different forms of media for communicating news. In pairs, think of one advantage and one disadvantage of each form.

magazines

the internet

mobile phone

television

newspapers

radio

B 🎧 You are going to listen to eight people complaining about forms of media and communication. First listen and decide which of the things from A they are talking about.

Speaker 1 .... Speaker 5 ....
Speaker 2 .... Speaker 6 ....
Speaker 3 .... Speaker 7 ....
Speaker 4 .... Speaker 8 ....

How do you learn about what's happening in the world?
Are people of your age interested in the news? Why/Why not?

C 🎧 Listen again and choose the best answer.

1 You hear a woman talking about the media. Who does she think is treated unfairly?
A the public
B celebrities
C editors

2 You hear a man talking about local media. Why is he unhappy?
A There are too many radio stations.
B There are too many commercials.
C There isn't enough variety.

3 You hear a woman talking about a problem with her daughter. Why is she unhappy?
A She doesn't like what her daughter watches on TV.
B Her daughter watches too much TV in general.
C Her daughter plays her TV too loudly.

4 You hear a man expressing his opinion. He believes that people shouldn't
A play their radios in public places.
B believe what they hear on the radio.
C have their televisions playing loudly.

5 You hear a woman expressing her opinion. What doesn't she trust?
A computers in general
B social networking sites
C online shopping

6 You hear a man talking about something his wife reads. Why doesn't he like it?
A It's too serious.
B It's too boring.
C It's too old-fashioned.

7 You hear a woman talking about her son. Why is she worried?
A He spends too much money on telephone calls.
B He may be damaging his health.
C He stays out late too often.

8 You hear a girl talking about the news. What opinion does she express?
A You can't trust the TV news.
B The TV news isn't very exciting to watch.
C The TV news is better than other news sources.

Speaking

A 👥 Look at the things mobile phones can do. Work in pairs. How useful are these things for you or your friends? Put the things in order of importance.

B What would these people want to use a mobile phone for? Tell your partner what you think.

C 🎧 Listen to Marcus talking about the two photos in B. Which uses of mobile phones from A does he mention?

Steps to success
- If you can't remember the exact word, try to describe what you mean with other words.

D 🎧 Listen to Marcus. What word is he looking for?

colleague ....
manager ....
texting / email ....
twins ....

E 👥 Work in pairs. Take turns describing these things to each other without using the actual words for them.

F 👥 Work in pairs. Student A look at the photos below. Student B look at the photos on page 165. Talk for a minute about the photos. Make sure you answer both parts of the question. Use the expressions in the Language chunks box.

Student A's photos:

Compare the photos and say why these people are using computers.

Language chunks

Talking about similarity
similarly ...
likewise ...
in the same way ...

Talking about difference
in contrast ...
on the other hand ...
whereas ...
however ...

Say it right!

Long and short vowels: /ɑː/, /æ/ and /ʌ/

G 🎧 Listen and circle the words that have the same vowel sound as the word you hear.

dad /æ/	bad	rat	late
bar /ɑː/	father	stamp	cart
cup /ʌ/	mop	pup	monkey

H 🎧 Now listen, check and repeat.

7

Grammar 2

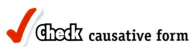 causative form

See page 148 for information about causative form.

Which of these sentences uses causative form? What is the difference in meaning?

1
a I've had a lot of work to do on the house recently.
b I've had a lot of work done on the house recently.

2
a Dad's got to repair the car.
b Dad's got the car repaired.

3
a She wants to have photos taken in her garden.
b She wants to take photos in her garden.

4
a Mr Jones is getting his painting framed.
b Mr Jones is getting a frame for his painting.

5
a He must have fixed the computer.
b He must have the computer fixed.

A Find and correct the mistakes in the sentences.
1 We're going to have got our portraits painted.
2 I've cut my hair at that new hairdresser's.
3 The police have had the man arrested.
4 The mechanics have had a good job done on my car.
5 I'd stolen my phone in the park.
6 We damaged the roof during the storm.

B Complete with the causative form.
1 Where .... you .... your hair .... ? It always looks great. (cut)
2 Next week I .... a new computer .... (deliver)
3 We should .... the new radio station .... by someone famous. (open)
4 James .... his music video .... 5,000 times so far. (download)
5 .... you .... your subscription for *Metal Monthly* .... last month? (renew)
6 I'm afraid there isn't a TV in the lounge. We .... it .... at the moment. (repair)

C Complete these thoughts with the causative form of words from the boxes.

costumes • crew • film • lead role • music

compose • direct • fly • make • play

If I could make a film I would ...

1 ....have.... the ..film directed.. by Steven Spielberg.
2 .... the .... by a famous Italian designer.
3 .... the .... by Kate Winslet.
4 .... the .... by Coldplay.
5 .... the .... to Brazil for the filming.

Quick chat
What about you? If you could make a film, how would you have it done?

7

Practise your English

A Look at the picture. What kind of show is this? Are these shows popular in your country? Can you name any winners?

Would you like to be famous? Why/Why not?

Steps to success
When choosing the best way to complete a gapped text, remember to:
- read the whole text to understand the gist.
- read the whole sentence before you choose.
- think about grammar as well as vocabulary.

B Quickly read this article about the way talent shows have changed over the years. What three changes does the writer mention?

People have been (**1**) .... talent shows for years. When I was a child there was a show on TV called *Opportunity Knocks*. Contestants included (**2**) .... comedians, singers or magicians all hoping for (**3**) .... Most of them were quite good at what they did, but nothing special. After they (**4**) .... their brief moment of fame and a small prize, they generally disappeared forever.

Today things could hardly be more different. Programmes like the *X Factor* are seen by millions of (**5**) .... in the UK alone, and the shows (**6**) .... exported to dozens of countries around the world. On offer is a one million pound recording contract as first prize, and many successful singers (**7**) .... serious careers started by such shows.

What's more, today's talent shows spread beyond TV. The shows have website channels with millions of (**8**) .... and newspaper (**9**) .... seem to love them. Stories about contestants' private lives and fighting between the shows' judges make the (**10**) .... every week. These programmes, it seems, have become more than a show. They're a way of life.

C Read the text again. Choose the best answer.

	A	B	C	D
1	watching	seeing	viewing	looking
2	professional	vocational	amateur	full-time
3	stars	stardom	star-studded	starring
4	had been given	had given	got given	gave
5	watchers	spectators	viewers	audience
6	have	had been	been	have been
7	had have	are having	have had	have been
8	amateurs	editors	subscribers	buyers
9	articles	editors	subscribers	viewers
10	critics	titles	headlines	headers

D Complete the second sentence so that it has a similar meaning to the first sentence. Use the word given.

1. Alexander Graham Bell invented the telephone.
   BY
   The telephone .... Alexander Graham Bell.
2. The director asked an artist to copy the *Mona Lisa*.
   COPIED
   The director .... by an artist.
3. Someone has stolen Alan's MP3 player.
   HAD
   Alan .... stolen.
4. We were told an awful story.
   THEY
   .... an awful story.
5. Some people believe that newspapers may disappear eventually.
   IS
   .... newspapers may disappear eventually.
6. They published my mum's letter in *Chatterbox Magazine*!
   HAD
   My mum .... published in *Chatterbox Magazine*.
7. My uncle presents a music show on the local radio.
   DISC
   My uncle .... on the local radio.
8. Let's not lose contact with each other.
   TOUCH
   Let's .... each other.
9. The story has been in all the newspapers.
   HIT
   The story ....
10. I'm so upset that I missed last night's episode of *Coronation Street*.
    DIDN'T
    I'm so upset .... last night's episode of *Coronation Street*.

7

Writing: Film review

A What makes a good film? Work in pairs. Put these things in order of importance.

.... a famous cast   .... the directing
.... the special effects   .... the plot
.... the acting   .... the scenery
.... the costumes   .... the musical score

B Quickly read this review. Which of the things from A does it mention?

When I heard that *The Golden Compass* had been turned into a film, I was so excited. I went last Saturday night to see it with my friends at the local cinema. The film is based on my favourite book, *Northern Lights*. The book is the first in a series of three books called *His Dark Materials*. They're great books, and I would recommend them. Unfortunately, the film was a great disappointment.

The plot is all about Lyra, an orphan who lives in Oxford. Lots of children start disappearing. When Lyra's best friend is kidnapped, she goes on a journey to rescue him and to solve the mystery. Along the way she meets lots of other characters, such as some people called the Gyptians and a talking bear.

It's an exhilarating story. However, I wasn't convinced by the actors. The film has a star-studded cast, and that's the problem. Nicole Kidman was too beautiful to be a villain. Every time I saw Daniel Craig I was reminded of James Bond! Actually, I think his performances in James Bond films are much better, especially in the latest one. There was some intelligent acting from Dakota Blue Richards, who is only 14 years old and comes from Brighton, as Lyra, but I'm afraid she couldn't save the film.

My verdict? There were some astonishing special effects. The costumes were sumptuous and the music was lovely. However, if you enjoyed that fabulous book as much as I did, you're better off avoiding this film.

Steps to success
- A review should not be longer than 180 words. Don't try to tell the whole story; that's not necessary or interesting. Make sure everything you write is relevant and don't forget that a review is about your opinions.

C Read the review again and cut out any irrelevant parts. Try to reach 180 words. Compare with a partner. Did you cut the same things?

Have you seen *The Golden Compass*? What did you think of it?
What kind of films do you like?

Skills development

Organization

D Here are two plans for a review. Which one matches the review on page 80?

Plan A

Introduction, with a surprising opening sentence
Brief outline of the plot and characters
Your opinion in more detail
Summing up and recommendations

Plan B

Introduction with a brief description of what the film is about
The good points
The bad points
Sum up with your overall view

Language

E Find adjectives in the review on page 80 to describe these things:

1 the original book ....
2 the cast ....
3 the plot ....
4 the costumes ....
5 the music ....
6 the acting ....

F Can you think of more adjectives, positive and negative, for the things listed in E?

G Here are some useful expressions from the review on page 80. Match each expression (1-5) with its opposite (A-E).

Language chunks

1 … you're better off avoiding this film.
2 I wasn't convinced by …
3 … a star-studded cast,
4 … couldn't save the film.
5 … a great disappointment.

A … rescued the film.
B I'd thoroughly recommend it.
C … a pleasant surprise.
D … was totally believable.
E … little-known actors,

Planning and writing

H You recently saw this notice in an English-language magazine:

Reviews wanted!
Loved it or loathed it, we want to hear. If you've seen a film recently that you loved or hated, write a review for us and you could be published in next month's edition of *Movie Monthly*.
Write your review.

I Before you write, complete the planner so that you know what will be in each paragraph.

Planner

Film title: ....

Paragraph 1: ....

Paragraph 2: ....

Paragraph 3: ....

Paragraph 4: ....

quick check

Be sure to:
- choose a film that you have strong opinions about.
- start with a surprising statement.
- plan before you write.
- use plenty of adjectives.
- give your opinions throughout.

Do not:
- just tell the story.
- write irrelevant information.

J Now write your review. Write between 120 and 180 words. Use the planner and the Language chunks to help you.

8 The world of sport ... and leisure

A Work in pairs. How much do you know about sport and leisure? Do this quiz and find out.

Sport and leisure quiz

1 Name three team sports beginning with B.

2 Name two extreme sports?

3 What sport are these professional sports people famous for?
a Tiger Woods   c Lucas Leiva
b Serena Williams d Michael Phelps

4 Which of the following is not a board game?
a *Monopoly* b *Chess* c *Blackjack* d *Scrabble*

5 What would you be doing if you were skydiving?

 Now, check your answers on page 175.

Reading

B You are going to read about extreme sports. Read the article quickly and label each picture with a name and an activity.

Steps to success
- In a multiple matching task, accuracy and speed are important. Don't waste time reading the whole text in detail.
- Skim or scan the text for specific information. Check that the part of the text you have located says the same thing as the information in the question.

1

What will they think of next?

A Gerry

I'm not really an athletic person and I've never been into sports but I think if I took up a sport, I'd like to do something unusual. A few weeks ago I was watching a TV programme about unusual interests and sports and I saw something that looked strange enough for me to try. It's called extreme ironing. The people who do it claim it's more than just an extreme sport. They like to call it a performance art! Personally, I think it looks like a lot of fun. What happens is you take an ironing board to a remote place (for example, to the top of a mountain, to a desert or even under the sea!) and iron a few items of clothing on it. I must admit, I really like the idea of combining the excitement of an extreme outdoor activity with the satisfaction of a well-pressed shirt. Whacky!

B Penny

I've been doing free running for some time now and I really love it. Some people call it an extreme sport, but I like to think of it as an art you do with your body. In fact, it's more similar to dance than to regular running. It's usually done in cities and it involves performing different movements to get over buildings and walls. Movements like running, jumping, acrobatics, dance – anything that will keep you moving. As you run, you focus on freedom and beauty. The aim is to create a beautiful way of moving. We practise in gymnasiums and in any city areas that are full of obstacles like buildings, cars, walls, trees, etc. It can be quite dangerous and injuries are very common. But if you train well and warm up before you run, it's not as unsafe.

2

C Claire

I've always loved the sea and have tried many different sea sports. I've been water-skiing, windsurfing and of course swimming. But last summer, on a trip to Spain, I tried wave jumping. It was amazing! I saw people doing it during a storm off the coast of Cantabria. They were using their windsurf boards, but you can actually use anything that <u>floats</u> – a surfboard, a jet ski, or even an air mattress! Obviously, you can only do this sport if the weather conditions allow for it. There have to be fairly large waves. The higher the wave the higher you can jump and, of course, the harder you fall! This can be a dangerous sport as the sea and the waves are very <u>unpredictable</u>. But if you're careful, you'll be fine and if you start with small waves, you can slowly progress to bigger waves.

D Will

I suppose most people would call me crazy. You see I've always been fond of extreme, adrenaline-raising activities. You name it, I've probably tried it! I've been bungee jumping, hang-gliding, skydiving and rock climbing. What I'd like to try next though is ice climbing. I've been <u>reading up</u> on it and plan to try it this winter. It involves climbing up steep ice formations. Like rock climbing, you need to use ropes if you want to do it the safe way – and I don't plan to do it any other way. I'm going to try it on icy cliffs in the Canadian Rockies, but you can do it on frozen waterfalls, rock slabs covered in ice, or any <u>vertical</u> icy surface. Like mountain climbers, many ice climbers risk losing their toes and fingers to frostbite, but that's really only if you do it regularly. I'm not sure yet if I'll want to do it a second time. It will all depend on how the first time goes!

C For questions 1-6, choose from the people (A-D).

A Gerry **B** Penny **C** Claire **D** Will

Who …

does not usually do a sport? 1 ....

says their sport can be considered an art? 2 ...., 3 ....

says their sport is pleasing to watch? 4 ....

enjoys doing anything extreme? 5 ....

isn't planning to start a new sport? 6 ....

D For questions 1-6, choose from the sports (A-D).

A Extreme ironing **C** Wave jumping
B Free running **D** Ice climbing

Which sport(s) …

is usually done in any isolated place? 1 ....

can cause serious damage to parts of your body if not done with care? 2 ....

can you do with a variety of different equipment? 3 ....

can you only do in certain weather? 4 ...., 5 ....

requires special equipment to make it safe? 6 ....

Work it out!

E Match the words and expressions underlined in the text with a definition.

1 doesn't sink ....
2 started ....
3 straight up and down position ....
4 things that get in your way ....
5 unexpected ....
6 far away and difficult to get to ....
7 ironed ....
8 studying ....

F Scan the article again and write down the names of all the sports and extreme sports.

Quick chat

Do you think these activities should be considered sports? Why/Why not?

8

Grammar 1

✓ Check zero, first and second conditionals

See page 148 for information about zero, first and second conditionals.

Match the extracts with the use of each conditional.

1 But if you train well and warm up ... , it's not that unsafe.
2 ... I think if I took up a sport, I'd like to do something unusual.
3 ... if you're careful, you'll be fine ...

a The **zero conditional** is used to talk about situations that are generally true. ....
b The **first conditional** is used for a situation that is real or likely in the future. ....
c The **second conditional** is used for a situation that we can imagine, but probably won't happen. ....

A Three of these sentences contain mistakes. Find them and correct them.

1 If Rafael Nadal will win Wimbledon, we'll all be very happy.
2 If Pete is lucky, he'll be picked for the team.
3 Rock climbing is not a dangerous sport if you will take precautions.
4 If you don't train, you don't improve.
5 If I could try any sport, I'd try snowboarding.
6 If I'd win this match, I'd get a chance to play in the finals.

B Complete the dialogue with the correct form of the verbs.

Sara: Good luck in the game today!
Alice: Thanks. If I (1) .... (play) well I think I (2) .... (win). But if I don't then I (3) .... (be) terribly upset.
Sara: If I (4) .... (be) you, I (5) .... (take) a deep breath and try to think positively. You're certainly good enough to win.
Alice: I (6) .... (be) more confident if I (7) .... (be) good enough to win, but I just don't think I'm as good as Kate.
Sara: Whenever you (8) .... (put) yourself down like that, it (9) .... (make) me mad. You are good enough and that's that!
Alice: Thanks, Sara. If I (10) .... (believe) in myself, I'd probably be a better player.

C Use this information about Alice to make six conditional sentences.

(1) play well: get a university scholarship
(2) not play well: study hard for university
(3) have more confidence: play better
(4) do better at school: more time for tennis
(5) not do well: does not know what to do
(6) have boyfriend: feel happier

- has an important tennis tournament coming up
- not confident in herself
- not doing very well at school
- doesn't have a boyfriend

If Alice had more confidence in herself, she would play better.

Alice would play better if she had more confidence in herself.

D Work in pairs. Continue one of these sequences until you can't think of anything else to say.

If it's a sunny day, I'll go to the park.
If it's raining, I'll stay at home.

If it's raining, I'll stay at home.

What will you do if you stay at home?

If I stay at home, I'll invite my friends over.

Vocabulary
Sport and leisure

A Match the sports descriptions to the words in the box. Then describe the objects in the pictures.

> athletics • basketball • boxing • deep-sea diving
> football • tennis

1 You play in a **ring**. Each person **punches** his/her opponent wearing special **gloves**. ....
2 You play on a **track**. It includes all **track and field** events. For example, running, long jump, etc. ....
3 You do this in the sea. It involves **diving** under water wearing **flippers**, a **wetsuit** and a **snorkel** or an **oxygen tank**. ....
4 You play this on a **court**. You **throw** a ball into a **hoop**. ....
5 This team sport is played on a **pitch**. You score by **kicking** a ball into a **goal**. ....
6 You need a **net**, a **racket**, a ball and two players. It's played on a **court**. ....

B Complete the table.

Sport/Hobby	Verb	Person
baseball	play baseball	baseball player
chess		
fishing		
gardening		
gymnastics		
hockey		
ice-skating		
photography		
sailing		
skateboarding		
swimming		

C Now add the sports from A to the table. Which sports or hobbies do you do in a team? Which do you do individually?

D Circle the correct option.
1 Federer **beat** / **won** Nadal very easily, but he had already **beat** / **won** the last two sets. He **defeated** / **won** him in three straight sets.
2 Your **competitor** / **opponent** is the person or team you are playing against.
3 Someone who takes part in sports competitions is called a(n) **competitor** / **opponent**.
4 Sometimes a **spectator** / **viewer** at a baseball match will get injured by a ball.
5 In a tennis match, the person who makes sure the game is played fairly is called a(n) **umpire** / **referee**. In a football match this person is known as the **umpire** / **referee**.
6 The game ended in a(n) **draw** / **equal**. There was no winner.

E Complete the gaps with *come* or *go* in the correct form.
1 I hope your dream of winning a medal .... true.
2 Jess .... second in the race.
3 Our team's colours .... well together.
4 If we lose the match, I'll .... mad!
5 How did the game .... ?
6 They lost! I wonder what .... wrong?

Phrasal verbs

F Match the phrasal verbs with the verbs from the box.

> come • eliminate • exercise • spend time socially • start

1 Many people **take up** a sport at school. ....
2 A lot of kids **hang out** in fast food restaurants after school. ....
3 **Working out** at a gym makes a big difference to your fitness. ....
4 Joe didn't **turn up** for training last night. ....
5 To win the match a boxer needs to **knock out** his opponent. ....

8

Listening

A Have you ever played chess? What do you know about the game?

B You are going to hear an interview with a young chess champion. Which of the following words or phrases do you think you will hear?

- chess pieces ☐
- check ☐
- checkmate ☐
- competition ☐
- opponent ☐
- tournament ☐
- chess players ☐
- draw ☐

C 🎧 Listen to the interview. Tick the words or phrases in B that you hear.

D Read the gapped sentences below. How many answers can you remember from the first time you listened?

Dalita Zadian: teen chess champion

Dalita is 16 years old and she started playing chess when she was (1) ....
She started (2) .... her father at chess by age ten.
Dalita was born in Armenia, but (3) .... to the USA when she was nine.
Dalita started entering chess tournaments when she was (4) ....
She (5) .... chess for an hour and a half a day.
She enjoys playing speed chess two to three times a (6) ....
In a game of speed chess, each player is given only (7) .... to complete a game.
The players use a (8) .... to time their moves.
The player that (9) .... of time before checkmate or draw is achieved loses.
Dalita says that people enjoy what they're (10) .... at.

Steps to success
- When you have to write a word or short phrase in a gap, write exactly what you hear.
- After listening, read through the sentences and make any changes necessary to the words to make the sentences grammatically correct.

E 🎧 Listen again and complete the sentences with a word or short phrase.

Quick chat

Which would you enjoy more, speed chess or traditional chess?
What do you think life would be like for a young chess champion? Talk about:
- their studies
- their free time
- their friends
- their family

Speaking

A Look at the results of a class sports survey. What do they show about students' preferences?

> What students prefer:
> team sports – 75%
> individual sports – 50%
> extreme sports – 20%
> water sports – 45%
> walking or hiking – 45%
> snow sports – 60%

B 🎧 Listen to three students talking. What are they trying to decide?

C 🎧 Listen to the students again. Tick the expressions in the Language chunks box the speakers use.

Language chunks

Interrupting another speaker	
Excuse me.	☐
Sorry, … , but …	☐
May I say something?	☐
Sorry for interrupting …	☐

Acknowledging the interruption	
Of course.	☐
Please do.	☐
That's all right.	☐
Go ahead.	☐

Steps to success
- When you're having a discussion, it's all right to interrupt as long as you do it politely and don't do it too often!

D Work in pairs. Take turns to give your opinion on the statements below. Interrupt your partner after 30 seconds using the Language chunks. Remember to acknowledge the interruption.
- Everyone should find the time to play sport.
- It is important to have leisure time.
- Students today have very little free time.
- Playing board games is better for children than playing computer games.

E Work in pairs or small groups to discuss the holiday packages below.

Imagine your class would like to go on a three-day adventure trip. Discuss the advantages **and** disadvantages of each holiday package. Then decide which package would best suit the class. Use the class survey in A for information about the class preferences.

Package 1
whitewater rafting
hiking
bungee jumping
tennis

Package 2
kitesurfing
windsurfing
wave jumping
beach volleyball

Package 3
hiking
skiing
snowboarding
ice hockey

Word stress

F 🎧 Underline the syllable that carries the main stress in these words. Then listen and check.

1. fishing
2. cinema
3. gardening
4. photograph
5. photography
6. opponent
7. opposite
8. tournament
9. skiing
10. competitor

G Practise saying the words. Pay special attention to the unstressed syllables.

Grammar 2

✓ Check conditional links

See page 148 for information about conditional links.

Choose the correct conditional links and then answer the questions below.

1 **Unless / As long as** it snows in the next few days, we'll have to call our skiing trip off.
2 I'll try any new sport **unless / as long as** it's safe.
3 **Suppose / Provided (that)** you practise, you'll do well in the competition.
4 **Suppose / Provided** you lost, what would you do?
5 **What if / Unless** you lost? What would you do?

a Which links mean *if* and *only if*? ....
....
b Which link means *except if*? ....
c Which links are only used in questions?
.................., ...

A Complete the second sentence so that it has a similar meaning to the first sentence. Use the word given.

1 If the referee made a bad call, what would you do?
   IF
   What .... made a bad call? What would you do?
2 I wouldn't go skydiving because I think it isn't safe.
   PROVIDED
   I'd go skydiving .... was safe.
3 If the waves are high enough, we can go wave surfing.
   AS
   We can go wave surfing .... the waves are high enough.
4 I won't tell Justine unless you want me to.
   IF
   I won't tell Justine .... want me to.
5 Ian will practise if you ask him to.
   UNLESS
   Ian .... you ask him to.
6 Suppose things don't go as planned, what will you do then?
   IF
   What will you do .... go as planned?

✓ Check *like* and *as*

See page 148 for information about *like* and *as*.

Circle the correct option.

1 He works **as / like** a football coach.
2 She plays volleyball **as / like** a professional player.
3 He looks **as / like** David Beckham.
4 He used his hand **as / like** a bat.
5 **As / Like** any professional athlete, table tennis players have to train a lot.

B The reading text on pages 82 and 83 contains many examples of the different uses of *like* and *as*. Scan it and underline all the different examples you find.

C Match the questions with the different uses of *like* with the answers.

1 What do cats like?
2 What are cats like?
3 What does your cat look like?
4 How is your cat?

a He's fine, thanks.
b They're cute and furry.
c It's black and white and a little chubby.
d They like to play and they like to eat fish.

D Four of these sentences contain mistakes. Find them and correct them.

1 Sally's working as a yoga instructor.
2 That looks nice. I'll have the same like you.
3 American football looks a bit as rugby, don't you think?
4 What's the new goalkeeper like? Have you seen him?
5 He's very fast, as most people in the team.
6 I wish I could play as you. You're fantastic!

Practise your English

A Choose the best answer.

1. My favourite track and .... event is the 100-metre sprint race.
   A pitch   C race
   B field   D court

2. The .... all cheered when their team finally scored a goal.
   A spectators   C listeners
   B viewers   D referees

3. When we scored our second goal, the .... blew his whistle to indicate that the player had been offside.
   A umpire   C referee
   B coach   D player

4. The chess player looked at his .... as he made his final move.
   A competitor   C opposite
   B player   D opponent

5. Barcelona .... Liverpool to secure their place in the Champions League final.
   A won   C beat
   B defeat   D win

6. Nobody won. The game ended in a ....
   A equal   C draw
   B win   D defeat

7. Callie .... first in the hurdle race.
   A came   C went
   B come   D go

8. How did your night .... ?
   A go   C come
   B went   D came

9. Have you ever .... fishing?
   A played   C gone
   B done   D came

10. I've been throwing the ball all morning, but I can't get it to go in the ....
    A hoop   C pitch
    B net   D racket

B Discuss these questions in pairs.

1. Do you know the names of any world swimming champions?
2. The photo shows a junior swimming champion called Troy. How many hours of training do you think he does every week?

C Read the text quickly to find answers to the questions in B.

Junior champ

I'm a junior swimming champion and (1) .... any athlete, I spend most of my 'free' time training. The competition is tough and (2) .... I give it 100%, I will never get to world championship level. I often get asked what it's (3) .... to be a teenage swimming champion. I tell people that in many ways, my life (4) .... be the same even if I wasn't a swimmer. I go to school, I have my friends, I even have hobbies. But the truth is that, in one important way, it is very different. (5) .... a champion swimmer, I will eventually train for at least 30 hours a week, which will mean five hours a day, six days a week. At the moment, I'm only training 18 hours a week, but (6) .... I ever want to be as good as someone (7) .... Ian Thorpe or Michael Phelps, this will have to change. People often ask me, '(8) .... if you don't succeed? What (9) .... you do then?' I tell them that in my opinion, I've already achieved a lot more (10) .... most people will ever achieve. The truth is you never really know if you will ever become good enough for the Olympics or any other world championship competition. But hey, where's the fun in knowing?

D Read the text again and write one word in each gap.

Quick chat

Do you think Troy is right to say his training is worth all the sacrifice even if he never gets to the Olympics? Why/Why not?

Writing: Article (2)

A Read the following writing task. In pairs, make a list of all the benefits of playing team sports. Then compare your list with the class.

You have seen the following announcement in an international teen magazine.

The benefits of team sports
Tell us what you think the benefits of taking part in team sports are for children and young people.
We will publish the most interesting articles next month.

The benefits of team sports:

B Read the article. Are any of your ideas mentioned?

Team sports:
why should we play?

There's no doubt that most people are aware of the physical benefits of taking part in team sports. But can playing team sports offer us any other benefits?

The answer is, yes. To begin with, it's a fact that if you exercise, you have more energy and you feel better about yourself. As a member of a girls' basketball team, I've noticed that teenagers who play team sports are more active in general. What I mean is, they have more interests, they do more and they even study more!

I think another important benefit is that when you are in a team and work closely with other people, you learn to co-operate and you improve your social skills. Because you learn to work together with others rather than competing against them, as a member of a team, you tend to make more friends.

As far as I'm concerned, playing a team sport can definitely offer many benefits. But perhaps the best thing about it is the fact that it's a lot more fun than staying at home!

Skills development

Making the article interesting

> **Steps to success**
> - An article should interest and engage the reader.
> - Use questions, have a personal angle, include a catchy title and get the reader's attention from the very first paragraph.
> - It doesn't matter if it is informal or neutral in style as long as it is consistent.

C Which of the following features does the article in B have?
- A catchy title
- The use of direct or indirect questions
- The writer's opinion
- A personal angle
- An example

D Is the article written in a neutral or informal style? How do you know?

Developing ideas

E Underline the explanations the writer uses in the article to develop these points.

Being a member of a team …
1. makes you more active.
2. teaches you to co-operate with others and to improve your social skills.

Organization

F How is the article organized? What does the writer include in each paragraph? Make notes.

Paragraph 1 *Introduction with question*
Paragraph 2 ....
Paragraph 3 ....
Paragraph 4 ....

Language chunks

Giving your opinion
To begin with …
I think another important benefit …
As far as I'm concerned …
What I mean is …

Planning and writing

G Read this writing task and, in pairs, make a list of all the benefits you can think of associated with having a hobby. When you have finished, compare your list with the rest of the class.

You have seen the following announcement in an international teen magazine.

> **The benefits of having a hobby**
> Tell us what you think the benefits of having a hobby are for young people. Write an article of between 120 and 180 words.
> We will publish the most interesting articles next month.

H Complete the planner.

Planner

Title: ....
Paragraph 1: ....
Paragraph 2: ....
Paragraph 3: ....
Paragraph 4: ....

I Now write your article. Use the Language chunks to help you.

quick check

Be sure to:
- write four paragraphs.
- talk about one topic only in each paragraph.
- develop your ideas with explanations or examples.
- use linking words/phrases to link your ideas and paragraphs.
- be consistent in style (eg informal or neutral).
- make it interesting by asking questions, giving your opinion, using a personal angle and/or giving examples.
- give it a title.

Check your knowledge 4

A Use the clues to complete the crossword puzzle.

Down

This person …
1 decides what stories to print in a newspaper.
3 plays against you in a game.
6 writes reviews about movies. (4, 6)

Across

This person …
2 plays music on the radio. (4, 6)
4 presents a chat show.
5 is the referee in a game of tennis.
7 is in the crowd at a football match.
8 has signed up for a service.

B Write one word to complete the sentences.

1 Email is a great way to keep in ....
2 Every week the match ends in a ....
3 How did last week's game .... ?
4 I know that John won the race, but where did you .... ?
5 Sometimes it takes ages to download ....
6 The next day the news hit the ....

C Choose the best answer.

1 If the car ...., our planet would be a much cleaner place.
   A didn't exist   B don't exist   C won't exist   D existed
2 This is where the Prime Minister has ....
   A cut his hair   C his hair cut
   B been cut his hair   D hair cut
3 When you .... water to 100 degrees, it boils.
   A are heating   B heat   C will heat   D heated
4 It .... that Noel Best is going to join the team next month.
   A has said   B is said   C is being said   D says
5 When we throw plastic in the sea, it .... marine life.
   A harmed   B would harm   C is harming   D harms
6 Fiona's dream of becoming a pilot has finally .... true.
   A come   B turned   C gone   D been
7 Beaches .... much cleaner if people didn't throw their cigarettes on the sand.
   A would be   B will be   C are   D get
8 They .... new store opened by a celebrity next week.
   A are having their   C are have their
   B have had their   D will have had
9 If life existed on other planets, what .... be like?
   A it would   B would it   C won't it   D will it
10 Excuse me, is there a telephone here? I need to .... a call.
   A phone   B do   C take   D make

D Find and correct the mistakes in these sentences.

1 Unless you try hard, you might be chosen for the team.

2 She cuts her hair at the same hairdresser's as me.

3 I wonder what we would find if we can travel to another solar system.

4 If dogs don't get regular exercise, they became unfit and restless.

5 The car was broken down again yesterday.

6 Builders have had the new football stadium completed.

E Complete the second sentence so that it has the same meaning as the first sentence. Use the word given.

1. I'll only climb up there if you come with me.
   AS
   I'll climb up there .... with me.
2. Builders came last week to fix our roof.
   HAD
   We .... last week.
3. This plant will only grow if it gets enough light.
   UNLESS
   This plant won't .... enough light.
4. Someone has revealed that Britney Spears is going to play in London.
   IT
   .... that Britney Spears is going to play in London.
5. If we keep going, we should reach the village before it gets dark.
   THAT
   .... keep going, we should reach the village before it gets dark.
6. Families don't talk to each other because they watch so much television.
   DID
   If .... so much television, they would talk to each other more.
7. What would you do if you won a million euros?
   SUPPOSE
   .... a million euros, what would you do?
8. Tim is a security guard at a bank.
   WORKS
   Tim .... security guard at a bank.
9. If you get an hour's exercise at the gym every day, you can lose weight quickly.
   OUT
   If .... an hour a day at the gym, you can lose weight quickly.
10. Mike's football playing is as good as a professional's.
    LIKE
    Mike .... professional.

F Complete each gap with one word.

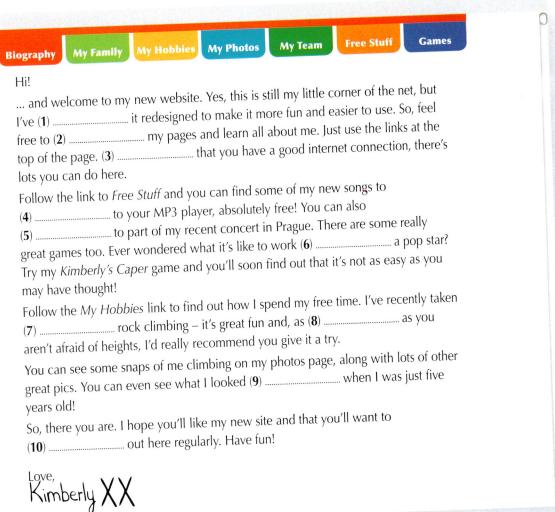

Hi!
... and welcome to my new website. Yes, this is still my little corner of the net, but I've (**1**) .... it redesigned to make it more fun and easier to use. So, feel free to (**2**) .... my pages and learn all about me. Just use the links at the top of the page. (**3**) .... that you have a good internet connection, there's lots you can do here.

Follow the link to *Free Stuff* and you can find some of my new songs to (**4**) .... to your MP3 player, absolutely free! You can also (**5**) .... to part of my recent concert in Prague. There are some really great games too. Ever wondered what it's like to work (**6**) .... a pop star? Try my *Kimberly's Caper* game and you'll soon find out that it's not as easy as you may have thought!

Follow the *My Hobbies* link to find out how I spend my free time. I've recently taken (**7**) .... rock climbing – it's great fun and, as (**8**) .... as you aren't afraid of heights, I'd really recommend you give it a try.

You can see some snaps of me climbing on my photos page, along with lots of other great pics. You can even see what I looked (**9**) .... when I was just five years old!

So, there you are. I hope you'll like my new site and that you'll want to (**10**) .... out here regularly. Have fun!

Love,
Kimberly XX

9 It's a weird, wonderful world

Dive in!

A Work in pairs. Which one of these 'amazing facts' is not true?

True or false … ?

1 Dolphins sleep with one eye open.
2 Ants can lift 50 times their own weight.
3 An ostrich's eye is bigger than its brain.
4 Bats have two noses.
5 A starfish doesn't have a brain.
6 A hippo can run faster than a man.

Check your choice was correct on page 175.

B Work in pairs. Look at the pictures. Which of these strange creatures do you think really exist?

Reading

C You are going to read about animal life in the world's oceans. Skim the article. Which animals from the pictures are mentioned?

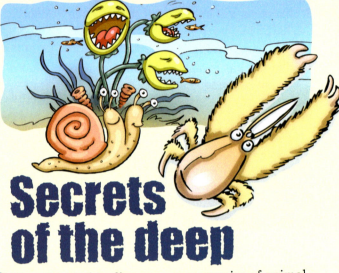

Secrets of the deep

1 If you wanted to discover a new species of animal, where would you look? The rainforests might be a good place to start. The deserts could hold secrets under the sand. But your best bet would be the oceans. The oceans cover nearly three quarters of the Earth's surface. They are so <u>vast</u> and so deep that scientists have only just begun to learn what lives there. And the creatures they do know about are so <u>bizarre</u> they look like visitors from another world.

2 'The oceans are a place of extremes,' says Professor Sally Fishwick of Bristol University, 'they are home to the biggest creatures on our planet.' And she's right! Take the blue whale, for instance. Growing to over 30 metres long, weighing around 180 tonnes and with a heart the size of a car, it is the biggest animal that has ever lived. These monsters of the ocean are an example of a phenomenon called deep-sea gigantism. 'We don't know why,' explains Professor Fishwick, 'but when some species <u>evolve</u> deep under the sea, they become huge.' The colossal squid is another example. This bizarre <u>beast</u> can grow to ten metres in length, weigh nearly half a tonne and has the largest eyes of any known animal.

3 But it's not just giants that make the oceans so special. Almost every day scientists are finding creatures that are, in the words of Sally Fishwick, 'just plain weird.' The 'Yeti crab' is a good example. Discovered two and a half kilometres below the surface, this blind beast is covered in white fur and is part-crab, part-lobster and part … <u>alien</u>! Another

Steps to success

Be careful! The choices given in the questions may be correct facts or commonly held opinions about the topic of the text. Make sure these facts or opinions are actually stated *in the text*!

recent discovery is the 'Dumbo octopus', so called because of the large <u>fins</u> growing out of its head that look like an elephant's ears.

4 Some discoveries have left scientists <u>utterly</u> confused. Deep under the icy waters of Antarctica, for example, researchers have found animals that look like flowers. They stand, like tall glass tulips in a field, feeding on tiny creatures called plankton. Some creatures are so different from any other animal that biologists need to create a new category for them.

5 If you live several kilometres below the surface of the sea, you have to be pretty <u>tough</u>. 'The pressure down there is like having several jumbo jets on top of you,' explains Professor Fishwick. 'Yet some creatures can actually survive there.' Other amazing organisms have been discovered near undersea volcanoes where the temperature <u>exceeds</u> 400 degrees Celsius. These are exciting discoveries. They show us that we needn't spend millions on space exploration in order to find new forms of life. As Fishwick points out, 'If life exists in such places on Earth, then it must exist elsewhere in the universe.'

6 Until recently, however, the depths of the ocean were just as mysterious as the <u>distant</u> planets. The colossal squid, for example, lives so deep in the sea that it has never been seen alive. If fishermen hadn't accidentally caught them over the years, we would never have known they existed. 'If people could see what lives there, they would be amazed,' says Fishwick. Now the latest technology is helping to do just that.

7 But it's a race against time. Global warming and the careless way we treat the ocean is threatening this mysterious undersea world. If you think that the extinction of species is something that only happens in the rainforest, you'd better think again. 'We ought to remember that the oceans are full of life, too, and that they need our protection,' urges professor Fishwick.

8 We should see the story of the blue whale as a warning to us all. If governments hadn't banned the hunting of this beautiful animal in the 1960s, it would have become extinct. Professor Fishwick's words are worth remembering. 'We must put the damage right, or we will lose a world that has only just been discovered.'

D Read the text and choose the best answer (A, B, C or D).

1 According to the writer, why is the ocean the best place to find new species?
A It is easy to explore there.
B It is such a large place.
C It is difficult for animals to hide there.
D It is rich in plants and food.

2 What **don't** scientists know about deep-sea gigantism?
A what it is   C where it happens
B what causes it   D which animals demonstrate it

3 In paragraphs three and four, what does the writer want to emphasize about ocean creatures?
A their strangeness C their size
B their number   D their usefulness

4 Why are the creatures described in paragraph five so exciting?
A They are so large. C They come from outer space.
B They can fly.   D They live in extreme conditions.

5 Scientists know about the colossal squid because
A dead ones have been seen.
B scientists can dive to great depths.
C live ones have been seen on rare occasions.
D fishermen catch them frequently.

6 What does the writer mean by 'it's a race against time'?
A Scientists are too busy to explore properly.
B The blue whale is threatened by hunters.
C Some species may disappear before we find them.
D Ocean life changes too quickly for science to record it.

7 What does the word *they* refer to in paragraph seven?
A all sea creatures   C the oceans
B blue whales   D the rainforests

E Match the words underlined in the text with a definition.

1 a fish's 'arms'   ....   6 more than   ....
2 big   ....   7 strange   ....
3 change over time   ....   8 strong   ....
4 far away   ....   9 totally   ....
5 not from Earth   ....   10 ugly creature ....

Did anything in the text surprise you?
Do you think there may be life on other planets? Why/Why not?

9

Grammar 1

 modals

See page 149 for information about modals.

Match these extracts with an explanation.

1 The rainforests **might be** a good place to start.
2 ... some creatures **can** actually **survive** there.'
3 ... you **have to be** pretty tough.
4 The deserts **could hold** secrets under the sand.
5 ... it **must exist** elsewhere in the universe.'
6 We **should see** the story of the blue whale as a warning to us all.
7 'We **must put** the damage right ...'

This expresses ...
a possibility .... , ...
b certainty ....
c ability ....
d obligation ....
e necessity ....
f advice ....

A Which modal *can't* be used to complete these sentences?

1 If we want to stop global warming, we really .... stop consuming so much.
a must   b ought to   c might
2 A giant tortoise .... live for over 150 years.
a must   b can   c may
3 One day we .... find life on another planet.
a might   b can   c could
4 This .... be a new discovery!
a must   b might   c ought to
5 I think you .... recycle more.
a could   b should   c may
6 Nothing .... live in the middle of a volcano.
a can   b could   c ought to

B Circle the correct option.

The Bloop

The oceans are full of mysteries, but the story of the Bloop **(1) must / has be** one of the most mysterious. In the summer of 1997, marine scientists in the Pacific detected a sound on their equipment. The sound was so loud that it **(2) might / could** be heard over a 5,000 km area. Scientists studied the sound and decided that only some kind of animal **(3) could / had to** make such a noise. But if it was an animal, it **(4) must / had to** be several times bigger than a blue whale – the biggest known creature on the planet. We **(5) may / should** never know what the Bloop really was ... or is, but if you're ever swimming in the Pacific, you **(6) don't have to / shouldn't** go too deep!

Quick chat

What do you think the Bloop might be?

C Complete the second sentence so that it has the same meaning as the first sentence. You can use up to three words in each gap.

1 It's not necessary for you to buy so many things.
You .... to buy so many things.
2 It's illegal to smoke in public places.
You .... in public places.
3 I wish I did more to be environmentally friendly.
I .... to be environmentally friendly.
4 The law in some countries makes people pay for the rubbish they throw away.
In some countries people .... for the rubbish they throw away.
5 I'm sure that travelling by plane is not good for the environment.
Travelling by plane .... good for the environment.
6 You don't have to use plastic bags from the supermarket. You can use your own.
You .... plastic bags from the supermarket. You can use your own.
7 We shouldn't forget to take our rubbish with us when we leave.
We'd .... to take our rubbish with us when we leave.
8 I'm sure that this is the dirtiest beach I've ever seen.
This .... the dirtiest beach I've ever seen.

Vocabulary

The environment

A Match to make sentences.
1 Animals and plants that live in a **wildlife**
2 Siberian tigers are examples of **endangered**
3 Paper bags are more **environmentally**
4 Factories pollute the air and this can cause **acid**
5 Scientists say that **global**
6 Every day a different animal or plant is **becoming**

a **extinct** because of our behaviour.
b **friendly** than plastic bags.
c **rain** to fall over a large area.
d **reserve** are protected by law.
e **species** that may disappear in the future.
f **warming** is making the sea levels rise.

B Now match the words in bold from A with a definition.
1 a safe place for animals and plants ....
2 animals and plants we may lose forever ....
3 disappearing forever ....
4 kind to the environment ....
5 polluted water ....
6 the heating of the planet over time ....

The weather

C Match these words for extreme weather conditions with the pictures.

blizzard • drought • flood • heatwave
hurricane • tornado

D Circle the correct options to complete the weather forecast.

Tomorrow's going to bring some pretty unpleasant weather to most parts of the country. In the north you can expect **(1) freezing / frozen** temperatures, nearly eight degrees **(2) under / below** zero on high ground. To the west there will be **(3) soft / light** showers in the morning, but this will turn to **(4) heavy / thick** rain by the afternoon. In the east the day will begin with a **(5) light / bright** breeze, but by evening there will be gale- **(6) force / strength** winds. In short, wherever you live, you'd better stay at home!

Weather idioms

E With a partner, decide what the idioms in bold mean.

1 When I heard the news, well! It was like **a bolt from the blue**.

2 They're so happy together. They're **on cloud nine**.

3 Don't worry. I'll be there to help, **come rain or shine**.

4 When I forget my homework, Mrs Grimm has **a face like thunder**.

5 I don't know what the fuss is all about. It's just **a storm in a teacup**.

6 I'm not going out tonight. I feel **a bit under the weather**.

How does the weather affect your mood?

9 Listening

A Match these words with the type of weather shown in the photos. Some words may go with more than one type of weather. Explain the connection.

> bang • bend • blow • burn • deep • electricity
> flash • freezing • gust • pouring • puddles • scorching
> shade • slip • soaked

Steps to success
In a listening exercise like this:
- read the choices carefully and look for clues.
- use your imagination to *guess* what you will hear before you listen.

B These people are talking about accidents caused by the weather. What do you think happened to each of these people? Tell another student.

- **A** I lost something.
- **B** I had to be rescued.
- **C** I was late.
- **D** I had something damaged.
- **E** I felt ashamed.

C 🎧 Now listen to five people talking about the accidents. First, listen and match each person with a picture from A. What words helped you choose?

D 🎧 Now listen again and match the speakers with the speech bubbles in B.

Speaker 1 ....
Speaker 2 ....
Speaker 3 ....
Speaker 4 ....
Speaker 5 ....

Do you prefer sun or snow? Why?

Speaking

A Many fish in our seas are endangered because of over-fishing. Here are some suggestions for dealing with the problem. Which solutions do you think would be best?

- Government Choose to Do Nothing to Protect Endangered Fish
- 200 Fish Farms Created as Alternative to Fishing
- **Fish Threatened with Extinction**
- Fishing Banned for Five Years
- Fish to Be Protected in New Marine Sanctuaries

B 🎧 Listen to two students talking about the problem. Which two solutions do they talk about?

Steps to success
- Whenever you express your opinion, give your reasons for it.
- Remember! The discussion is not only about your opinion. Listen and react to your partner's opinion too.

C 🎧 Now listen again. Tick the expressions in the Language chunks box that the speakers use.

Language chunks

Supporting your opinion
- That's because … ☐
- The reason I say that is … ☐
- For that reason … ☐
- So … ☐
- Since … ☐
- As … ☐

Reacting to opinions
- I see what you mean. ☐
- I understand what you're getting at. ☐
- You've got a point there. ☐
- That's a good idea. ☐
- Do you think so? I'm not so sure. ☐

D 👥 Work in pairs or small groups to discuss how to reduce litter.

Here are some ideas to stop people throwing litter away carelessly. Discuss the advantages and disadvantages of each idea and then choose the idea which will work best. Remember to use some of the expressions from the Language chunks box.

Say it right!

Sentence stress / silent letters

E Underline the words which are most stressed when these sentences are spoken.

I can ride a bike, but I can't ride a horse.

My mum can't speak English, but she can speak French.

F 🎧 Now listen, check and repeat. Can you think of a rule for when *can* is stressed?

G 🎧 Sometimes letters 'disappear' when we speak at normal speed. Listen to these sentences. Which letter disappears?

I must get up early tomorrow because I mustn't be late for school.

I mustn't eat so much chocolate and I must eat more fruit.

Grammar 2

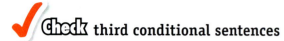 third conditional sentences

See page 149 for information about third conditional sentences.

Look at this sentence and decide if the statements that follow are true or false.

If governments hadn't banned the hunting of the blue whale in the 1960s, it would have become extinct.

1 This is about the present. **True / False**
2 The government banned the hunting of the blue whale. **True / False**
3 The blue whale became extinct. **True / False**

A Match the sentences that have the same meaning.

1 If Dr Botany hadn't gone to the jungle, he wouldn't have made a new discovery.
2 If Dr Botany had gone to the jungle, he would have made a new discovery.
3 If Dr Botany had gone to the jungle, he wouldn't have made a new discovery.

a Dr Botany made a discovery because he didn't go to the jungle.
b Dr Botany didn't go to the jungle and he didn't make a new discovery.
c Dr Botany went to the jungle and made a new discovery.

B Find and correct the mistakes in these sentences.

1 If we had protected tigers sooner, they wouldn't become so rare.
2 The house wouldn't have flooded if it is better built.
3 I wouldn't crashed the car if there hadn't been ice on the road.
4 We could have saved the building if we acted sooner.

C Choose the best way to complete each sentence.

1 If the car .... invented, our planet wouldn't have become so polluted.
a hadn't been   b wasn't   c isn't
2 Jane's fish .... have died if she had looked after them better.
a won't   b would   c wouldn't
3 Our holiday .... much nicer if the beaches had been cleaner.
a would be   b would have been   c wouldn't have been
4 If we had tried harder, we .... the Yangtze river dolphin from extinction.
a can save   b could save   c could have saved
5 If the wind .... so strong, the forest wouldn't have burnt so quickly.
a wasn't   b hadn't been   c had been
6 If we hadn't remembered to bring an umbrella, we .... soaking wet.
a would have got   b wouldn't have got   c will have got

D Make third conditional sentences about these situations.

1 There was a hole in the roof and the bedroom flooded.
   If there hadn't been ....
2 There were no litter bins near the beach and it got covered in rubbish.
   If there ....
3 The snow got very deep and I couldn't go to school.
   If the ....
4 We discovered fossil fuels and we created global warming.
   If we ....
5 We didn't look after the forests and they burnt down.
   If ....

Quick chat

Think about your life. How might things have been different if ...
• you had never been to school.
• you had lived in a different town.
• television had never been invented.

Practise your English

A Look at these photos of freak weather conditions. Do they really happen? What causes them?

B Read the news article quickly and answer these questions.
1 Which freak weather picture from A does it describe?
2 What cause is suggested?

Great balls of ... ice

We talk about (1) .... rain, but it's just an expression, right? Well, (2) .... better think again! The weight of some objects falling to Earth recently is very worrying. The objects are huge balls of ice and they have been crashing to the ground all over the place.

The biggest ice ball yet recorded fell in Brazil. This bolt from the (3) .... weighed 200 kilos, was the size of a fridge and landed in a car showroom. 'If I (4) .... seen it with my own eyes,' said Fabio Souza, a cleaner at the showroom, 'I wouldn't have believed it. It's a miracle that no one was hurt.' The same is true for pensioner Jan Kenkel. If she had been in her living room when a 22 kilo chunk of ice fell on her house in Iowa, she may (5) .... killed.

Scientists, who have called the balls 'megacryometeors', are (6) .... confused by the phenomenon. First of all, you don't (7) .... live in cold countries to get one in your back garden. They have fallen in parts of Africa that never experience (8) .... temperatures. What's more, they often fall from clear blue skies.

So what's going on? Some people think that these balls (9) .... form naturally because they are just too large. They think the balls (10) .... form on aeroplanes high overhead, then break off and fall to Earth. Whatever the cause, it looks like we now have one more extreme weather condition to worry about.

C Now read the text again and choose the best answer.

1 **A** big	**B** heavy	**C** deep	**D** thick
2 **A** you had	**B** you are	**C** you'll	**D** you would
3 **A** red	**B** green	**C** yellow	**D** blue
4 **A** haven't	**B** wasn't	**C** didn't	**D** hadn't
5 **A** was	**B** have been	**C** had been	**D** be
6 **A** certain	**B** wholly	**C** a lot	**D** utterly
7 **A** have to	**B** must	**C** need	**D** needn't
8 **A** freezer	**B** frozen	**C** freezing	**D** freeze
9 **A** don't have to	**B** must	**C** can't	**D** shouldn't
10 **A** need to	**B** can	**C** ought to	**D** must

Quick chat

Do you ever get strange weather in your country? If you do, why do you think it happens?

D Use the word in capitals to form one word that fits each sentence.

1 There are many .... species in the world which need our protection.
DANGER

2 Using a bike is a very .... friendly way to travel.
ENVIRONMENT

3 Fumes from factories and vehicles cause .... warming.
GLOBE

4 The blue whale nearly became .... in the 1960s.
EXTINCTION

5 Do you believe that people .... from apes?
EVOLUTION

6 I was .... amazed when I saw the damage from the storm.
UTTER

7 The colossal squid can often .... nine metres in length.
EXCESS

8 One day in the future people may be able to travel to .... planets.
DISTANCE

9 The climbers were surprised by the .... of the winds at the top of the mountain.
STRONG

10 The animals living in wildlife .... are protected by local governments.
RESERVATION

Writing: Formal letter

A Read the newspaper article below and discuss the following:
- what are the causes of this problem?
- what can we do to prevent it?

Forest fires rage out of control

Another day, another fire. Firefighters are battling to control the fifth forest fire that has started this week. Another huge area of forest land has been totally destroyed, and the fire is fast approaching homes. 'The situation is out of control,' said fire service chief Angelos Katrakis.' We need to stop this happening.'

B Note your ideas down. Use the headings to help you. Think about:
- who is responsible?
- what actually makes the fires start?
- are these accidents or deliberate?
- what can the government do to help?
- what can we do to help?

Why do forest fires happen?

How can forest fires be prevented?

C Now read this letter that a reader sent to the newspaper. Does she mention any of your ideas?

Dear Sir/Madam,
Your reports on the forest fires last week made me so sad. However, I am sure we can stop this happening again if we understand the two main causes: nature and our own carelessness.

It is true that forest fires sometimes happen naturally. Nevertheless, we can still prevent these if there are more foresters cleaning up the dry wood and leaves from the ground. In addition, there should be more firefighters near the forests so they can reach fires quickly.

The second main cause is people's carelessness. It goes without saying that people shouldn't light fires in the middle of the forest. Furthermore, visitors often leave litter behind. When the weather is hot, paper and bottles can cause fires to start. We need to teach people about these things. Without a doubt, last week's fires would not have happened if people had known how to treat the forest properly.

Some people think there's nothing we can do to protect our forests. On the contrary, I believe the solutions are very simple, but we must make an effort. Let's get started!

Yours faithfully,
Paula Pringle, Pinkerton

Quick chat

Do you agree with the writer? Why/Why not?

Skills development

Organizing the whole letter

D This kind of letter describes the causes of a problem and suggests possible solutions. There are two ways you can organize this. Which way matches the letter on page 102?

Plan A
Introduction, say why you're writing.
List the causes of the problems.
List the solutions.
Sum up with a call to action.

Plan B
Introduction, say why you're writing.
Describe one cause, give solutions for it.
Describe another cause, give solutions for that.
Sum up with a call to action.

Organizing each paragraph

Steps to success
You should have a 'mini plan' for *each paragraph* before you write it. Your ideas in each paragraph should be organized in a clear way.

E These words and phrases can help connect your ideas in a paragraph. Put them under the correct heading.

furthermore • however • in addition • in contrast
likewise • on the contrary • on the other hand

Joining similar ideas:
....

Joining opposing ideas:
....

Language chunks

Expressing certainty
Without a doubt …
It goes without saying …
There's no question that …

Introducing other people's opinions
It's often argued that …
Some people believe that …
It's thought that …

Planning and writing

F Read this task and note down ideas for your letter.

The Trumpet
Protests over dump plans

Hundreds of protesters gathered outside the village of Little Haven yesterday to show their anger. They are furious about council plans to open a new rubbish dump near the village. 'It will ruin our beautiful village, and who knows what health problems it will cause?' complained one local resident. However, the council argue they have nowhere else to put the waste.

You have read articles in *The Trumpet* newspaper about the problem of what to do with the rubbish. Write a letter to the editor saying what you think should be done about it.

G Now choose your best ideas to complete the planner.

Planner

Paragraph 1: ....
Paragraph 2: ....
Paragraph 3: ....
Paragraph 4: ....

H Write your letter. Try to use some of the expressions from the Language chunks box.

quick check

Be sure to:
- start by clearly mentioning the news article you are responding to.
- decide how to organize the whole letter.
- use linking words and phrases to connect your ideas logically.
- finish off with a strong statement of what you believe and a 'call to action'.

10 Food for thought

Dive in!

A Work in pairs. Decide if these common beliefs about food and health are true.

- a Drinking warm milk makes you sleepy. ....
- b An apple a day keeps the doctor away. ....
- c Chocolate gives you spots. ....
- d Carrots can help you see in the dark. ....
- e If you listen to music too loudly, you go deaf. ....
- f We use only ten per cent of our brains. ....
- g Reading in dim light or sitting too close to the TV damages your eyes. ....

Reading

B You are going to read about some common beliefs. Skim the article and match a paragraph to each common belief in A.

C Read the article a little more carefully. Are the common beliefs in A right or wrong?

Is there any truth to old wives' tales?

1

Like most people, I grew up believing the more chocolate I ate, the more spots I would get. **(1)** .... I wish I'd known that then! Research hasn't found any ingredients in chocolate that can either <u>trigger</u> acne or make existing acne worse. Acne is thought to be <u>associated with</u> the body's reaction to hormones rather than to what we eat.

2

What about reading in poor light or sitting too close to the TV? What does it do to your sight? Nothing, apparently. **(2)** .... In fact, you can't harm your eyes by using them, unless you stare into the sun. With the size of most TV sets today, you won't be able to see <u>the set</u> properly if you sit too close to it anyway.

3

Watch out MP3 users, this one is true. It is especially the case for music heard loudly through earphones. So, either keep the sound down low, or stop using earphones. The maximum volume of most MP3 players is around 120 decibels, which, I'm told, is about the level of a jet aeroplane taking off! **(3)** .... The government has <u>set a limit</u> of 100 decibels in MP3 players, and companies have had to make <u>adjustments</u>.

4

Funnily enough, this is a myth almost everyone believes. But scans have shown that we do in fact use 100 per cent of our brain! Each thing we do when we're awake (and even when we're asleep) uses a different part of the brain. **(4)** .... But even if we were to look at it from an evolutionary point of view, it is unlikely that larger brains would have developed if they weren't necessary.

5

Surprising as it may seem, it is true: eating apples every day can keep the doctor away. **(5)** .... Apples contain large amounts of phenols, which work as strong antioxidants and protect cells from damage. As we all know, there is plenty of evidence to suggest that antioxidants not only keep us looking young, but also protect us from disease.

6

Carrots contain high levels of a compound known as beta-carotene. It is what gives the vegetable its colour. It is also this substance, together with other essential vitamins, that can improve eyesight in later years. So, it is true that eating carrots does your eyes a lot of good, but can it help us see in the dark? The answer to this question is no, it can't. **(6)** .... If you want to see in the dark, you will need to get yourself a pair of night vision glasses!

7

This one is true, but you probably already knew that. **(7)** .... Warm milk contains an amino acid called tryptophan. Your body changes this into melatonin and serotonin, both of which cause a feeling of sleepiness. So, for those who have problems sleeping, a glass of warm milk before going to bed should ensure that you fall asleep as soon as your head hits the pillow.

Steps to success
- When deciding which sentence best fits a gap, read the text after the gap as carefully as the text before the gap.
- Once you have decided on a sentence for the gap, check that the text after it follows logically.

D These sentences have been removed from the article. There is also one extra sentence. Choose from the sentences (A-H) the one which fits each gap (1-7).

A In France, they're taking this very seriously.
B Nothing you eat or drink can do that.
C But now we are told that, in fact, there is no evidence that has been able to link it to skin problems.
D But does chocolate, which is a well-known antioxidant, really do that?
E Apart from all the useful fibre it contains, this common fruit lowers the risk of getting certain types of cancer.
F The question is why.
G These activities may strain or tire your eyes, but permanently damage them they will not.
H So, in the course of a day, all of it is used.

E Match the words and expressions underlined in the text with a definition.

1 important and necessary
2 changes
3 substances that slow down damage to our bodies
4 allowed a maximum level
5 a way of looking at something
6 connected with
7 the TV
8 cause

Did anything in the article surprise you? What's your opinion of these common beliefs regarding the common cold?
1 Going outside with wet hair causes colds.
2 Chicken soup will cure a cold.
3 The best treatment for the common cold is large doses of vitamin C.

 Find the answers on page 175.

Grammar 1

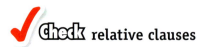 relative clauses

See page 150 for information about relative clauses.

Read these sentences and answer the questions that follow.
1 ... , in fact, there is no evidence that has been able to link it to skin problems. ....
2 ... this is a myth almost everyone believes. ....
3 Your body changes this into melatonin and serotonin, both of which cause a feeling of sleepiness. ....

Which sentence(s):
a uses a relative clause to give extra information? ....
b contain relative clauses that give necessary information? .... , ...
c separates the relative clause from the main clause with a comma? ....
d contains a relative clause but no relative pronoun? ....
e use or could use the relative pronoun *that*? .... , ...

Now decide whether sentences 1-3 are defining (D) or non-defining (ND) relative clauses.

A Circle the correct option.
1 The chef **who / which** makes the pasta is Italian.
2 I want a kitchen **where / which** is bigger than the one I have now.
3 The reason **why / which** they go there is because the food is excellent.
4 The café, **which / where** good quality coffee is served, closed.
5 We had hot chocolate at Angelina's every day **when / where** we visited Paris.
6 Donna, **who's / whose** mother owns a cake shop, is a fabulous cook.
7 The recipe **on which / which** this dish is based, was my grandmother's.
8 The chefs, both **of whom / whom** specialize in vegetarian food, are world famous.

B Decide if the gaps in these sentences are more likely to be filled with a defining or non-defining relative clause.
1 People .... have healthier lives.
2 My brother Ben .... is also coming to lunch.
3 I was speaking to someone ....
4 Is this the drink .... ?
5 I'm looking for a cookbook ....
6 Louise .... made it for me.

C These sentences contain the information missing from the clauses in B. Match them and rewrite them as relative clauses, using commas where necessary. Omit the relative pronoun if it is not necessary.
a Her carrot cake is excellent.
b You met him last year.
c It contains a lot of vitamins.
d She was telling me about the benefits of super foods.
e It has vegetarian recipes.
f They don't smoke.

D Join these pairs of sentences using non-defining relative clauses.
1 This cookbook is from the 19th century. It has a lot of interesting recipes.

2 Many people eat fast food. It is high in calories.

3 I eat pasta three times a week. I make it myself.

4 Helen needs to lose weight. She doesn't eat anything but pizza.

5 On Saturdays, I go to George's café. I always order their iced coffee.

6 On Friday nights we always go to The Jumping Bean. It's my favourite restaurant.

E Work in pairs. Write six quiz questions. Use each of these relative pronouns:
that, which, whose, when, who, where.
When you finish swap your questions with another pair.

Name the artist who painted the *Mona Lisa*.

Vocabulary
Health and diet

A Match to make phrases. Which of these things have ever happened to you? Tell the class.

1	cut	a	an ankle
2	sprain	b	a bone
3	break	c	a muscle
4	pull	d	yourself
5	get	e	your arm/leg in a cast
6	graze	f	your knee
7	have	g	a black eye / a bruise

B Complete the sentences with the correct form of a phrase from the box.

> cut down on • get over • go off
> put on • take care of

1 Can you smell this milk? I think it's ....
2 I've .... weight. I'll have to lose a bit if I want this dress to fit me again.
3 If you want to be healthy, you need to .... yourself better.
4 Drink this. It will help you .... your cold.
5 To lose weight, you'll need to .... the amount of junk food you eat.

Food and drink

C Circle the correct option from each pair of opposite adjectives.

1 I love pizza and burgers because they're very **tasty / bland**.
2 Ripe grapes are **sweet / sour**, but unripe grapes can be as **sweet / sour** as lemons.
3 Indian food is hot and **spicy / mild**.
4 I prefer to drink **sparkling / still** water or tap water. The bubbles in **sparkling / still** water go up my nose.
5 Carrots are fresh if they are **crisp / soft**.
6 Strong black coffee is quite **sweet / bitter**, unless you add sugar.
7 If you're watching your weight, a salad or **light / heavy** lunch is better.
8 I'd like my steak **rare / well-done**, please. I don't want to see any blood when I cut into it.
9 Salads can provide more vitamins because the vegetables are **raw / cooked**.
10 **Salty / Sweet** foods such as crisps are good in the summer.

D Read the two recipes. Find words and phrases connected with food preparations, quantities and food. Write them in the table below.

Vegetarian pizza

Ingredients
1 20 cm pizza base
1 tablespoon of tomato paste
100 grams of cheese
(or 1 cup of grated cheese)
1 pepper
6 mushrooms
1 onion
1 tablespoon of olive oil
some olives
some basil leaves

Method
Slice the onion into rings and fry it in some olive oil until golden. Put it aside. Spread the pizza base with the tomato paste. Grate the cheese and sprinkle it onto the pizza base. Add the onion. Slice the pepper and mushrooms and add them to the pizza together with the basil leaves. Cut the olives and remove the pip. Add them to the pizza. Bake the pizza in a hot oven for about ten minutes. Serve with a fresh green salad.

Jelly with fruit

Ingredients
1 packet of jelly crystals
2 cups of water
some fruit

Method
Put the jelly crystals into a bowl. Boil the water and pour it into the bowl with the jelly crystals. Stir the mixture until the crystals have completely dissolved. Chop the fruit into bite-sized pieces and add it to the jelly. Refrigerate until set.

Verbs connected with food preparation	Quantities	Food
slice	1 tablespoon	pizza base

E In pairs, talk about …
- a recipe for a dish you can make.
- a tasty meal you've had.

10

Listening

A Match the adjectives in the box to the first four sets of pictures in D.

> boiled • cooked • fattening • fried • grilled
> nutritious • raw • roast

B Now look at the last four sets of pictures. For each set, think of three words or phrases that you expect to hear. What is the topic of conversation likely to be in each extract?

Steps to success

The extracts are very short and you will hear them once only. You should:
- use the pictures to predict information before you listen.
- listen very carefully from the beginning.
- try to work out who the speakers are and what they are talking about.

C 🎧 Listen to the first extract and answer these questions.
- Where are the speakers?
- What is their relationship?
- What are they talking about?

D 🎧 You are going to hear eight extracts. After each extract, there is a question. For each question choose the correct picture, A, B or C.

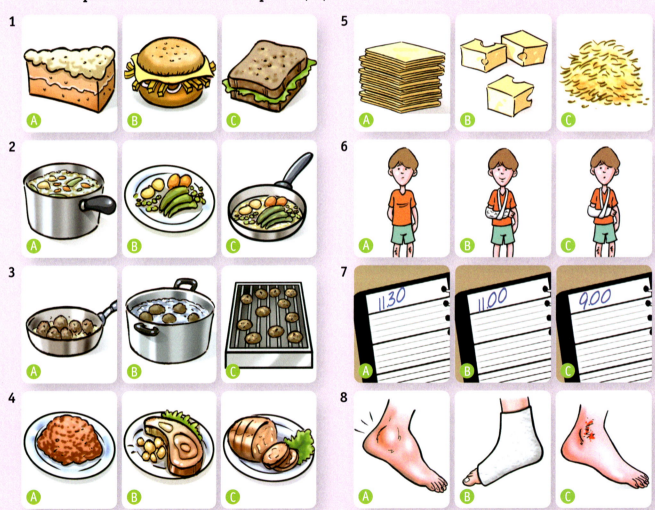

Quick chat

Which foods or ways of cooking are healthier?
Which foods should you try to eat less of or avoid?

Speaking

A Imagine you are organizing a party. What sort of things do you need to consider?

B 🎧 Listen to two friends organizing an end-of-term party. Which of the following do they talk about?

- food ☐
- drink ☐
- times ☐
- music ☐
- invitations ☐
- extra features ☐
- cleaning up after the party ☐
- plates, glasses and cutlery ☐
- the cost ☐

Steps to success
- When you have to talk about preferences, use phrases like the ones in the Language chunks box to vary the way you express yourself. Remember to invite your partner to express his/her preferences too.

C 🎧 Listen again and tick the expressions you hear.

Language chunks

Asking about preference
Do you prefer X or Y? ☐
What would you rather have, X or Y? ☐
Which do you think is best? ☐
Which do you prefer? ☐
Would(n't) you rather … (than)? ☐

Expressing preference
I'd prefer (not) to … ☐
I prefer X to Y … ☐
I'd rather do X than Y … ☐
I'd rather not have … ☐

D 👥 Work in pairs or small groups. Imagine you are responsible for planning an end-of-term party for the students in your year at school. You only have money for four of the following. Decide which you will choose for the party. Say why you have rejected the others.

E 👥 In pairs or small groups discuss these questions.
1 Do you like going to parties? Why/Why not?
2 What kind of celebrations (eg parties, weddings, etc) have you been to in the last year? What did you like/not like about them?
3 How do **you** usually celebrate a special occasion (eg your birthday)?
4 Do you prefer to celebrate a special occasion with your friends or your family? Why?

Sentence stress

F 🎧 Words that carry meaning, are stressed more than articles, auxiliary verbs, prepositions, conjunctions and pronouns. Listen to these sentences and underline the words that are stressed.
1 Which would you prefer, Madonna or the Black Eyed Peas?
2 Do you prefer going to a wedding or to a dinner party?
3 I think I'd prefer finger food to a buffet.
4 I'd rather not have house music at the party.
5 I've got a good recipe for fruit punch.

G 🎧 Listen again and repeat.

Grammar 2

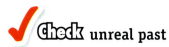 unreal past

See page 150 for information about the unreal past.

Match the sentences to their meaning.
1 I wish I'd eaten less at the party.
2 If only I was smarter.
3 I wish you wouldn't smoke.
4 I wish I was going to Sally's party on Saturday.
5 I'd rather you didn't smoke.
6 It's about time you started eating better.

a a wish or preference about the present ....
b a wish about the future ....
c a regret about the past ....
d a complaint about the present .... , ...
e advice about the present ....

What tense is used when the unreal past statement refers to

1 the past?
   past perfect / past simple or continuous
2 the present?
   past simple or continuous / present simple or continuous
3 the future?
   past simple or continuous / present simple or continuous

A Circle the correct option.
1 I'd love to be able to wear these jeans. If only they **would fit** / **had fit**.
2 I wish I **had** / **have** more time to exercise.
3 If only I **could give up** / **gave up** junk food.
4 I'd rather we **didn't** / **don't** have to walk home.
5 It's time you **started** / **start** going to the gym.
6 I wish I **hadn't eaten** / **ate** all that chocolate. I feel sick now.

B Write sentences about each situation beginning with the words given.
1 If I'd gone to the party, I would have had a really good time.
   If only ....
2 My sister falls over all the time. It's annoying!
   I wish ....
3 You're always complaining! You really should stop complaining so much.
   I wish ....
4 I regret not telling Georgia the truth.
   If only ....
5 I really regret not going to Denise's party on Saturday.
   I wish ....
6 I really hate being sick. When will I get better?
   I wish ....
7 Watching so much television can't be good for you.
   It's time you ....
8 I don't like you eating so much chocolate.
   I'd rather you ....
9 You never eat any fruit.
   It's time you ....
10 Please don't open the window. It's cold!
   I'd rather you ....

C Write four sentences about things that could be better in the town or city where you live. Use *I wish*, *If only*, *I'd rather*, *It's time*.

I wish there was less pollution.

D What do they wish? Write sentences with *I wish*, *If only*, *I'd rather*, *It's time*.

I wish I had straight hair.

Practise your English

A Fast food is often called junk food. Why do you think that is?

B Read the text quickly. What experiment did Morgan Spurlock conduct and what was the result of it?

Isn't it time we **(1)** .... caring about what we eat? This is the question **(2)** .... the documentary film-maker, Morgan Spurlock, asked himself before making *Super Size Me*. The film, **(3)** .... shocked audiences worldwide **(4)** .... it came out in 2004, documents Spurlock's life for 30 days on a diet of junk food. Horrified at the obesity rate in the USA, Spurlock, **(5)** .... generally leads a healthy life, decides he will start eating the diet of the average American in the USA. For 30 days he will eat a diet of high-fat burgers, fries, milkshakes and fizzy drinks, all of **(6)** .... are high in calories and lacking in nutrition. The experiment almost kills Spurlock, **(7)** .... health gets worse day-by-day. By the end of the 30 days on a junk food diet, he has **(8)** .... 11.1 kilos, often feels depressed and has done severe damage to his liver. We are told at the end of the film that it takes Spurlock 14 months to **(9)** .... the weight he has gained and to get his health back. The reason **(10)** .... he puts his own health at risk is to show people that what they are eating is in fact killing them. Spurlock proves beyond a doubt that there is a lot of truth in the saying 'You are what you eat'.

C Read the text again and write one word in each gap.

Do you agree with the saying 'You are what you eat'? How often do you eat junk food? Do you think you need to change your eating habits? Why/Why not?

D Complete the second sentence so that it has a similar meaning to the first sentence. Use the word given.

1 I would love to be able to give up junk food.
   STOP
   I wish .... eating junk food.
2 Things would have been better if I had not told Gemma the truth.
   TOLD
   If only .... the truth.
3 I would prefer it if you wouldn't call me every night.
   YOU
   I'd rather .... every night.
4 The soup needs more salt, it's rather bland.
   TASTY
   The soup needs more salt, ... enough.

E Choose the best answer.

1 Limes are as .... as lemons.
A sour B bitter C sweet D crisp
2 I can hardly move my right leg. I think I might have .... a muscle.
A broken B sprained C pulled D scraped
3 Polly's always falling over and .... her knees.
A pulling B spraining C breaking D grazing
4 I know a great .... for chocolate mousse.
A receipt B recipe C cook D cooker
5 I want to be healthier so I've decided to .... a diet.
A put on B lose C go on D go off
6 .... the cake in a hot oven for 45 minutes.
A Bake B Boil C Fry D Roast
7 It took Tom three weeks to .... his cold.
A take care of B get over C take over D get off
8 A good steak should be .... so there is a little blood.
A grilled B raw C rare D well-done

10

Writing: A letter of advice

A Read this letter that was sent to a problem page in a teen magazine. In pairs, come up with some suggestions for Mary.

Dear Rosanne ...

This year I'm in my final year at school. Up until last year I played in a volleyball team, but gave it up because I didn't have the time to attend all the games and the training. I spend my time studying for exams and I find myself snacking on crisps and anything salty. Mum keeps complaining that my eating habits will make me sick. What can I snack on instead and how can I keep fit without spending too much time doing so? Can anyone help?

Stressed-out, Mary

Suggestions:

B Now read this letter of advice for Mary. Were any of your suggestions mentioned?

Dear Mary,

A
I read your letter in *Teen Magazine* and I'd like to make some suggestions which I think could help you.

B
Firstly, you say you've given up playing sport this year because you don't have the time. It might be a good idea to take up some other physical activity otherwise, by the end of the year, you'll wish you had! You could try walking. A 20-minute walk every day is just as good as working out or playing a sport and it will also clear your head.

C
Secondly, instead of snacking on crisps, which are high in calories, you can snack on something healthier. If it's something salty or tasty you crave, try eating some sliced raw vegetables, like carrots or cucumbers, with some salt and vinegar on them. They're just as tasty as crisps, but more nutritious and lower in calories.

D
You'll find that exercise combined with a healthy diet will help you take care of yourself better and will also help you concentrate more on your studies.

E
Hope this helps and good luck with your studies this year.

Best wishes,
Rosanne

Steps to success

- When writing a letter of advice to someone you don't know, you need to be friendly, but not too direct or absolute. Using modals like *can*, *could*, *may* or *might* makes opinions and suggestions sound more polite.

Skills development

Appropriate register

C Look back at the letter and underline all the modals that are used.

D Use the modals that you have underlined in the letter to make the following suggestions sound less absolute or direct. Use each modal verb at least once.

1 Eat fewer snacks.
   It might be a good idea to eat fewer snacks.

2 Eat more fruit.

3 Work out three times a week.

4 People who don't exercise put on weight more easily.

5 Cut down on all the chocolate you're eating.

Organization

E Read the letter again and match each paragraph with a topic below.
- ending the letter with a friendly comment
- saying why you're writing
- advice about diet
- advice about exercise

Planning and writing

F Read this letter also asking for advice. In pairs, come up with some suggestions for Joaquim. Make notes in the planner.

I've heard that a healthy diet combined with regular exercise can make you look good, feel better and live longer. I think it's time I started eating a healthy diet and doing some exercise, but I'm not sure how to go about it. I don't have much time for breakfast or lunch and the canteen at school only sells junk food. Also, I hate going to the gym. Is there anything else I could do instead? Any suggestions would be welcome.
Many thanks,
Joaquim

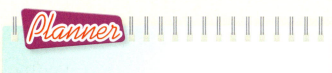

Planner

How are you going to start your letter? Dear .... ,

Paragraph 1: Why are you writing?

Paragraph 2: Make some suggestions about diet.

Paragraph 3: Make some suggestions about exercise.

Paragraph 4: End the letter with a friendly comment.

How are you going to sign off?

G Write your letter. Use some of the Language chunks to help you.

Letters of advice

Dear Mary,
I read your letter in …
You say …
It might be a good idea to …
Hope this helps.
Best wishes,

Be sure to:
- write four paragraphs.
- talk about one topic in each paragraph.
- use a friendly, but polite style.
- use *can*, *could*, *may* and *might* to be less direct and more polite.
- begin and end the letter appropriately.

Check your knowledge 5

A Use the clues to complete the crossword puzzle.

Down
1 Yesterday's snow .... left a metre of snow on the roads.
3 It was .... yesterday! The maximum temperature was only -5°C!
5 Pollution can result in acid ...., which damages forests.
9 In the .... reserve there are some rare birds.

Across
2 When water levels rise dangerously, a .... can occur.
4 If it doesn't rain for long periods, a .... occurs.
6 If a rare plant or animal is not seen for a long enough period of time, it is considered ....
7 In 2005, ... Katrina killed many people and destroyed the city of New Orleans.
8 Many plant and animal .... become endangered when their natural environment is destroyed.
10 Scientists believe that .... warming will result in more incidents of extreme weather.

B Complete the sentences with words from the box. There are four extra words.

add • bitter • cooked • cup • glass • pour • raw
refrigerate • slice • spicy

1 .... the onion into rings.
2 .... the milk into the saucepan slowly.
3 Thai food is just as .... as Indian food.
4 Isn't sushi made with .... fish?
5 .... the cheesecake for at least two hours or until it sets.
6 You will need a(n) .... of flour and three eggs.

C Match to make sentences.

1 I'm feeling a bit under the weather
2 When I heard the good news,
3 Nick needs to put
4 Gill has cut down
5 You really need to take
6 Seeing her was a

a bolt from the blue!
b so I think I'll stay in bed.
c on the amount of sweets she eats.
d I was on cloud nine.
e on three kilos.
f care of yourself a little more.

D Complete with a relative pronoun from the box. Then decide which relative pronouns can be a) omitted and b) replaced with *that*.

when • where • which (x 4) • who • why

Déjà vu

Have you ever been in a place (**1**) .... you know you have never been before, but (**2**) .... you have a strange feeling you have visited before? What about a situation (**3**) .... you know has not happened before, but you have the feeling you've already experienced? Well, you are not alone. Déjà vu, (**4**) .... in French means 'already seen', is the experience of being certain that you have lived or seen a new situation before. You feel as though the event (**5**) .... you are experiencing has already happened or is repeating itself. The feeling is quite strange and people (**6**) .... experience it are often very surprised at the moment (**7**) .... it happens. The reason (**8**) .... you may be experiencing déjà vu is not clearly understood. It may be attributed to a dream, but equally there could be other possible reasons for the experience.

E Circle the correct option.

1 If we want to slow down global warming, we really **have to / could** drive less.
2 One day the average lifespan of humans **might / must** reach 100.
3 People really **should / ought** buy products with less packaging.
4 We need oxygen to live, which is why we **can't / mustn't** live on any other planet.
5 That **mustn't / can't** be Bill you saw in London. He's in Spain at the moment.
6 People **could / need** definitely do more to protect the environment.

F Choose the best way to complete each gap in the text.

Dear Agony Aunt,

I am in desperate need of your advice. I am very accident-prone and I'd like to know what I **(1)** .... do to be less so. Let me give you an example of what I mean. Last year, I **(2)** .... my ankle. I suppose I should count myself lucky I didn't break it. Earlier this year, I fell down some stairs and broke two **(3)** .... in my right arm. Last month, I walked into a door and **(4)** .... a glowing black eye. Last week, during karate training, I **(5)** .... a muscle. This afternoon, as I was preparing a salad for lunch, I cut **(6)** .... with the knife. My doctor **(7)** .... believe how many accidents I have had. He told me I **(8)** .... to be more careful. But I **(9)** .... see how. I'm always so careful! What do you think I **(10)** .... to do? Can you help, please?

Desperately yours,
Patricia

1	A should	B ought	C must	D have
2	A broke	B sprained	C pulled	D cut
3	A bones	B muscles	C elbows	D wrists
4	A had	B got	C made	D had got
5	A grazed	B sprained	C broke	D pulled
6	A my	B me	C myself	D mine
7	A can't	B mustn't	C shan't	D shouldn't
8	A should	B need	C must	D can
9	A needn't	B mustn't	C can't	D couldn't
10	A must	B should	C ought	D have

G Find and correct the mistakes in these sentences.

1 Charlie, who's dad is a chef, is learning to become a pastry chef.
2 The cake, that you made for Tina's birthday, was delicious.
3 This brownie recipe, who I downloaded from the internet, is the best I've ever tried.
4 The flat I live has a huge kitchen.
5 The restaurant which we went for dinner last night was really cheap.
6 If it hadn't been so cold yesterday, we could gone out.
7 You don't need recycle everything you use, but you should at least make an effort.
8 Television programmes should to promote green living.

H Complete the second sentence so that it has a similar meaning to the first sentence. Use the word given.

1 It wasn't warm enough to go swimming.
HAVE
If it had been .... gone swimming.
2 It rained all day and flooded the streets.
RAINED
If it .... the streets would not have been flooded.
3 Many people died because of the heatwave.
BEEN
Many people would not have died if there .... a heatwave.
4 Stop complaining!
WOULD
I wish .... complaining.
5 I don't like the fact that you drink so many fizzy drinks.
RATHER
I'd .... drink so many fizzy drinks.
6 Staying up so late every night isn't good for you.
WENT
It's time .... earlier.
7 I regret having told Sue about our plans.
WISH
I .... Sue about our plans.
8 I regret not ordering something cheaper.
ORDERED
If only .... something cheaper.

11 Vanished without a trace!

A 🎧 These people have mysteriously disappeared. Listen and complete the fact files.

1
Name: The crew of the *Mary Celeste*
Year of disappearance: ....
Where last seen: ....

2
Name: Amelia Earhart
Year of disappearance: ....
Where last seen: ....

3
Name: Lord Lucan
Year of disappearance: ....
Where last seen: ....

Kidnap <u>ruled out</u> on ghost yacht

Police investigating the case of the Australian ghost yacht, *Zak III* say they do not believe the crew were kidnapped.

The disappearance of Bob Hatton (56), Peter Dunstable (69) and his brother Jim (63) has <u>baffled</u> police since April 2007. They said goodbye to friends at the East Coast port of Airlie Beach and were planning to sail to Townsville. They never got there. Their empty boat was found off the Australian coast and when police went on board, they expected to find a murder scene. Instead, they found a scene of <u>eerie</u> calm.

The <u>abandoned</u> boat was neat and tidy. The men's clothes were folded on their beds. The table was laid for dinner. They can't have been planning to go anywhere because a laptop was being recharged and there was a cup of coffee next to it. It must have been just another normal day on board when tragedy struck. But what kind of tragedy?

'There were no signs that anyone had boarded the vessel,' said a police spokesman. 'They must have fallen <u>overboard</u> and drowned.' But Jean Gregory, Hatton's niece, doesn't accept the police's view of things. 'It just doesn't <u>add up</u>,' argues Miss Gregory, 'They were experienced sailors. They can't have fallen over … not all three of them!'

The police say there may have been a sudden storm that knocked the crew off, but Gregory doesn't believe that theory either. 'They couldn't have been in any immediate danger,' she says, 'because their lifejackets were still folded up in the cabin.' Some think pirates may have boarded the ship and kidnapped the crew. 'There's no <u>evidence</u> to support such a theory,' said the police spokesman. 'Perhaps it is simply that they should have been more careful.'

FACT FILE 1
Name(s): ....
Year of disappearance: ....
Where last seen: ....

Reading

B You are going to read about two more mysterious disappearances. Read the newspaper articles quickly and complete the fact files.

Steps to success
• You have to find evidence in the text to support your answer. If you cannot find evidence for your choice, it is probably wrong.

Farmer's discovery could solve 40-year-old mystery

A parachute unearthed by a farmer's tractor last week could be a clue to one of the world's great unsolved crimes.

In 1972, a man calling himself Dan Cooper boarded flight 305 in Portland. Once in the air, he passed a note to the flight attendant which read, 'I have a bomb. You are being hijacked'. Cooper forced the pilot to land in Seattle. Once on the ground, he demanded $200,000 and four parachutes. The authorities agreed to his demands, Cooper let the passengers go and the plane took off again.

Shortly after take-off, Cooper asked the pilot to keep flying south, towards Mexico. When they were flying somewhere over the state of Washington, he made the flight attendant go to the flight deck with the pilots. That was the last time he was ever seen. Despite flying through the middle of a storm, Cooper opened the back door of the plane and jumped out. Of course, he took the ransom with him. A huge police search was carried out and investigations lasted for years afterwards, but Cooper — or whoever he was — had disappeared without a trace. Until now.

Police are examining the parachute, but haven't yet decided if it is Cooper's. But even if investigators do decide it's his, the mystery still remains: is he dead or alive? Some say that Cooper couldn't possibly have survived such a jump through a thunderstorm. Others say he can't have died, because his body ought to have been found. It never was.

Over the years there have been countless theories about who Cooper was. The police have a suspect list with over 1,000 names. Perhaps the farmer's discovery will help solve the mystery.

FACT FILE 2

Name(s): ....

Year of disappearance: ....

Where last seen: ....

C Now choose the best answer (A, B, C or D). Find evidence in the text.

1 *Zak III* was found
A on its way to Airlie Beach.
B sailing round the coast of Australia.
C in Townsville.
D floating at sea.

2 When they got on the yacht, the police were surprised because
A it was in a terrible mess.
B everything looked normal.
C it looked like a murder scene.
D there were no clothes.

3 What were the crew probably about to do before they disappeared?
A eat B swim C sleep D send an email

4 According to Jean Gregory, the lifejackets prove that
A the men were experienced sailors.
B there wasn't a storm.
C the men were kidnapped.
D the men fell overboard.

5 Who saw Cooper jump?
A the pilots   C no one
B the flight attendant   D the passengers

6 Some people think Cooper didn't survive because
A he forgot his parachute.
B of the weather.
C he was never seen again.
D his parachute didn't open.

7 Some people believe that Cooper survived because
A his parachute has been found.
B his body was never found.
C all the money disappeared.
D he has been seen in Mexico.

D Match the words underlined in the articles with a definition.

1 confused
2 looking closely at something
3 don't think is a possibility
4 left empty
5 make sense
6 strange and spooky
7 over the side of a ship
8 people who solve a crime
9 proof
10 money paid to kidnappers

How would you explain the mysteries you have just heard and read about?

11

Grammar 1

✓ Check modal perfect

See page 151 for information about modal perfect.

Match the extracts with their use.
1 '... they **should have been** more careful'.
2 ... there **may have been** a sudden storm ... .
3 They **can't have been planning** to go anywhere ...

Modal perfect forms can be used to express:
a possibility about the past ....
b certainty about the past ....
c criticism about past actions ....

A What do these sentences express? Choose the correct option.
1 They can't have been planning to go anywhere.
a They weren't able to plan.
b I am sure they didn't plan.

2 There may have been a sudden storm.
a I'm not sure, but it's possible there was a storm.
b I'm certain there was a storm.

3 They must have had a meeting.
a I'm certain they had a meeting.
b It was necessary for them to have a meeting.

4 They ought to have called the police.
a They called the police and that was a good idea.
b They didn't call the police and that was a mistake.

B Write sentences about these situations. Use the modal perfect form and the verb given.
1 It isn't raining now, but the ground is wet. (must / rain)

2 You're expecting a call from your friend. The phone rings, but you don't answer it in time. (may / be)

3 Your brother didn't work hard for his exams and he failed them all. (should / study)

4 You heard a noise like thunder outside, but it's a beautiful sunny day with no clouds in the sky. (can / be)

C Complete these sentences with a modal verb and the correct form of the verb in brackets.
1 The back door is open and my computer is missing. A thief .... (break in).
2 I think I had my keys in my pocket, but now they aren't there. I'm not sure, but I .... (drop) them.
3 Maria didn't arrive on time. She .... (catch) an earlier train.
4 Greg was insulted by what you said. You .... (be) so rude.
5 Helen only left an hour ago. She .... (arrive) in London yet.
6 My dad is brilliant at the piano. He .... (become) a musician.

D Work in pairs. Look at this picture of a crime scene. Talk about the burglars using modal perfect.

They must have had a dog.

Vocabulary

People and crime

A Match these people with the definitions.

detective • judge • jury • lawyer • suspect
victim • witness

1 a person who has suffered from a crime ....
2 a group of ordinary people who decide on a case in court ....
3 the person in charge of the court ....
4 a person who sees a crime happening ....
5 a special police officer who investigates crimes ....
6 the person police think is responsible for a crime ....
7 a person who defends or accuses in a court ....

B 🎧 Now listen and match each speaker to a person from A.

Crime and mystery

C Complete the text with words from the box.

alibi • clue • committed • cover-up • culprit
evidence • motive • weapon

The Grime (8.30pm, Channel 4)
The second in a new three-part series starring Max Bruce as detective Rudyard Barlow. Barlow now knows he's close to finding out who (1) .... the murder of the beautiful Audrey Mapp. All the (2) .... points to two possible suspects. However, there has been a clever (3) .... that baffles even Barlow. He finds the murder (4) .... in Julie Harrison's room, but it turns out to be a useless (5) .... Harrison's jealousy may be a likely (6) .... for the murder, but she has the perfect (7) .... She was with Barlow all that night. So who's the (8) .... ?
You'll just have to watch and find out!

D Write the adjective and adverb forms of these nouns.

Noun	Adjective	Adverb
crime		
dishonesty		
guilt		
innocence		
law		
mystery		

E Use the word in capitals to form one word that fits each sentence.

1 A man has been arrested for driving .... without a licence. LEGAL
2 James looked .... at his lawyer and said, 'It's not true!' GUILTY
3 I think this evidence proves that she's .... , don't you? INNOCENCE
4 Don't trust Ben. He's a very .... person. HONESTY
5 After leaving school he got involved in .... activities and eventually went to prison. CRIME
6 Holly disappeared .... one night and hasn't been seen since. MYSTERY

F Match to make sentences.

1 The manager was **accused**
2 A man and a woman have been **charged**
3 The gang were **sentenced**
4 The gang **got away**
5 The police have been **blamed**

a **for** not acting quickly enough.
b **of** stealing money from the company.
c **to** five years in prison.
d **with** murder.
e **with** nearly two million pounds.

Has anyone you know been the victim of a crime? What happened?

11

Listening

A Can you match the crimes to the picture?

> arson • burglary • pickpocketing • robbery
> shoplifting • vandalism

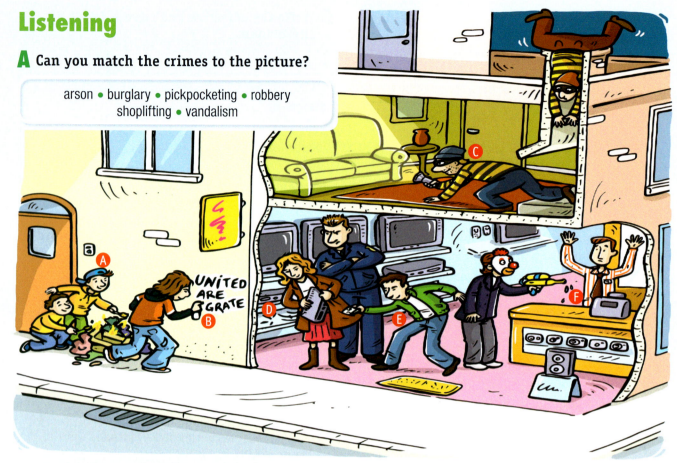

B 🎧 You are going to hear a radio interview about crimes that have gone wrong. Listen and tick the crimes from A that are mentioned.

Steps to success
- Sometimes the 'wrong' choices in questions include words that are used by the speakers. Don't make your choice just because you see a word that you heard spoken. It may be a trap!

C 🎧 Now listen again and choose the best answer for each question.

1 What couldn't David Davies explain?
A how he got stuck in a chimney
B why he was on the roof
C what his friends were doing

2 Who first found Davies?
A a police officer
B a firefighter
C a supermarket employee

3 Why didn't the bank robber speak to the clerk?
A He wasn't able to speak.
B He was wearing a mask.
C He didn't want anyone to recognize his voice.

4 What information did the bank robber give?
A his name   B his telephone number   C his address

5 Which of these things did the Californian teenagers *not* damage?
A schools   B cars   C shops

6 Why did the teenagers use MySpace?
A to get other friends involved
B to show how proud they were
C to plan more crimes

7 How did the police find out about the pair?
A They received an email.
B They received a telephone call.
C They searched the internet.

D Check your answers with your teacher. Can you explain why the other answers are not correct?

Which of the crimes in the picture do you think is the worst?

What sort of punishment is best for each of the crimes? Choose from the list:
- a fine
- a prison sentence
- community service
- other ... what?

Speaking

A Work in pairs. Put *four* of these pictures in order to make a story about a crime. What is your story? Which picture *didn't* you use?

B Now listen to two students doing the same task. Was their story the same as yours? Which picture did they leave out?

Steps to success

Remember! It is not a problem if you don't understand what someone says, even in an exam. Just ask politely for clarification.

C Listen again. Which of the expressions in the Language chunks box do you hear?

Language chunks

Asking for clarification
Could you explain what … means? ☐
I'm not sure what you mean. ☐
Would you mind repeating that, please? ☐
Could you say that again, please? ☐

Expressing agreement
Aha … ☐
I think you're right. ☐
Hmm. That's true. ☐
Absolutely. ☐
Exactly. ☐
I see what you mean. ☐

D These pictures show evidence that was left at a crime scene. The crime was the theft of a valuable painting from a museum. Work in pairs. Decide what each of the clues might tell the police about the crime.

Say it right!

Sentence stress
We often stress certain words in a sentence in order to make our point clearer.

E Look at these sentences. Which word do you think is stressed the most?

I don't like crime stories, but I love mysteries.
It wasn't a ghost. It was just a trick.

F Now listen, check and repeat.

G Work in pairs to say sentences using the correct stress. Student A look at page 165. Student B look at page 175.

Rome is in France.
Rome isn't in France. It's in Italy.

11

Grammar 2

✓ **Check** infinitives and -ing forms

See page 151 for information about infinitives and -ing forms.

A Choose the sentence, a or b, that means the same as the one given.

1 I was doing something else and then I started reading instead.
 a I stopped reading.   b I stopped to read.

2 Fiona hasn't forgotten that she met me.
 a Fiona remembers meeting me.   b Fiona remembered to meet me.

3 Graham was watching TV, but then he decided to do something else instead.
 a Graham stopped watching TV.   b Graham stopped to watch TV.

4 Alex needed to post the letters, but he didn't remember.
 a Alex forgot to post the letters.   b Alex forgot posting the letters.

B Circle the correct option to complete the story.

Sleepwalking into crime

Jonathan Kipp was a regular sleepwalker. He was taking medicine (1) **stopping / to stop** it. One night, however, he forgot (2) **taking / to take** his pills. At about three in the morning, Kipp got out of bed and got dressed, still fast asleep. Without waking, he went (3) **getting / to get** his car keys and walked out of the house. Amazingly, he even remembered (4) **locking / to lock** the door behind him. Then he got into his car and drove into town. Still asleep, he stopped (5) **buying / to buy** petrol and then kept driving towards the town centre. Police officer Rob Berry remembers (6) **seeing / to see** him. 'He didn't stop (7) **driving / to drive**, even when the traffic lights turned red,' said Berry. PC Berry followed Kipp and couldn't believe his eyes when Kipp eventually got out of his car, walked to a jeweller's window and tried (8) **smashing / to smash** it. Kipp was arrested and at that moment, so he claimed, he woke up. Later in court, Kipp said he didn't remember (9) **doing / to do** anything that night. Unfortunately for Kipp, the judge was not convinced!

Quick chat
Do you believe Kipp was sleepwalking? Why/Why not?

C Use the correct form of a verb from the box to complete each sentence.

buy • look • persuade • steal • wear

1 He tried .... the police that he was innocent.
2 I bet she really regrets .... those CDs.
3 The thieves forgot .... gloves, and they left fingerprints everywhere.
4 When they stopped .... something to eat, the gang was arrested.
5 They've tried .... everywhere, but they can't find Cooper.

✓ **Check** make, let and allow

See page 151 for information about make, let and allow.

D Make sentences from the notes.

1 my parents / not / let / go out / tonight
 ....

2 they / not / allow / dogs / enter / the park
 ....

3 Miss Pringle / made / do / my essay / again
 ....

4 they / let / you / eat / in here?
 ....

E 🎧 Listen and complete the sentences so that they are true according to what you hear. Use up to three words, including the word in brackets.

1 Angela didn't .... (remember) me.
2 Dad didn't .... (us) out.
3 Dad .... (me) my room.
4 They don't .... (go) into the zoo.

Practise your English

A You are going to read an article about two strange events. Read it quickly. What happened?

B Read the article again. Use the word in brackets to form one word that fits each gap.

The Bennington Triangle

You may have (**1**) .... (HEAR) of the Bermuda Triangle, but do you know about the Bennington Triangle? Bennington is a small village in Vermont, USA. Between 1920 and 1950 Bennington hit the headlines due to a number of unexplained (**2**) .... (DISAPPEAR). In 1949, for example, a man called James Tetford was on a bus near Bennington. There were 14 other passengers on the bus at the time. Later they all told (**3**) .... (INVESTIGATE) that they had seen Tetford asleep in his seat. However, when the bus reached Bennington, there was no sign of him. Where could Tetford have (**4**) .... (GO)? To this day, nobody knows.

Equally (**5**) .... (MYSTERY) is the story of 18-year-old Paula Weldon. In 1946 she went walking in the countryside near Bennington. Another couple walking just behind Weldon remembered (**6**) .... (SEE) her go round a bend in the path. But when they went round the same bend, the girl had vanished. Despite carefully (**7**) .... (EXAM) a wide area, the police never found any sign of Weldon or any (**8**) .... (EVIDENT) which could explain what happened to her.

Quick chat
What could have happened to the people in Bennington?

C Complete the second sentence so that it has a similar meaning to the first sentence. Use the word given.

1 Your behaviour was criminal.
   BEHAVED
   You ....

2 The police said that they would help us.
   AGREED
   The police .... us.

3 The judge ordered him to pay for the damage.
   MADE
   The judge .... for the damage.

4 My parents won't let me go out after ten.
   ALLOW
   My parents won't .... out after ten.

5 I'm sure that was a UFO.
   HAVE
   That .... a UFO.

6 I'm certain that wasn't a ghost.
   HAVE
   That .... a ghost.

7 Jane should have done her homework, but she forgot.
   FORGOT
   Jane .... her homework.

8 Tony met me last year and he hasn't forgotten.
   REMEMBERS
   Tony .... last year.

D Choose the best answer.

1 The judge gave the .... a day to make a decision.
   A jury   B lawyer   C culprit   D suspect

2 The police have arrested two ....
   A suspects   B culprits   C witnesses   D victims

3 The .... who investigated the case gave his evidence in court.
   A judge   B jury   C detective   D suspect

4 Police are asking for any .... who saw the crime to come and speak to them.
   A culprits   B victims   C suspects   D witnesses

5 Robert James couldn't have committed the crime because he has a perfect ....
   A culprit   B weapon   C alibi   D motive

6 Very often the .... for crimes is money.
   A victim   B weapon   C motive   D alibi

11

Writing: A story (2)

A Look at this writing task. In pairs, tell each other what you would write about.

> You have decided to enter a short story competition. The competition rules say you must write a story of between 120 and 180 words with the title, 'My mysterious experience'.
>
> Write your story.

B Look at the story a student wrote for the competition. Put the parts of the story in the correct order.

A I must have gone very pale, because Anne asked, 'Are you OK, Maude?' When I'd recovered, I told her my strange story.

B A few days later I was looking at an old photo album with my sister, Anne. I'd never seen it before. Suddenly, I found a photo that made my stomach feel strange. There was an old black and white photo of my grandma at primary school. Next to my grandma, staring at me, was the woman from the bus. She had an eerie, sad look on her face.

C This is the strangest, most mysterious thing that has ever happened to me. It happened many years ago, but whenever I think about it, I still get a shiver down my spine.

D I was on a bus in the city centre. A middle-aged woman was sitting opposite me. I felt uncomfortable because she had started to stare at me. She looked confused about something. Eventually I said, 'I'm sorry. Do I know you?' The woman, in a very soft voice, answered, 'I remember teaching you.'

C Strong emotions usually cause physical feelings too. Can you find examples of this in the story?

D Match these situations with the physical feelings in the Language chunks box.

1 I saw the train rushing towards me.
2 I heard someone whisper my name.
3 My eyes fell on the word 'FAIL'.
4 In front of me was a dish of spinach and snails.

Language chunks

Physical feelings

I felt a chill down my back. ☐
My heart sank. ☐
My body froze. ☐
My stomach turned. ☐

Have you ever had any of these feelings? Why?

Skills development

Adjectives

E You can make your story more memorable by using good vocabulary. Match the adjectives on the left with the more dramatic ones on the right.

1. surprised
2. annoyed
3. embarrassed
4. happy
5. frightened
6. sad

a. ashamed
b. astonished
c. delighted
d. furious
e. heartbroken
f. terrified

F Write five sentences, each with a dramatic adjective from E.

Direct speech

> **Steps to success**
> - Including some direct speech in your story is a way to bring your story to life. It makes your characters more 'real' and helps add drama. However, don't include too much direct speech — don't forget that you're writing a story, not a dialogue!

G Can you find three examples of direct speech in the story on page 124?

H Add the correct punctuation to this paragraph. Pay particular attention to the direct speech.

I thought I was alone but suddenly a voice from the next room whispered what are you doing Mark it sounded familiar but strange at the same time is it my stupid brother playing games again I thought is that you John I called as there was no answer I walked angrily into the next room stop playing games I said as I walked in but to my amazement the room was empty

Planning and writing

I Look at this writing task. In pairs, brainstorm ideas for a story. Use the mind map to help you.

> Write a short story for your school magazine. The story must include the words,
> 'It's a mystery,' she said.
> Write between 120 and 180 words.

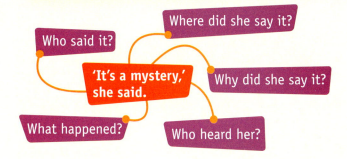

J Organize your story using the planner and some of the Language chunks. Then write your story. Write between 120 and 180 words.

Planner

Paragraph 1: Introduction – when and where did this happen? ....

Paragraph 2: Set the scene and describe the characters. ....

Paragraph 3: What happened next? ....

Paragraph 4: How did the characters feel? ....

quick check

Be sure to:
- describe feelings as well as events.
- include some dramatic adjectives.
- include some direct speech.
- check your punctuation.

12 Big spender

Kathy　　　Paula

Dive in!

A Work in pairs. How much do you know about shopping? Do the quiz and find out.

1 Which country has the largest shopping mall?
a China　　b the USA　　c France

2 Which of the following is not an accessory?
a jewellery　　b a belt　　c a cardigan

3 What is the spending money given to children or teenagers called?
a pocket money　　b bank account　　c money box

4 Where would you haggle over the price of an item?
a a department store　　b a street market
c a high street shop

5 What can you buy at the butcher's?
a fruit　　b magazines　　c meat

 Now check your answers on page 175.

Reading

B You are going to read about consumerism. Skim the article. What do you learn about each person in the pictures?

Steps to success
- Limit the possible options in a missing sentence task. First work out what the paragraph or section is talking about (eg *what, who, where* and *when*).
- Look at linking devices such as articles, pronouns, conjunctions, etc in order to make your decision.
- Reread the paragraph with the missing sentence in place. Does it make sense?

C These sentences have been removed from the article. Which are in the first person and which are in the third person? How can this help you with your choice?

A Trying to look trendy is listed as her main hobby.
B I don't spend all my money on myself.
C To the poorhouse if we're not careful.
D How is that different from Paula, you ask?
E She shows me her shoes and a picture of a similar pair at ten times the price.
F Max and Paula are very similar.
G So much so, in fact, that some people might even say she is frugal.
H But today, things are different.

Teenage consumerism

Consumerism is the term used today to describe our obsession with buying things. Some would say that it has become a way of life. In fact, for many people, spending money equals happiness. Is it any wonder then, that young people have also been affected? Years ago, the pocket money teenagers got would not allow them to buy an iPod, a trendy outfit or anything more expensive than some sweets, magazines and perhaps even a record. (1) .... We interviewed three teenagers about their consumer habits and this is what they had to say.

Paula, 16, is a fashion victim, she admits it herself. (2) .... 'I spend at least six hours a week shopping for clothes and shoes. I love it! I wouldn't want to spend my time doing anything else.' Where does Paula find the money to spend on so many clothes when she's only 16, you ask?

'I have a part-time job working as a cashier in a local supermarket on Friday nights after school and on Saturday mornings. Also, I always ask for cash presents for my birthday and for Christmas. I buy most of my clothes when the sales are on, that way I can buy more with my money. I spend so much time window-shopping that I can compare prices from one store to the next. I know where to get the best bargains.'
(3) .... 'I got these shoes for only £30, the real thing would have cost me over £300! I know I could be doing other things with my time, but I find it hard to resist!'

Paula may spend hours a week shopping, but most of that time she is only window-shopping as she does not have the money to do much else. Max on the other

Max

hand is a shopaholic. (**4**) .... Well, Max, 18, buys something every time he goes shopping and he goes shopping every day!

'I'm happiest when I'm shopping. I do most of my shopping online. I find it such a pleasure. (**5**) .... I get presents for friends, my family and even my dog.' A day does not go by when Max hasn't spent some money on clothes, games, music or the latest electronic gadget. Retail therapy is very real for Max. He is only happy when he is spending money.

You probably couldn't find two more different people than Max and Kathy. Kathy, 15, is careful with her money. (**6**) .... 'I don't like spending my money needlessly. I don't need to buy lots of jeans and shoes to be happy. I have hobbies, family and friends for that. I save money and spend it when I absolutely have to.' Kathy says she is sensible with money and that everyone else is a consumer victim. She says we need to find other things that make us happy because this is something that will end up costing us more than we bargained for. Spending leads to debt. Debt leads to misery. 'I don't want to be one of those people who cannot see that there are other things in life that can make you happy. Every day more and more shopping malls are popping up around us. Why aren't we building parks instead?'

Where will all this spending lead us? (**7**) .... As Kathy wisely points out, 'It's a trap. Fashion changes every year and so, to keep up, you have to buy more things every year. Perhaps if we weren't so fashion conscious or so easily influenced by fashion magazines, we could see past it for what it really is – a spending trap. Money doesn't grow on trees and the sooner we realize that the better.'

D Choose from the sentences (A-H) in C the one which fits each gap (1-7). There is one extra sentence which you do not need to use.

E Find these words and phrases in the text. Choose the correct definition for each one.

1 trendy outfit
a a fashionable set of clothes worn together
b trendy clothes that fit

2 sales are on
a when things are for sale
b when shops reduce the price of the goods they sell

3 bargains
a agreements
b things bought more cheaply than usual

4 window-shopping
a looking at things displayed in shop windows
b shopping for windows

5 find it hard to resist
a it is difficult to stop doing it   b it is difficult

6 retail therapy
a shopping to make yourself feel happier
b therapy for an illness

7 frugal
a very careful with money   b wastes money

8 debt
a money that is owed   b to question something

9 keep up
a to continue at the same pace
b to keep something up high

10 fashion conscious
a to be aware of what is in fashion and to dress accordingly
b to not follow the fashions

F Complete the sentences with words from E.
1 I bought some real .... in the sale. Everything was under ten pounds.
2 Jill is really fashion conscious. She wants to .... with all the latest trends.
3 I borrowed money and now I'm in ....
4 .... is great. There's no need to buy, you can just look.
5 Tina always feels better after some ....

What advice would you give to Kathy, Paula and Max?

12

Grammar 1

✓ Check countable and uncountable nouns

See page 152 for information about countable and uncountable nouns.

Match each word in bold with the type of noun it is.

1 ... or so easily influenced by fashion **magazines** ...
2 **Money** doesn't grow on trees ...
3 I buy most of my **clothes** when the sales are on.

a uncountable noun
b countable noun
c plural uncountable noun

Circle the best option to complete the rules.

1 We usually use **many** / **much** for countable nouns and **many** / **much** for uncountable nouns, but they are usually only used in **negative** / **positive** statements and questions.
2 We can use **a lot of** / **many** for both countable and uncountable nouns.

A Circle the correct option.

1 My house needs new **furniture** / **furnitures**.
2 I don't have **much** / **many** cash on me.
3 This store sells electrical **goods** / **good**.
4 I bought two **pairs of jeans** / **pair of jeans**.
5 We spend **many** / **a lot of** money on food.
6 The sales are only on for **a few** / **few** days.

✓ Check so / such and so many / so much

See page 152 for information about so / such and so many / so much.

Read the extracts and match the rules below.

1 I spend **so much** time window-shopping **that** I can compare prices ...
2 **So** careful, in fact, **that** some people might even say she is frugal.
3 Where does Paula find the money to spend on **so many** clothes ...
4 I find it **such** a pleasure.

| adjective • countable noun • noun • uncountable noun |

a *so* + ...
b *such* + ...
c *so much* + ...
d *so many* + ...

B Find and correct the mistakes in these sentences.

1 This top is such nice that I think I'll buy two!
2 There was so many traffic that it took two hours to get to work!
3 These jeans are so much expensive that Mum will never agree to buy them.
4 I've never seen so much books before!
5 This is so nice car. Is it new?
6 Some actors have so many money they don't know what to do with it!

✓ Check too and enough

See page 152 for information about *too* and *enough*.

Match the sentences with meanings a or b.

1 These trousers are *too* expensive.
2 These trousers are expensive.
3 These trousers aren't cheap *enough* for me.

a These trousers cost more than I can afford and so I won't buy them. ...., ...
b These trousers cost a lot, but I still might buy them. ....

C Complete the sentences with *too*, *enough*, *so* or *such*.

1 I don't have .... money for a car like this.
2 We had .... a good time shopping yesterday.
3 Those trousers are .... small for you. You need a bigger size.
4 This department store is .... big – it takes ages to get around!
5 These earrings are pretty, but they're .... expensive. They're not even silver!
6 I spent .... much on these boots that I can't go out for the rest of the month!

12

Vocabulary

Clothes and accessories

A Match the words and phrases from the box with the picture.

> belt • bracelet • denim jacket • earrings • high heels
> leggings • necklace • nosering • waterproof jacket
> ring • scarf • sweater • tracksuit • trainers

B Circle the correct option.
1 These shoes don't **fit / suit** – they're too small. What **size / number** are they?
2 That colour really **fits / suits** you. You look good in green.
3 Can you help me **do up / take up** my zip? I can't reach it.
4 Those jeans are really **loose / tight**. Can you breathe at all?
5 Those trousers are too **loose / tight**, you should get them **taken in / taken up**.
6 Because I'm short, new skirts or trousers usually need to be **taken in / taken up**.
7 Would you like to **take it back / try it on**? The changing rooms are this way.

Shopping and money

C In pairs, list three things that you can buy in each of these shops.
1 Claire's Accessories ....
2 Selfridges Department Store ....
3 Witfield's Newsagent's ....
4 Virgin MegaStore ....
5 Sainsbury's Supermarket ....

D Complete the sentences with words or phrases from the box.

> brand • buy • cash desk • logo • product
> receipt • take it back

1 This CD keeps jumping. I've still got the ...., so I think I'll ....
2 This skirt looks really good. Why don't you .... it!
3 I'd like to pay for this. Where is the .... ?
4 What's your favourite .... of trainers?
5 This designer label has a little crocodile as its ....
6 This advert is funny, but what .... is being advertised?

E Match to make sentences. Then match the idioms in bold with their meanings below.

1 John **has more money**
2 I think we've just **been ripped**
3 I can't afford to buy a thing,
4 I can't lend you any more. I'**m not made**
5 You must **be loaded**

a I**'m broke**!
b **than sense**. I can't believe he paid £500 for those boots!
c if you own five houses.
d **off**. We paid far more than we should have.
e **of money** you know!

1 get cheated ....
2 have unlimited amounts of money ....
3 be very rich ....
4 wastes money ....
5 have no money ....

Quick chat

What clothes, shoes and accessories do you like to wear?
What kind of things do you like to buy when you have money?
What's your favourite shop?

12

Listening

A Work in pairs. How far do you agree with the following statements?

> Your hairstyle is an expression of who you are and how you feel.

> I don't enjoy shopping.

> It's important to keep up with hair fashions.

> With clothes, being comfortable is more important than looking smart.

> Credit cards can make you spend more money than you earn.

B Read the multiple choice questions in C and match them to the pictures.

Steps to success
- Before you listen, read the questions carefully, because they contain a lot of information about the content of the listening extract.
- The first time you listen to each extract, listen to it all **before** choosing an answer. Choose your answer during the pause and check it the second time you listen.

C You will hear people talking in eight different situations. For questions 1-8, choose the best answer, (A, B or C). You will hear each situation twice.

1 A girl is discussing her hairstyle. Why does she say it's important for her to style it herself?
A It is an expression of how she is feeling.
B It is cheaper than getting it done by a hairdresser.
C Only she knows how she wants it to look.

2 You hear two boys talking about hair. What does one of the boys want to do?
A Dye his hair a dark colour.
B Dye his hair blonde.
C Dye his hair blue or violet.

3 You hear a mother and a daughter talking. What's the problem?
A The daughter needs a new pair of jeans.
B The daughter spends more than she earns.
C The daughter buys clothes she doesn't need.

4 You hear a girl talking about clothes. What does her mother tell her?
A That she looks better in formal clothes.
B That she needs to dress more smartly.
C That no one takes her seriously.

5 You hear a man talking with a sales assistant. What is the dress code at his work?
A The employees have to wear a suit and tie.
B The employees are smartly dressed.
C The employees can wear anything they like.

6 You hear a man talking about online shopping. What does he like about shopping online?
A He finds it convenient.
B He finds it fun.
C He can buy anything online.

7 You hear a man talking about buying a home. What does he say people should do first?
A Talk to the bank about a loan.
B Put a 10% deposit on the house.
C Start saving as soon as they start working.

8 You hear a man and a woman talking about something the man has bought. How does the woman feel about his purchase?
A She does not approve.
B She is impressed.
C She is envious.

Would you ever buy anything online? Why/Why not?

12

Speaking

A Imagine you won €1,000,000 in the lottery. What would you spend it on? Make a list.

B 🎧 Now listen to two dialogues with students talking about the same topic. What do the four students say they would spend the money on?

1 .... 3 ....
2 .... 4 ....

Steps to success
- When you're pausing to think of ideas, don't drag out words or pause for too long. Fill your hesitations with expressions like the ones in the Language chunks box.
- If you're having a conversation, make sure you show you're listening to your partner(s). You can do this by expressing interest, surprise, etc in what your partner says.

C 🎧 Listen again and tick the expressions you hear.

Language chunks

Hesitating
Umm … ☐
Let me think … ☐
Just a minute … ☐
Let's see … ☐
How shall I put it, … ? ☐

Expressing interest in what your partner says
Really? ☐
That sounds great/wonderful/nice/good. ☐
I know what you mean … ☐
I see … ☐
I can understand that … ☐
Wow! ☐
Why's that? ☐
That's interesting! ☐

D How would you express interest in the following statements? Use language from the Language chunks box.

I do most of my shopping online.
— That's interesting.

1 I'm not sure I like shopping online.
....

2 I go shopping every day.
....

3 I think shopping centres are a waste of space.
....

4 I never shop in large department stores.
....

5 I'm trying to save for a trip around the world.
....

E 👥 In pairs or small groups, tell each other what you have decided to spend your lottery winnings on. Give reasons for your choices. Remember to express interest in what your partner says.

F 👥 How important are the following things for a happy life? Rate them in order from the most important (1) to the least important (10). When you've finished, in pairs or small groups, decide on a common ranking.

☐ money   ☐ fashion
☐ love   ☐ career
☐ friends   ☐ fame
☐ family   ☐ free time
☐ health   ☐ good grades

Say it right!

/iː/ and /i/

G 🎧 Listen and circle the number you hear. Practise saying the numbers.

1 sixty / sixteen   4 ninety / nineteen
2 fifty / fifteen   5 forty / fourteen
3 thirty / thirteen

H 🎧 Listen and write the number(s) you hear.

1 ....   4 ....
2 ....   5 ....
3 ....

12

Grammar 2

✓ Check both ... and, neither ... nor, each, every, all, none

See page 153 for information about *both ... and, neither ... nor, each, every, all, none.*

Match to make six sentences.

1 Neither
2 Both
3 None
4 All
5 Each / Every

a of the clothes were cheap.
b the dress **and** the shoes were on sale.
c the prices **nor** the service was acceptable.
d the presents I bought were expensive.
e person in the store bought something.

A Complete the sentences with words from the box.

all • and • both • each • every • neither
none • nor

1 .... of the clothes I tried on suited me, so I didn't buy anything.
2 .... these shoes .... those fit me properly. Are you sure they're a size 39?
3 .... the dress .... the jacket fit beautifully. Are they in the sale?
4 .... person I know is mean with their money.
5 She spent .... the money she won in a week!
6 .... of us has bought something online.

B Work in pairs. Discuss the six items in each group and write sentences describing similarities and differences. Use *all, each / every, none, both* or *neither*, as shown in the example.

1 jeans, trousers, top, blouse, shirt, jacket
2 currency, money, dollars, cash, love, friendship
3 chair, sofa, table, desk, bookshelf, lamp
4 bird, bee, fly, parrot, horse, sheep
5 films, music, DVD player, dishwasher, television, washing machine

Both jeans and trousers are plural nouns.
All these goods can be worn.

✓ Check indeterminate pronouns

See page 153 for information about indeterminate pronouns.

Complete the table of indeterminate pronouns.

someone/ somebody		everyone	
somewhere			anywhere
	nothing		

C Circle the correct option.

1 Is there **anybody** / **somebody** home?
2 Are we going **somewhere** / **anywhere** this evening?
3 Why are you crying? Did I do **anything** / **something** to upset you?
4 **Someone** / **Anyone** told me you spent a lot of money yesterday. Is it true?
5 I'm bored. There's **nothing** / **something** to do.
6 **Everyone** / **Someone** loves my new boots. I'm so glad I bought them.

D Complete with indeterminate pronouns.

On Boxing Day last year, I made the mistake of going to the Boxing Day sales. As (1) .... knows, on the 26th December, all the shops have huge discounts on (2) .... (3) .... queues for hours outside the shops so that they can be the first to find the best bargains. The sales really are amazing – (4) .... you buy is 50% off! The problem is that (5) .... knows about the sales and they all go (6) .... to shop. As a result, all the shops are very crowded and if it's clothes you want to buy, you'll be disappointed because it's difficult to try (7) .... on. In the end, I didn't buy a thing. I've made a promise never to go again. Take my advice, if you're looking for (8) .... to do next Boxing Day, don't go shopping!

Practise your English

A Read the text quickly and answer these questions.
- What is eBay?
- What was the first thing ever sold on eBay?

eBay is the world's largest online auction and shopping website. It is a marketplace where (**1**) .... who wants to buy or sell anything can go. All over the world, (**2**) .... individuals and businesses trade (**3**) .... on eBay every day. It caters for everyone: buyers, sellers, browsers and collectors. As a place to buy, you can find (**4**) .... you need or want at (**5**) .... prices. It is also a place to sell your unwanted items. New or old, you can sell almost (**6**) .... on eBay. You can be sure there is (**7**) .... out there who wants to buy it. The first thing that ever sold on eBay (**8**) .... it first started in 1996 was a broken laser pointer. The story goes that the seller warned the buyer that the laser pointer was broken and the buyer said that he was, in fact, a collector of broken laser pointers! Proving that there is (**9**) .... you cannot sell on eBay. Finally, it is a place for collectors. It is the world's largest market of rare, hard-to-find items. Whether it's stamps you collect or vintage cars, you'll find it on eBay. It has been (**10**) .... a success that its website claims that there are more than 100 million users of the site worldwide!

B Now read the text again and choose the best answer (A, B, C or D).

1	**A** nobody	**B** anything	**C** anywhere	**D** anyone
2	**A** both	**B** neither	**C** and	**D** all
3	**A** good	**B** goods	**C** shopping	**D** product
4	**A** something	**B** nothing	**C** anything	**D** anywhere
5	**A** expensive	**B** bargain	**C** cheaply	**D** high
6	**A** something	**B** nothing	**C** anything	**D** anywhere
7	**A** anyone	**B** everyone	**C** someone	**D** anybody
8	**A** who	**B** that	**C** where	**D** when
9	**A** something	**B** nothing	**C** anything	**D** anywhere
10	**A** such	**B** so	**C** many	**D** much

Quick chat
Is there anything you would be interested in buying or selling on eBay? What?

C Complete the second sentence so that it has a similar meaning to the first sentence. Use the word given.

1 I can't afford this coat.
TOO
This coat is .... for me.

2 I don't have a lot of money, you know.
MADE
I'm not .... , you know.

3 She's very happy. She sings all the time.
SO
She's .... sings all the time.

4 I love the way she does her hair.
AMAZING
Her .... , don't you think?

D Choose the best answer.

1 Your new outfit is amazing! It really .... you.
A goes **B** fits **C** suits **D** matches

2 I have a huge .... I owe more than €1,000.
A borrow **B** lend **C** debt **D** doubt

3 Sorry, I can't lend you any money. I'm ....
A broke **B** ripped **C** ripped off **D** loaded

4 That top looks too big. You should ....
A get it in **B** put it up **C** take it up **D** take it in

5 .... can make an outfit look better.
A Clothes **B** Noserings **C** Necklaces **D** Accessories

6 There are always lots of bargains in the shops when the sales are ....
A in **B** up **C** on **D** at

7 I don't have .... money for this. Can you lend me some?
A enough **B** too **C** many **D** so

8 I have .... money left. How much do you need?
A a lot **B** much **C** a little **D** a few

9 It's .... cold to go swimming. We'll freeze!
A too **B** very **C** so **D** enough

10 You're jeans .... really nice.
A are **B** is **C** be **D** was

12 Writing: A letter of application

A Discuss these questions.
1. Do students in your country have part-time or summer jobs?
2. Have you ever had a part-time or summer job?
3. What kind of part-time or summer job would you like to have?

B Read the advertisement and answer these questions.
1. What is the position?
2. Should the letter be formal or informal? Why?
3. What do you need to mention in your letter?

City Lights Café

Are you looking for a summer job?

We are looking for enthusiastic people to work in our busy café for the summer. If you would like a summer job, we'd like to hear from you. You must be at least 16 years old to apply.

Apply in writing. Please include information about:
- your current situation
- your level of English
- why you would like to work in a café over the summer

C Read this letter of application. Does the letter do all of the things below?

A letter of application should:
- be formal. ☐
- be separated into paragraphs. ☐
- begin and end appropriately. ☐
- mention the information asked for in the advertisement. ☐
- if necessary, ask for further information. ☐

Dear Sir or Madam,

I am writing in response to your advertisement. I would like to apply to work in your café for the summer.

I am a 16-year-old student in year ten at secondary school. I have been studying English for six years now and my level of English is good. I am free for the summer and would like to do something useful with my time. I believe this job will give me both valuable work experience, and the opportunity to practise my English.

I would like to ask for some information, which the advertisement does not give. I would appreciate it if you would let me know whether the job is full-time or part-time. I would also be grateful if you could tell me the exact dates the job will be available for.

Please do not hesitate to contact me if you require any further information or to arrange an interview.

I look forward to hearing from you.

Yours faithfully,
Giordano Piccirilli

Skills development

Style, content and organization

D A letter of application should be formal. Match the formal phrases (1-8) to the informal phrases (a-h).

Language chunks

1. Dear Sir or Madam,
2. I am writing in response to …
3. I am a 16-year-old student …
4. I believe this job will …
5. I would like to ask for some information.
6. I would appreciate it if you would let me know …
7. I look forward to hearing from you.
8. Yours faithfully,

a. Best wishes,
b. Please get back to me ASAP.
c. Hi!
d. I want to know something …
e. I'm 16.
f. Please tell me …
g. I think this job will …
h. Just a quick note to …

Steps to success
- In a letter of application, make sure you include all the information about yourself that the advertisement asks for. Remember, you would really like to get the job, so be positive!

E Underline the parts of the letter on page 134 that mention the necessary information.
- the applicant's current situation
- the applicant's level of English
- why the applicant would like to work in a café over the summer

F What information does the writer include in each paragraph?

Paragraph 1 ....
Paragraph 2 ....
Paragraph 3 ....
Paragraph 4 ....

Planning and writing

G Imagine you would like to apply for the job below. Read the advertisement and complete the planner.

Planner

Paragraph 1: reason for writing ....

Paragraph 2: your current situation / why you would like to work in a souvenir shop ....

Paragraph 3: any previous work experience you have (including voluntary work) or don't have ....

Paragraph 4: any questions you have ....

City Souvenirs

Are you a teenager looking for something to do over the summer?

We are looking for enthusiastic people to work in our souvenir shop over the busy summer months. If you are eager to gain work experience and would like to work with other people your age, we'd like to hear from you. You must be at least 16 years old to apply.

Apply in writing. Please include information about:
- your current situation
- why you would like to work in a souvenir shop
- any previous work experience (including voluntary work)

H Write your letter in 120-150 words.

quick check

Be sure to:
- use a formal style.
- talk about your current situation.
- say why you would like to work in a souvenir shop.
- mention any previous work experience you may have.
- organize your letter into paragraphs.
- use indirect questions if you'd like to ask for information.
- begin and end the letter appropriately.

Check your knowledge 6

A Circle the correct option.

1. Why hasn't Julie called yet? She should **have arrived / arrive** home by now.
2. Janice claims **being / to be** the fastest runner in her class.
3. The police won't allow anyone **go / to go** into the house.
4. I'd like to buy this shirt, but I don't have **much / a lot** cash on me.
5. It was **such a / so** good restaurant that we decided to book a table for the following week.
6. That's a nice jacket, but it's far **too / so** expensive.
7. Neither Seb **nor / either** Alison can come with us tomorrow.
8. I enjoy **either / both** jazz and pop music.
9. Don't work so hard. **Everyone / Someone** needs a rest sometimes.
10. We don't have **nothing / anything** to cook for lunch today.

B Complete the sentences with words from the box.

alibi • brand • clues • logo • motive • products sense • witnesses

1. Police have asked for .... who may have seen the crime to contact them.
2. I find it silly to pay more for clothes just because of the .... name.
3. Justin spends so carelessly. Sometimes I think he's got more money than ....
4. The .... for Mercedes-Benz cars is one of the most famous in the world.
5. It's difficult to understand the .... for crimes like arson.
6. Apart from a few fingerprints, the police haven't found any other ....
7. What kind of .... does your shop sell?
8. Jones might have committed the crime, but he has a perfect ....

C Complete with a preposition.

1. A 39-year-old man has been accused .... arson.
2. Excuse me, can I try .... this dress?
3. Alan was unfairly blamed .... breaking the computer.
4. These new trousers are too long and need to be taken ....
5. This skirt is too loose. I need to have it taken ....
6. A couple from London have been charged .... robbery.
7. One hundred euros for two tickets! I think you've been ripped ....
8. I don't like this hat that I bought. I think I'll take it ....

D Use the word in capitals to form one word that fits each sentence.

1. Don't look at me so .... I know you're the culprit. — INNOCENCE
2. If you want to return an item to the shop, you'll need a .... — RECEIVE
3. I wouldn't trust him. He looks like a .... to me. — CRIME
4. My uncle Robert is so .... that he's got his own aeroplane. — LOAD
5. There's a great new shop nearby that sells .... like bracelets, earrings and scarves. — ACCESS
6. One thing I really hate is .... — HONEST
7. I can't afford to go out tonight. I'm totally .... — BREAK
8. You can't park here. It's .... — LEGAL

E Find and correct eight mistakes.

Dear Sir/Madam,

I recently ordered some jeans from your catalogue. When it arrived I found that one leg was short enough and the other was torn. I have tried speaking to one of your representatives about this, but no one answers the phone. For this reason, I have decided writing an email.

Over the years I have spent much money with your company. Generally, your goods is excellent quality and I have had a few problems. However, I have been very disappointed by this latest purchase. I would like either a refund or a replacement.

I hope hearing from you soon.

Yours faithfully,
Ann Grey

F Complete the second sentence so that it has the same meaning as the first sentence. Use the word given.

1. I'm sure that Polly didn't see us earlier.
   CAN'T
   Polly .... us earlier.
2. My mum doesn't allow me to wear make-up.
   LET
   My mum .... make-up.
3. It was such a heavy bag that it took two of us to carry.
   SO
   The .... that it took two of us to carry.
4. I don't think these trousers are long enough.
   TOO
   I think these trousers ....
5. Both the colour and the size were wrong.
   NOR
   .... the size were right.
6. There is nothing we can do to help her.
   ISN'T
   There .... do to help her.
7. Andrew has forgotten that he borrowed my CDs.
   REMEMBER
   Andrew .... my CDs.
8. This shirt is too small for me.
   DOESN'T
   This .... me.

G Choose the best answer to complete the text.

Investigations are still underway into yesterday's (1) .... of a jewellery store in Foley town centre. Thieves got away with £10,000 worth of gold, diamonds and famous (2) .... watches. Police have cordoned off the corner of Market Street near Bewley's department (3) .... and (4) .... is currently allowed (5) .... the area. (6) .... believe that an employee may be one of the (7) .... 'The thieves couldn't (8) .... about the shop's side entrance unless an employee had told them it was there,' said Detective Mike Holmes. Holmes also believes there must (9) .... three members of the gang, with one waiting outside. A (10) ...., Mrs Hazel Nutt, remembers seeing a suspicious car parked near the store at the time of the robbery. However, she can't remember (11) .... the driver's appearance or the vehicle's number plate. The police are still examining the area and it is (12) .... early to say just when Market Street will reopen to the public.

1	A theft	B robbery	C arson	D burglary
2	A brand	B logo	C product	D receipt
3	A shop	B centre	C market	D store
4	A anyone	B everyone	C someone	D no one
5	A entering	B entered	C to enter	D enter
6	A Investigations	B Investigates	C Investigators	D Investors
7	A victims	B culprits	C alibis	D witnesses
8	A know	B knowing	C knew	D have known
9	A be	B were	C have been	D had been
10	A suspect	B witness	C culprit	D clue
11	A neither	B either	C or	D nor
12	A too	B enough	C so	D such

Grammar reference

Unit 1

Present simple

positive		negative			questions		
I You We They	live … .	I You We They	do not (don't)	live … .	Do	I you we they	live … ?
He She It	lives … .	He She It	does not (doesn't)	live … .	Does	he she it	live … ?

We use the present simple to talk about:
- a general truth or fact.
  Penguins **live** in the South Pole.
- a habit.
  I **get up** at seven thirty every morning.
- a state, situation or feeling.
  You **don't look** well.
- a timetabled or scheduled event in the future.
  The train for Paris **leaves** at 10.50.

Adverbs of frequency

We often use the present simple with these adverbs *always, usually, often, sometimes, rarely, never* to show how frequently something happens.
  It **never snows** in July.
  Liam **doesn't always get** to school on time.
  Is Kelly **often** late for meetings?

Present continuous

positive			negative			questions		
I	am ('m)		I	am not ('m not)		Am	I	
You We They	are ('re)	living … .	You We They	are not ('re not) (aren't)	living … .	Are	you we they	living … ?
He She It	is ('s)		He She It	is not ('s not) (isn't)		Is	he she it	

We use the present continuous to talk about:
- a temporary situation.
  That new James Bond film **is playing** at the Odeon this week.
- an activity taking place around the time of speaking.
  I**'m helping** my dad to decorate the living room today.
- an activity taking place exactly at the time of speaking.
  Oh look! It**'s snowing** now.
- an annoying habit (with *always*).
  Ryan **is always leaving** his bedroom light on. It's such a waste.
- plans we have already made for the future.
  I**'m meeting** Tony at the cinema tonight.

be used to + *-ing* / noun

We use *used to* + noun or *used to* + *-ing* to show that something is no longer strange or difficult because we have done it so many times.
  Pilots **are used to flying**. They **are used to heights**. They aren't afraid.
  I**'m used to hearing** English. I**'m used to the sound** of it. It doesn't confuse me.

Stative verbs

We don't normally use stative verbs with continuous tenses because they don't describe actions.
  I **like** ice cream. **not** ~~I'm liking ice cream~~.
  This **doesn't belong** to me. **not** ~~This isn't belonging to me~~.

Stative verbs can be divided into the following categories:

- feelings: *love, hate, like, want, prefer*
- senses: *see, feel, smell, taste, sound, weigh*
- mental processes: *believe, imagine, know, mean, realize, recognize*
- relationships: *belong, include, involve, depend on, owe, own*
- appearance: *appear, seem, look like*

Some of these verbs can be used in both tenses, but the meaning changes. The present simple meaning is usually connected with the senses or with mental states, and the present continuous meaning is usually an action or process.

	present simple	present continuous
smell	These flowers **smell** lovely.	Why **is** your dog **smelling** my shoes?
appear	There **appears** to be a problem.	Melanie Spears **is appearing** at the Palladium theatre tomorrow.
feel	This material **feels** very soft.	Why **are** you **feeling** under the sofa? Have you lost something?
taste	My soup **doesn't taste** very nice.	I'm just **tasting** the sauce to see if it needs salt.
weigh	How much **do** you **weigh**?	I'm **weighing** your luggage to check it's not overweight.
think	I **don't think** that's a good idea.	What **are** you **thinking** about?
look	You **look** great!	What **are** you **looking** for?

Note: We use *can* with the verbs *see, hear* or *smell* to describe something happening now.
 I **can hear** someone coming up the stairs.

Unit 2

Past simple

positive		negative			questions		
I You He She It We They	lived … .	I You He She It We They	did not live … . (didn't)		Did	I you he she it we they	live … ?

We use the past simple to talk about:

- a repeated action in the past.
 My sister and I **fought** a lot as children.
- an action completed at a specific time in the past.
 Joe and I **didn't go out** last night.
- a state in the past.
 Did you **live** in Naples before moving to Rome?

Note: We can use adverbs of frequency and other present simple time words with the past simple: *often, sometimes, always, rarely, never,* etc.
 I **often went** to my friend's house after school.
 We **walked** to school together **every day**.

Past continuous

positive			negative			questions		
I He She It	was	living … .	I He She It	was not (wasn't)	living … .	Was	I he she it	living … ?
You We They	were		You We They	were not (weren't)		Were	you we they	

We use the past continuous to talk about:

- a temporary situation in the past.
  She **was staying** with me until the end of the summer.
- actions in progress at a point in the past.
  Were your family **travelling** at nine o'clock yesterday evening?
- an action or situation that was in progress when something else happened.
  While I **was watching** TV the doorbell rang.
- an annoying habit (with *always*).
  Liz **was always** complaining about homework when we were at school.

Time expressions in the past

We use:

- *during* with nouns not numbers.
  We went out a lot **during** her stay.
- *for* with a period of time.
  I went out with Heather **for** five years.
- *ago* after a period of time.
  My grandpa was still living in Germany 30 years **ago**.
- *when* for a point in time.
  When Emma was ten she had a bicycle.
- *as*, *when* and *while* to link two events that were happening or happened at the same time.
  I was doing the washing-up **when / while** you two were out having coffee.
  I saw them **as / while** I was walking home.

used to and *would*

We use *used to* and *would* to talk about past habits, especially in the distant past.
  I **used to / would** walk to school every morning.

Note: *used to* can be used to talk about states in the past, but *would* cannot.
  I **used to** live in Dublin. (✓)
  I **would** live in Dublin. (✗)

Negative and question forms

We use *used to* with *never* or *did / did not*.
  She **never used to** get angry.
  She **didn't use to** get angry.
  Did you **use to** be in my physics class?

We use *would* with *never* or with *not*.
  When I was younger I **would never** go out on a weeknight.
  When I was younger I **wouldn't** go out on a weeknight.
  Would he complain about everything?

Articles

We use *a/an* (indefinite article):

- with singular countable nouns when we talk about something specific.
  I saw **a** big flat and **a** small flat.
  If we eat **a** balanced diet, we stay healthy.
- with an example of a group.
  A house can have more than one storey.
  (or we can use the plural form of the noun: *Houses can have more than one storey.*)
- to describe jobs.
  She's **an** architect.

We use *the* (definite article):

- with singular, plural and uncountable nouns when we talk about something specific.
  The building on **the** corner is in **the** minimalist style.
  Are **the** guests in **the** garden?
  Where did you put all **the** money?
- with singular countable nouns when we talk about something in general.
  The forest is a dangerous place at night.
- when we talk about something unique.
  the Amazon rainforest, **the** world, **the** sun, **the** sky, **the** environment
- with rivers, seas and mountain groups.
  the River Severn, **the** Irish Sea, **the** Dolomites
- with names of buildings.
  the Guggenheim Museum, **the** Houses of Parliament

We don't use an article:

- when we are talking about plural and uncountable nouns in general.
  Houses aren't always bigger than flats.
  Sugar is not good for your teeth.
- with countries.
  Spain, Poland, Russia, Greece (but **the** United Kingdom and **the** United States of America)
- with cities, continents, planets and mountains.
  Moscow is a romantic city.
  Travelling through Asia is great fun.
  Jupiter is one of the larger planets.
  Mount Snowdon is in Wales.

Possessive pronouns and determiners

We never use *the* with possessive adjectives.
  That's ~~the~~ my house.

Determiners (possessive adjectives) are followed by nouns.

My Your His Her Its Our Your Their	house is large.

Possessive pronouns are not followed by nouns.

This flat is	mine. yours. his. hers. ours. yours. theirs.

Note:
  She's a friend of **mine**.
  Is that boy a cousin of **yours**?

Unit 3

Present perfect simple

positive			negative			questions		
I You We They	have ('ve)	been … . studied … . gone … .	I You We They	have not (haven't)	been … . studied … . gone … .	Have	I you we they	been … ? studied … ? gone … ?
He She It	has ('s)		He She It	has not (hasn't)		Has	he she it	

We use the present perfect simple:

- for an action in the recent past that has a result in the present.
  *She **has painted** her room.*
  *I **have bought** a puppy.*

- for a situation or state that was true in the past and is still true today.
  *Max **has known** me for years.*

- for an action completed repeatedly in the past at an unspecified time.
  *Michaela **has been** in detention three times this year.*

- to talk about an experience.
  I've been to Paris. Have you?

Present perfect continuous

positive			negative			questions		
I You We They	have ('ve)	been studying.	I You We They	have not (haven't)	been studying.	Have	I you we they	been studying?
He She It	has ('s)		He She It	has not (hasn't)		Has	he she it	

We use the present perfect continuous:
- for an action that started in the past and continues (without stopping) up to the present.
  *She **has been painting** her room this morning.*
  *I **have been waiting** for an hour.*

- for an action that first occurred in the past and has occurred again and again up to the present.
  *That squirrel**'s been visiting** our garden every day since the beginning of summer.*

- with *for* and *since*.
  *I've been working non-stop **since** eight this morning.*
  *The children have been playing in the garden **for** hours.*

have been or *have gone*?

Have been suggests that someone went somewhere, but has now come back.
  ***Have** you **been** to the shops today? No, I **haven't been** yet.*
  *I**'ve been** to America twice, but I**'ve never been** to New York.*

Have gone suggests that someone went somewhere, but has not come back yet.
  *Where**'s** Greg **gone**? He**'s gone** to the beach. (and he's still there)*

Present perfect and past simple

We use the past simple with:

- past actions or events that have no connection to the present.
  *Dinosaurs **died** out many millions of years ago.*

- past actions or events that took place at a specific, named moment in time.
  *I **bought** this mobile phone **last January** / **yesterday** / **in June** / **three days ago**.*

We use the present perfect simple or continuous with:

- past actions and events that have a result in the present or future.
  I've read that book. (so now I know what it's about)
  *I**'ve been watching** a lot of French films recently.* (so now I know more about them)

Time expressions with perfect tenses

* usually used with the present perfect simple only

	example	notes
for	We've lived here **for** ten years. I've been waiting **for** an hour!	***for*** + a period of time
(ever) since	Jane and I have been friends **ever since** we were small. I've been playing the piano **since** 2000.	***since*** + a point in time
so far	How many times have you eaten **so far** today?	* means 'up to now'
first / second / third time	This is **the second time** I've tried to pass this exam.	*
two / three / four times	I've read this book **four times**. I love it.	*
yet	Haven't you finished **yet**? Mum hasn't got back **yet**.	* usually negative or question form
already	I've **already** cooked dinner. You haven't finished **already**, have you?	*
just	Kevin has **just** gone out.	* something that has very recently occurred
still	They **still** haven't received your letter.	* usually negative form
ever	Have you **ever** eaten snails? This is the best book I've **ever** read.	* usually in questions about experiences or superlative sentences
never	I've **never** eaten snails.	*

Unit 4

Past perfect simple

positive			negative			questions		
I You He She It We You They	had ('d)	studied.	I You He She It We You They	had not (hadn't)	studied.	Had	I you he she it we you they	studied?

We use the past perfect:

- for a completed action that happened before another past event.
I **had** just **got** home when the phone rang.
She told her teacher that she **had** not **done** her homework.

- with words and expressions like:
before, after, when, already, as soon as, just, for, recently, still, yet, since, It was (not) the first time ... , etc

Past perfect continuous

positive			negative			questions		
I You He She It We You They	had ('d)	been studying.	I You He She It We You They	had not (hadn't)	been studying.	Had	I you he she it we you they	been studying?

We use past perfect continuous:

- for something that continued for some time up to another past event or situation.
  *The phone finally rang. I **had been waiting** for it to ring all day.*
  *I was excited. I **had been waiting** for something good to happen for a long time.*

- for a past action that continued over a period of time until another action interrupted it.
  *I **had been working** hard on the project when it was cancelled.*

- to show that an action was not complete.
  *I **had been trying** to call her all morning.*

Comparatives and superlatives

We use comparatives to compare two things. We use the words *more*, *less* or the ending *-er* and the word *than*.
  *It is **hotter** today **than** yesterday.*
  *This film was **more interesting than** her first one.*
  *These trainers are **less expensive than** your shoes.*

We use superlatives to compare more than two things. We use *most*, *least* or the ending *-est* and the word *the*.
  *Mount Everest is **the highest** mountain in the world.*
  *Nicole is **the most popular** girl in the class.*
  *Carol is **the least sporty** girl in the class.*

Regular adjectives

	comparative	superlative
short adjectives wide	-er wider	-est widest
short adjectives ending in -e nice	-r nicer	-st nicest
short adjectives ending in -y early	change -y to -i + -er earlier	change -y to -i + -est earliest
one syllable adjectives with one vowel and one consonant hot	double the last consonant + -er hotter	double the last consonant + -est hottest
long adjectives beautiful	more/less + adjective more beautiful	most/least + adjective most beautiful

Irregular adjectives

good	better	best
bad	worse	worst
far	further/farther	furthest/farthest

Regular adverbs

quietly	more/less + adverb more quietly	most/least + adverb most quietly
often	more/less + adverb more often	most/least + adverb most often

Irregular adverbs

badly	worse	worst
early	earlier	earliest
far	further/farther	furthest/farthest
fast	faster	fastest
hard	harder	hardest
long	longer	longest
near	nearer	nearest
well	better	best

Irregular determiners

little	less	least
much/many	more	most

We can also use (*not*) *as* + adjective + *as* to compare two things.
  *His second book is **as good as** his first.*
  (The first book and the second book are the same quality.)
  *This film is **not as bad as** her first one.*
  (Her first film was worse.)

We can also link two actions or situations using comparatives.
the + comparative + *the* + comparative
  ***The higher** a plane flies **the better**.*
  ***The more** I see her **the more** I like her.*

Unit 5

Future forms

will

We use *will* for:

- offers, promises or suggestions.
  I**'ll** do my homework. I promise I **won't** play computer games.
  My dad **will** give you a lift if you like.

Note: *shall* is used instead of *will* in the first person question form.
  Shall I bring in the shopping?
  Shall we lay the table?

- spontaneous decisions.
  Thanks for asking me to come. I**'ll** be there.

- predictions.
  I believe that one day I **will** travel to South America.

going to

We use *going to* for:

- intentions.
  I**'m going to** study abroad when I leave school.

Note: *intend to* is also used to talk about intentions.
  I **intend to** study abroad when I leave school.

- predictions based on what we know, believe, can see or hear.
  Look at the sun. It**'s going to** be another hot day.

Present simple

We use present simple to talk about timetables or scheduled events.
  The plane **leaves** at nine.
  Easter Sunday **falls** in April this year.

Present continuous

We use present continuous to talk about plans and arrangements.
  I can't go this weekend, I**'m having** a party.

Note: *plan to* is also used to talk about plans.
  I **plan to** visit Spain and Portugal when I'm in Europe next year.

about to

We use *about to* to talk about something that is going to happen very soon.
  Quick! The train is **about to** leave.
  It's nine o'clock and the film is **about to** begin.

Making predictions

Future continuous

positive			negative			questions		
I You He She It We You They	will ('ll)	be travelling.	I You He She It We You They	will not (won't)	be travelling.	Will	I you he she it we you they	be travelling?

Future perfect

positive			negative			questions		
I You He She It We You They	will ('ll)	have gone.	I You He She It We You They	will not (won't)	have gone.	Will	I you he she it we you they	have gone?

We use future continuous to make predictions about an activity that will be in progress at a certain time in the future.
  This time next month I**'ll be travelling** through Africa.

We use future perfect to make predictions about an activity that will be complete before a certain time in the future. We often use the word *by* with this tense.
  By the age of 30, I **will have travelled** widely.

Note: *may*, *might* and *could* are used to make predictions that we are less sure about.
  Jane **might** come hiking with us but, then again, she **might not**.
  By 2030, people **may** be holidaying on the moon.
  In the future, people **could** be flying in spaceships.

Time expressions with future forms

In sentences referring to the future, time expressions such as *as soon as*, *when*, *before* and *until* should be followed by present simple or present perfect simple tense.

*I'll do it **as soon as** I get home.*
*I'll ring you **when** I arrive.*
*Don't do a thing **before** I get there.*
*Please don't do anything **until** I've called you.*

Question tags

affirmative main verb	negative tag
You**'re** from Germany,	**aren't** you?

negative main verb	positive tag
You **aren't** from Germany,	**are** you?

If the main verb is *be*, then the verb in the tag is also *be* in the same tense.

*Jane **isn't** happy, **is** she?*
*You **were** at the cinema last night, **weren't** you?*

If the main verb includes an auxiliary verb or modal, then we use the auxiliary verb or modal in the tag in the same tense.

*You **don't** eat meat, **do** you?*
*It **isn't** raining, **is** it?*
*They **haven't** arrived yet, **have** they?*
*They **weren't** doing their homework, **were** they?*
*Mike**'s** been working all morning, **hasn't** he?*
*There **won't** be snow this year, **will** there?*
*She **must** arrive on time, **mustn't** she?*

If the main verb is in the present simple or past simple affirmative form, then we use the auxiliary verbs *do* or *did* in the tag.

*John **paints** well, **doesn't** he?*
*You **lived** in Norway, **didn't** you?*

We use question tags to:

- check that something is true.
*This is your book, **isn't it**?*
- check that someone agrees with us.
*This isn't a very good film, **is it**?*
- request something politely.
*You couldn't open the window, **could you**?*

Rising intonation means we are not sure about the answer.
It isn't time to go already, is it? ↗

Falling intonation means we are sure of the answer and we expect agreement.
You're Barbara's brother, aren't you? ↘

Indirect questions

We use indirect questions to be more polite.
Can you tell me *what time the next train gets here? (polite)*
I wonder if you could tell me *what time the next train gets here. (very polite)*

Some indirect questions need question marks. It depends on the first phrase.

with a question mark	without a question mark
Can/Could you tell me … ? Do you know … ? Do you think you can/could tell me … ? Would you mind telling me … ?	I wonder if you can/could tell me … I wonder if you could let me know … I wonder if you know … I would like to know …

All indirect questions need a question word or *whether/if*.

phrase	question word; whether/if	subject + verb
I wonder if you would/could tell me	how	long it will take.
Do you know	whether/if	any changes can be made to the ticket?
Would you mind telling me	what	the cost will be?

We do NOT use the question form in indirect questions.

Direct question: *What time **is it**?*

Indirect question: *Could you tell me what time **it is**?*

If the indirect question phrase is followed by a noun or noun phrase, a question word, *whether* and *if* are not used.

Could you please tell me the price of the holiday package?
not ~~Could you please tell me what the price of the holiday package?~~

If a question word is used, then a verb is needed.
*Could you please tell me **what** the price of the holiday package **is**?*

Unit 6

Reported speech

We can report what a person said using indirect or reported speech. When the reporting verb is in the past tense, eg he **told** me that ... , she **said** that ... , we change the tense of the direct speech and the pronoun.

direct speech	reported speech
'**I watch** TV every day,' said Karen.	Karen said (that) **she watched** TV every day.
'**I'm watching** TV,' said David.	David said (that) **he was watching** TV.
'**I watched** TV this morning,' said Greg.	Greg said (that) **he had watched** TV that morning.
'**I was watching** TV last night,' said Anne.	Anne said (that) **she had been watching** TV the night before.
'**I haven't watched** TV today,' said Mark.	Mark said (that) **he hadn't watched** TV that day.
'**I had finished** my homework by then,' said Mina.	Mina said (that) **she had finished** her homework by then.
'**They'll arrive** soon,' Mum said.	Mum said (that) **they would arrive** soon.
'**I'm going to be** famous one day,' my sister said.	My sister said (that) **she was going to be** famous one day.

Modal verbs

'**I must cut** the grass,' said Dad.	Dad said (that) **he must cut** the grass. Dad said (that) **he had to** cut the grass.
'**I wouldn't like** to be a pilot,' said Jane.	Jane said (that) **she wouldn't like** to be a pilot.
'**I couldn't swim** when I was ten,' said Mark.	Mark said (that) **he couldn't swim** when he was ten.
'**I can help**,' said Zoe.	Zoe said (that) **she could help**.
'**We have to tidy** the house,' said Liam.	Liam said (that) **we had to tidy** the house.

Time and place

'I went there **today**,' she said.	She said (that) she had been there **that day**.
'I went there **yesterday**,' she said.	She said (that) she had been there **the day before**.
'I went there **last week**,' she said.	She said (that) she had been there **the week before**.
'I went there three weeks **ago**,' she said.	She said (that) she had been there three weeks **before**.
'I'll go there **tomorrow**,' she said.	She said (that) she would go there **the next day**.

Reference words

'**This** is expensive,' said Jim.	Jim said (that) **that** was expensive.
'**These** cakes are nice,' said Dad.	Dad said (that) **those** cakes were nice.
'William lives **here**,' said Alan.	Alan said (that) William lived **there**.

Reporting pronouns

'I like **you**,' he said.	He said (that) **he** liked **me**.
'These sweets are **yours**,' my auntie said.	My auntie said that those sweets were **ours**.

Questions in reported speech

When reporting questions:

- we use normal word order (subject + verb) not question order.

'Where **is Timbuktu**?' asked Nina.	Nina asked where **Timbuktu was**.

- we don't use *do/did*.

'Where **do you live**?' asked Mike.	Mike asked where **I lived**.

- with *yes/no* questions, we use the reporting verb *ask* + *if*/whether.

'**Is** the cake nice?' Mum asked.	Mum **asked if** the cake was nice. Mum **asked whether** the cake was nice.
'**Does** Sue like tomatoes?' he asked.	He **asked if** Sue liked tomatoes. He **asked whether** Sue liked tomatoes.

- with *Wh-* questions (*where, when, why, how,* etc) we use reporting verb + question word + clause (normal word order).

'**Whose** are these things?' asked David.	David asked **whose** those things were.
Where does Helen live?' asked Paul.	Paul asked **where** Helen lived.

Reporting verbs *say* and *tell*

say + (**that**) + clause
 'Your dress suits you,' said Mandy.
 Mandy **said (that)** my dress suited me.

tell + object (pronoun or name) + **to** + infinitive
 'Meet me in the park at ten o'clock,' said Tim.
 Tim **told me** to meet him in the park at ten o'clock.

Other reporting verbs

verb + (**that**) + clause
admit, add, complain, deny, explain, suggest
 'I didn't steal the money,' he said.
 He **denied that** he had stolen the money.
 'We'll be a few minutes late,' they said.
 They **explained that** they would be a few minutes late.

verb + (**that**) + clause OR **verb** + **to** + infinitive
claim, promise, threaten
 'I'll call the police,' he shouted.
 He **threatened that** he would call the police.
 He **threatened to call** the police.

verb + object + **to** + infinitive
advise, ask, beg, invite, warn
 'Be more careful,' I said.
 I **advised her to be** more careful.

Unit 7

Passive voice

subject → James took this photo. ← object
         → This photo was taken by James. ← agent

The passive voice is formed with *be* + past participle of the verb.

present simple	This magazine **is published** twice a month.
present continuous	A new school **is being built** near the park.
present perfect	Their car **has been stolen**.
past simple	The pyramids **were built** thousands of years ago.
past continuous	Our house **was being painted** at the time.
past perfect	Their new album **had been released** a few months earlier.
will	We hope it **will be completed** by next year.
going to	It isn't **going to be delivered** until next week.
modal verbs	A little bit more sugar **can be added** if you prefer.

by + the agent

We use *by* + the agent to show who or what is responsible for an action.
 Dinosaur bones have been discovered in a field **by two farmers**.
 The forest was destroyed **by the fire**.

If we want to say something was done using an object, eg a tool, we use *with*.
 The photo was taken **with a digital camera**.

Sometimes it is not necessary to mention the agent.
 This house was built **(by builders)** in 1776.

We use the passive voice when:

- we don't know who or what is responsible for something.
 The fire **was started** some time yesterday afternoon.

- there are too many people to mention.
 Her newest album **has been bought** by over a million people.

- it's obvious who is responsible for an action.
 The gang **was arrested** a year ago.

- we want a more formal style.
 Members of the audience **are** kindly **asked** not to eat during the performance.

- to describe processes.
 First the wood **is cut** into small pieces and dried in the sun for two weeks.

- to report widely held opinions or beliefs.
 It **is believed** that the river dolphin has disappeared forever.
 It **is said** that the crime took place between three and four o'clock in the morning.

Sentences with two objects

Verbs like *give, bring, send, show*, can have two objects.

subject	verb	direct object	indirect object
The teacher	gave	John	a book.

To make sentences like these passive, there are two options. The first is most common.
 John was given a book (by the teacher).
 A book was given to John (by the teacher).

Note: Some verbs (intransitive) do not take an object and can't change into the passive voice.
 A man **appeared** from nowhere.
 The plane **rose** into the air.

Causative form

subject + *have* in the correct tense + object + past participle

*I **have** my hair **cut** once a month.*
*We're **having** our living room **painted** at the moment.*

Causative form is similar to passive voice. We often use it:

- when someone does something for someone else.
*I've **had** all the car tyres **replaced**.*

Note: For this use, we can sometimes use *get* instead of *have*.
*She **had / got** her portrait **painted** in Paris.*

- when someone has an unpleasant, unwanted experience.
*They've **had** their house **broken** into again.*

Unit 8

Zero, first and second conditionals

Zero conditional

(*if* + present tense + present tense)

A situation that is generally true.
***If** you **don't** sleep enough, you **don't feel** good the next day.*

Note: We can also use *when* or *whenever* to express something that is always true.
***When/Whenever** Jake **calls**, it's **always** bad news.*

First conditional

(*if* + present tense + *will/might/may/can/could/*etc + bare infinitive)

A situation that is real or likely in the future.
***If** I **see** Toby, I **will tell** him about the party.*
***If** you **tell** me what's wrong, I **can help** you.*

A situation that is certain in the future.
***When** I **see** Tom, I'**ll tell** him.*
***As soon as** I **get** home, I'**ll call** you.*
*We **won't start until** you **get** here.*

(*if* + present tense + imperative)

To give instructions about present or future situations.
***If** Harry **calls**, **tell** him about next week.*

Second conditional

(*if* + past simple or past continuous + *would/might/could* + bare infinitive)

A situation that is impossible, unlikely or hypothetical in the present or future.
***If** I **was** taller, I **would become** a model.*
***If** I **wasn't** so short, I **could become** a model.*

A situation that we can imagine, but probably won't happen.
***If** Madonna **came**, I **would** definitely go to see her.*

Be careful!

We can say *If I were ...* instead of *If I was ...*, eg *If I were rich, ...*

We can also say *If I were you, ...* to give advice.
***If I were you**, I **would** study more and go out less.*

We can also use *could* in the *if* clause.
*If I **could** meet anyone famous, I would meet Cristiano Ronaldo.*

Note: When the *if* clause comes first, it has a comma after it.
If you come to my house tonight, I will give you the books.

When the *if* clause comes second, we don't use a comma.
I will give you the books if you come to my house tonight.

Conditional links

Instead of *if*: provided that/as long as	***Provided (that)/As long as*** it's all right with you, I'll bring a friend to the party.
Instead of *if not*: unless	***Unless*** someone is late, the meeting will start on time.
for questions: suppose what if	***Suppose*** it rains, what will we do then? ***What if*** it rains? What will we do then?

like and *as*

We use *like*:
- to ask for descriptions or information about someone or something.
*What's she **like**?*
She's very nice.

- to say that people or things are similar or the same.
*She looks **like** Angelina Jolie.*
*She behaves **like** she was the queen.*

- to give an example.
*Some people, **like** Jane and Archie, had a really good time.*

We use *as*:
- to make comparisons (see Unit 4).
*Frank isn't **as** nice **as** his brother.*

- to describe a job or role.
*Debbie works **as** a PE teacher.*

Unit 9

Modals

Modal auxiliary verbs, *can, could, may, might, must, ought to, should, shall, will, would*:

- do not change form for person or tense.
- don't use *do* in questions.
- are followed by bare infinitive.
- are made negative using *not* or *n't*.
  I **might not** come tonight.
  You **shouldn't** drink too much coffee.
- do not have an infinitive form (you need to use another word or phrase).
  I plan to be able to come to the party.
  not ~~I plan to can come to the party~~

Note: *have to* and *need to* work in the same way as other verbs.
  Do you really **need to** buy that?
  I **didn't have to** get up this morning, but I did.

Expressing ability: *can, could* (in the past), *be able to*
  Josephine **can** really dance.
  I **could** play the piano when I was young.
  They **weren't able to** find any tickets.

Expressing possibility: *can, may, might, could*
  Athens **can** get too hot during July and August.
  It **may** rain later.
  They **might** get here a bit late.
  Could that be my old friend from school?

Expressing certainty: *can't, must* (based on some evidence)
  That **can't** be John over there. He's in London today.
  That **must** be a tasty cake. It's homemade.
  They **must** be eating out tonight. They're not answering.

Expressing obligation / necessity: *must* (personal obligation), *have to* (obligation from someone else, eg rules), *needn't*
  I **must** get more exercise.
  You **have to** be here at ten o'clock exactly.
  Do you **have to** wear that terrible dress?
  You **needn't** do the washing-up. I'll put them in the dishwasher.

Note: When we need to show tense or use an infinitive we use *have to*.
  We **had to** get to the port by 9am.

Mustn't means forbidden or not allowed but *don't have to* or *needn't* means not necessary.
  You **mustn't** eat anything before an operation.
  You **don't have to / needn't** eat your breakfast if you aren't hungry.

Giving or asking for advice: *should, ought to*
  You **ought to** get more rest.
  Should I take this bandage off?

Giving or asking for permission: *may, can, could*
(*may* is more polite than *can* or *could*)
  Can I go out tonight, Mum?
  May I take one of these delicious biscuits?
  Mum said I **could** come with you!

had better + infinitive

Had better is an expression which has a similar meaning to the modal verb *should*. It's usually used in the contracted form.
  It's late. We**'d better** get home.

Third conditional sentences

(*If* + past perfect + *would/could/may/might* + present perfect)

We use third conditional sentences to talk hypothetically about the past. We imagine situations or circumstances that didn't really happen, and wonder what might have been the result.
  If he **hadn't left** fingerprints, the police **wouldn't have found** him.
  If you **had got** here earlier, we **may have caught** the train.

Unit 10

Relative clauses

Relative clauses are introduced by relative pronouns:

who, that, whom (people)	People **who/that** live on islands eat a lot of fish. The woman to **whom** I spoke is sitting over there.
which, that (things)	The food **which/that** is in the fridge has gone off.
where (places)	The restaurant **where** I work serves all kinds of food.
when (times and dates)	I can't remember the birthday **when** we went to the beach.
whose (possessions)	My neighbour, **whose** mum is a chef, has invited me over for dinner.
why (reasons)	I can't understand **why** you don't learn to cook.

Defining and non-defining relative clauses

Relative clauses can be defining (1) or non-defining (2).

1 *The boy who is sitting next to the door is looking at you.*
2 *Harvey Jones, who is sitting next to the door, is looking at you.*

Defining relative clauses:
- tell us what exactly is being talked about (the boy next to the door).
- give us essential information that cannot be removed from the sentence.
- do not contain commas.
- **who** or **which** can be replaced by **that** (less formal). *The boy **that** is sitting next to the door is ...*
- don't need the relative pronoun if it is the object of the clause.
  That's the man who/that I told you about.
  That's the man I told you about.

Non-defining relative clauses:
- give us extra information that is not important to the meaning of the sentence.
- are separated from the rest of the sentence by commas.
- must contain a relative pronoun.
- cannot use the pronoun *that*.

Notes: *which* can refer to the entire previous clause.
*The food we ordered was very good, **which** pleased us immensely.*

Where can be replaced by *in/at/from which*.
*The restaurant **where** she had her dinner was expensive.*
*The restaurant **at which** she had her dinner was expensive.*
*The restaurant **which** she had her dinner **at** was expensive.* (less formal)

Other prepositions can also be used with relative pronouns.
*My friends, two **of whom** will be coming tonight, are all lovely people.*
*The person **to whom** I gave the parcel told me you weren't in.*
*The day **on which/when** we won our match was a day to remember.*

Unreal past

- We use the past simple to talk about hypothetical situations in the present and future after certain expressions.
  *I **wish** I **was** beautiful.*
  ***If only** we **didn't have to** do so much homework.*
  ***It's (high/about) time** we **started** going out more!*
  *I **would rather** you **didn't spend** so much money.*

- We can also use the past continuous with *wish* and *if only* to talk about a hypothetical situation in the future.
  *I **wish** you **weren't leaving** this Saturday.* (Fact: You are leaving this Saturday.)

- We use the past perfect with *wish* and *if only* to talk about something we regret doing or not doing in the past.
  *I **wish** / **If only** we **had not told** Tania about Steve.* (Fact: We told Tania about Steve.)
  *Bill **wishes** he **hadn't seen** / **If only** Bill **hadn't seen** her!* (Fact: Bill saw her.)

- We use *would* + bare infinitive with *wish* and *if only* when we want to criticize someone else's behaviour (but not our own).
  *I **wish**/**If only** George **wouldn't** have so many accidents.* (Fact: George often has accidents.)

- We only use unreal past with *I'd rather* when we are talking about someone else. When we talk about ourselves, we use bare infinitive.
  *I'**d rather** you **left** now.*
  *I'**d rather leave** now.*

- *I wish* is used for things we know are not true, but *I hope* is used for things we want to be true, and we think they are possible.
  *I **hope** I pass the exam.* (Fact: It's very possible I will pass the exam.)
  *I **wish** I was/were older.* (Fact: I'm not older.)

Unit 11

Modal perfect

Most modal verbs don't have a past form (apart from *can* and the semi modal *have to*). However, we can use modals to talk about the past by using this pattern:

subject + modal + *have* + past participle
I **should have gone** to the party last night.
They **must have arrived** home by now.

We can also use the continuous form of the modal perfect:

subject + modal + *have been* + *-ing*
I **should have been studying**.
They **must have been driving** too fast.

may, *might* and *could* for possibility

(To make guesses about what happened in the past, or about recently completed actions and events.)
They **may not have** received our letter yet.
I'm not sure, but John **might have** left this parcel for you.

must and *can't* for certainty

Someone **must have** stolen my wallet.
You **can't have** seen Sally yesterday. She's been in New York since last week.

should and *ought to* for criticism

You **ought to have** studied harder for your exams.
They **shouldn't have** bought that enormous house. It's too big for them.

should and *shouldn't* for regret

I **shouldn't have** been so rude to her.
We **should have** invited him to the party.

Unreal past

(To talk about things which we know didn't happen in the past, but which were possible.)
Be careful! You **could have broken** a window with that ball.
My mum **could have been** a ballerina, but she became a teacher instead.

Infinitives and *-ing* forms

These verbs are followed by the full infinitive (with *to*).

afford, agree, appear, arrange, ask, attempt, be able/pleased, etc, choose, claim, decide, expect, fail, happen, help, hope, intend, learn, manage, need, offer, plan, prepare, pretend, promise, refuse, seem, tend, want, wish, would like

This **appears to be** broken.
He **chose to stay** at home.

These verbs are followed by the *-ing* form.

admit, appreciate, avoid, be capable of, be good/bad at, be interested in, can't help, can't stand, consider, delay, deny, discuss, dislike, enjoy, feel like, finish, give up, imagine, involve, keep, look forward to, mention, mind, miss, practise, succeed in, suggest, talk about, think of

I **don't mind waking up** early.
I **finished eating** and then went to the shops.

These verbs can be followed by either full infinitive or *-ing*, with no change in meaning.

begin, continue, hate, intend, love, prefer, start

It **started raining**.
It **started to rain**.

Some verbs can be followed by either full infinitive or *-ing*, but there is a change in meaning.

stop
I **stopped to read**. = pause an activity to do something else
I **stopped visiting** my friend. = stop an activity

remember
He usually **remembers to buy** bread. = do something that was planned
He **remembers buying** fresh bread every morning. = a memory of doing something

forget
She **forgot to buy** milk. = not do something that was planned
She hadn't **forgotten living** in the country. = not remember a past event or experience (usually in negative form)

try
I **tried to cut** my own hair. = make an effort to achieve something
I **tried cutting** my own hair. = do an experiment

regret
I **regret to inform** you that the headmistress will be leaving. = (formal) be sorry to give bad news
I **regret going** to that hairdresser – my hair looks terrible. = be sorry about something that has happened

Modal verbs (*can, must, should,* etc) are always followed by the infinitive without *to* or perfect infinitive:
They **must wear** seat belts.
You **should have called** me.

make, *let* and *allow*

Make means 'force' someone to do something.
subject + *make* + object + infinitive (without *to*)
Dad **made** me **tidy** my room.

let / allow

Let and *allow* are similar in meaning, but we use them with different verb patterns.
subject + *let* + object + infinitive (without *to*)
My parents **let** me **watch** the film.

subject + *allow* + object + *to* infinitive
My parents **allowed** me **to watch** the film.

Unit 12

Countable and uncountable nouns

There are two different kinds of nouns:

- countable nouns which have a singular and a plural form.
  *I have two **cars**.*

- uncountable nouns which do not usually appear in a plural form.
  *You always give good **advice**.*

We use a singular verb with uncountable nouns. They are usually objects that are 'masses' and difficult to count, or abstract things. Eg *accommodation, cash, chocolate, coffee, fruit, furniture, garlic, hair, milk, money, news, pepper,* (as in *salt and pepper*), *rubbish, salt, shopping, sugar, traffic, water, window-shopping*

Some nouns can be both countable and uncountable, eg
  *Melted **chocolate** is used for making cakes.* (chocolate mass)
  *Have a **chocolate** – they're delicious.* (one chocolate from a box of chocolates)

We use different articles and determiners with countable and uncountable nouns.

article/determiner	countable nouns	uncountable nouns
a/an	✓	
the	✓	✓
one, two, three	✓	
some/any	✓	✓
a lot of	✓	✓
lots of	✓	✓
a few / few	✓	
a little / little		✓
(how) many	✓	
(how) much		✓
plenty of	✓	✓
a number of	✓	
an amount of		✓
a piece of		✓

We use *many* for countable nouns and *much* for uncountable nouns, but they are usually only used in negative statements and questions.
  *Do you have **much** money on you?*
  *I don't have **many** ideas.*

Few means not many, but *a few* means the same as *some* or *a small number of*.
  *I have very **few** friends. I wish I had more.*
  *I have **a few** very close friends. I don't need any more.*

Note: Some uncountable nouns only appear in the plural form, eg *clothes, glasses* (spectacles), *goods, jeans, scissors, trousers*

They are followed by a plural verb and use determiners and quantifiers for plural nouns.
  *Your **jeans are** on the washing line.*

so / such ... that ...

We use *so / such ... that ...* for emphasis.

  (*so* + adjective + *that* ...)
  *This dress is **so** beautiful **that** I can't stop looking at it.*

  (*such* + noun phrase + *that* ...)
  *It was **such** a good play **that** I've decided to see it again.*

so many / so much

We use *so many* for emphasis with countable nouns and *so much* for emphasis with uncountable nouns.
  *There were **so many people** that there was nowhere to sit.*
  *I have never eaten **so much food** before.*

too and enough

too + adjective / adverb / determiner
Too means 'more than enough', 'more than necessary' or 'more than is wanted'. It is different from *very*.
  *She is **too lazy** to work.*
  *She walks **too quickly**. I can't keep up.*
  *You've given me **too much** money. It didn't cost that much.*
  *There are **too many** people here. There's nowhere to sit.*

(not) adjective / adverb + *enough* (to)
  *Ruth is **good enough** to get into university.*
  *She's not **fast enough** to compete against others.*

(*enough* + noun)
  *Have you got **enough** money?*

both ... and, neither ... nor, each, every, all, none

We use *both ... and* to talk about two things in a positive way.

Both the food **and** the deserts are great at this restaurant.

I read two different books over the holidays. **Both** books were good.

We use *neither ... nor* to talk about two things in a negative way.

Neither Shelly **nor** Heather were at the party. (Shelly and Heather didn't go to the party.)

Shelly wasn't at the party. **Neither** was Heather.

Each person I know **is** a good person. (focuses on the members of a group)

Every person I know **is** a good person. (talks about members of a group in a general way)

Each of the people I know **is** a good person.

All (of) the people I know **are** good people. (talks about all members of a group)

Most (of) the people I know **are** good people. (talks about a large number of a group)

None of the people I know **are** good people. (talks about all the members of a group as a whole, but in a negative way)

Indeterminate pronouns

	negatives and questions	affirmative sentences
anyone	Has **anyone** seen my keys?	**Anyone** interested in acting lessons, call this number.
anywhere	Did you go **anywhere** yesterday?	
anything	Did you see **anything** interesting at the museum?	If you're rich, you can buy **anything** you want.
no one		**No one** likes Sally.
nowhere		There's **nowhere** to sit – we'll have to stand.
nothing		There's **nothing** here for me. I'm leaving.
someone		**Someone** told me you're moving house.
somewhere		I know I left my keys **somewhere** in my room.
something		There's **something** moving under the bed!
everyone		I knew **everyone** at the party.
everywhere		I've looked **everywhere** for my keys – they're nowhere to be found.
everything		Put **everything** away, please!

Note: All the pronouns with *-one* can use *-body* instead.

someone – somebody
anyone – anybody
no one – nobody
everyone – everybody

When we need a pronoun after using *-one* or *-body* words, we use **they**/**them**.

If **someone** calls, tell **them** I'm busy and that I'll call them back.

Anybody can do it if **they** know how.

Vocabulary file

Unit 1
What's my line?

Jobs
builder (n)
chef (n)
firefighter (n)
interpreter (n)
journalist (n)
lawyer (n)
model maker (n)
nurse (n)
office worker (n)
postal worker (n)
teacher (n)
translator (n)
vet (n)
zoo-keeper (n)

Describing people
aggressive (adj)
arrogant (adj)
big-headed (adj)
bossy (adj)
cheerful (adj)
creative (adj)
efficient (adj)
energetic (adj)
hard-working (adj)
imaginative (adj)
moody (adj)
outgoing (adj)
patient (adj)
reliable (adj)
responsible (adj)
selfish (adj)
sociable (adj)
(well-)organized (adj)

Negative prefixes *un-, im-, in-, ir-, dis-*

un	im	ir
unambitious	impatient	irresponsible
unattractive	impolite	
unimaginative		
unreliable	**in**	**dis**
unselfish	inconsiderate	disorganized
unsociable	inefficient	

curly (adj)
dark (adj)
fair (adj)
long (adj)
pointed (adj)
round (adj)
straight (adj)
thick (adj)
thin (adj)
turned-up (adj)
wavy (adj)

Other words
anxious (adj)
careers officer (n)
dull (adj)
for ages (adv)
irritated (adj)
It doesn't appeal to me (phr)
It had never occurred to me (phr)
occupation (n)

Unit 2
A place to call home

Town and village
block of flats (n)
country house (n)
farmhouse (n)
field (n)
garden (n)
gym/sports centre (n)
industrial area (n)
multiplex cinema (n)
multi-storey car park (n)
public garden/park (n)
rural (adj)
shopping centre / mall (n)
skyscraper (n)
urban (adj)
busy (adj)
dangerous (adj)
depressing (adj)
dull (adj)
exciting (adj)
green (adj)
historic (adj)
interesting (adj)
lively (adj)
lovely (adj)
modern (adj)
noisy (adj)
peaceful (adj)
pleasant (adj)
polluted (adj)

quiet (adj)
safe (adj)

House and home
be home (v phr)
homeless (adj)
homemade (adj)
homesick (adj)
hometown (n)
household (n)
housewarming (n)
housewife (n)
housework (n)
leave home (v phr)
play (match) at home (v phr)
do the cooking (v phr)
do the household shopping (v phr)
do the ironing (v phr)
do the laundry (v phr)
do the washing-up (v phr)
lay the table (v phr)
load the dishwasher (v phr)
make your bed (v phr)
take the rubbish out (v phr)
tidy your room (v phr)
walk the dog (v phr)
water the plants/garden (v phr)

Phrasal verbs
come over
do up
drop by
drop in
stay in
throw out

Describing buildings
ceiling (n)
colourful (adj)
decorative features (phr)
impressive design (phr)
roof (n)
staircase (n)
the inside (n)
the outside (n)
wall (n)

Other words
appreciate (v)
creepy-crawlies (pl n)
grow accustomed to (v phr)
hunting (n)
luxury (n)
reassured (adj)
shelter (n)
wilderness (n)

Unit 3
Learning for life

School and education
do well (v phr)
follow rules (v phr)
get into trouble (v phr)
get suspended (v phr)
lose interest (v phr)
pass exams (v phr)
pay attention (v phr)
play truant (v phr)
show interest (v phr)
work hard (v phr)
costume (n)
deadline (n)
evening classes (pl n)
finish line (n)
individual (adj)
lesson (n)
occupational (adj)
open day (n)
private school (n)
public school (n)
season (n)
state school (n)
term (n)
uniform (n)
vocational (adj)
adolescent (n)
age group (n)
assistant (n)
head (n)
helper (n)
peers (pl n)
principal (n)

sibling(s) (n)
teenager (n)

Phrasal verbs
break up
get marked down
give back
hand in
hand out
take up

Other words
addicted (adj)
far-flung (adj)
state-of-the-art (adj)
stroll (n)
the only requirement (phr)
the possibilities are endless (phr)
They're history. (phr)
virtual (adj)

Unit 4
The world of science and technology

Science
amount (n)
astronomy (n)
biology (n)
breakthrough (n)
cell (n)
chemical (n)
chemistry (n)
conduct (v)
discover (v)
discovery (n)
earthquake (n)
experiment (v) (n)
gas (n)
geology (n)
height (n)
invent (v)
invention (n)
laboratory (n)
length (n)
liquid (n)

litre (n)
mathematics (n)
measure (v)
physics (n)
planet (n)
powder (n)
research (n)
rock (n)
scientific (adj)
solar system (n)
solid (n)
space (n)
star (n)
stone (n)
theory (n)
volume (n)
weight (n)
width (n)

Technology
access (v)
desktop (computer) (n)
document (n)
email (n) (v)
enter (v)
illegally (adv)
insert (v)
internet (n)
key (n)
keyboard (n)
laptop (computer) (n)
make a copy (of) (v phr)
mouse (n)
moveable (adj)
online (adj)
portable (adj)
press (v)
printer (n)
scanner (n)
screen (n)
surf (v)
the Web (n)

Phrasal verbs
back up
click on
hack into
log into
plug (sth) into
set up

Other words
creature (n)
evolution (n)
fossil (n)
question (v)
rate (n)
scar (n)
sceptical (adj)
species (n)

Unit 5
Holidays with a difference!

Travel
boarding pass (n)
check in (v)
jetlag (n)
journey (n)
line (n)
lorry (n)
peak hour traffic (n)
queue (n)
rickshaw (n)
semi-trailer (n)
traffic jam (n)
travel (n)
trip (n)
voyage (n)
yacht (n)

Sights
ancient ruin (n)
archaeological site (n)
castle (n)
cathedral (n)
church (n)
monument (n)
museum (n)
palace (n)

Accommodation
apartment (n)
bed and breakfast (B & B) (n)
campsite (n)
double room (n)
eat in (phr v)
eat out (phr v)
en suite (bathroom) (n)
equipped (adj)
five-star hotel (n)
guest (n)
guesthouse (n)
luxury (adj)
rough it (phr)
self-catering (adj)
single room (n)
sleeping bag (n)
stay (v)
tent (n)
youth hostel (n)

Travel and transport

catch	bus/train	ferry/ship
drive	car/coach	
ride	bike/bicycle	motorbike
sail	sailing boat	yacht
get on/off	bus/train/coach/the Underground	ferry/ship
get in/out of	car/taxi/cab	(small) boat

bike helmet (n)
bike ride (n)
bus ride (n)
bus station (n)
bus stop (n)
bus ticket (n)
foreign country (n)
guided tour (n)
hotel room (n)
motorbike (n)
private tour (n)
private transport (n)
railway station (n)
train station (n)
train ticket (n)
walking tour (n)

by bus (prep phr)
go abroad (v phr)
go on holiday abroad (v phr)
go sightseeing (v phr)
go to a foreign country (v phr)
miss the bus (v phr)
on foot (prep phr)
set off (phr v)
sights (pl n)
spend your holiday in/at … (v phr)
start off (phr v)

Other words
enlighten (v)
inspire (v)
lurk (v)
make your way back (v phr)
off-the-beaten-track (adj)
spine-chilling (adj)
tale (n)

Unit 6
Serious fun

Books
children's literature (n)
children's picture book (n)
fairy tale (n)
fantasy (adj)
horror (adj)
mystery (n)
romance (n)
science (n)
science fiction (n)

Entertainment
art gallery (n)
audience (n)
choir (n)
composer (n)
concert hall (n)
conductor (n)
exhibition (n)
keyboards (n)
landscape (n)
portrait (n)

sculptor (n)
sculpture (n)
actor (n)
actress (n)
award (n)
cast (n)
comedy (n)
costume (n)
credits (n)
criticize (v)
director (n)
dramatic (adj)
location (n)
make-up (n)
outfit (n)
part (n)
performance (n)
plot (n)
practice (n)
practise (v)
rehearsal (n)
rehearse (v)
role (n)
set (n)
setting (n)
stage (n)
story (n)
writer (n)

Phrasal verbs with *out*
bring out
carry out
go out
look out
sell out
sort out
speak out
turn out

Other words
author (n)
debut (n)
delightful (adj)
gripping (adj)
illustration (n)
take a sinister turn (v phr)

Unit 7
Turn on, tune in

Media and communications
browse (v)
connect to the internet (v phr)
contact friends (v phr)
correspondent (n)
documentary (n)
editor (n)
find information (v phr)
follow the news (v phr)
headline (n)
image (n)
report (n)
reporter (n)
share photos (v phr)
text (n)
title (n)
viewer (n)
chat show (n)
chat show host (n)
disc jockey (n)
film critic (n)
game show (n)
make-up artist (n)
reality show (n)
sitcom (n)
soap opera (n)
sound engineer (n)
web designer (n)
download files (v phr)
glance (v)
hit the headlines (v phr)
keep in touch (v phr)
lose touch (v phr)
make a call (v phr)
search engine (n)
search the net (v phr)
social networking site (n)
surf the net (v phr)
take a call (v phr)
upload files (v phr)

Other words

amateur (n)
any number of (phr)
clip (n)
download (v)
exhilarating (adj)
fabulous (adj)
hilarious (adj)
revolution (n)
stardom (n)
star-studded (adj)
subscriber (n)
sumptuous (adj)

Unit 8
The world of sport ... and leisure

Sport and leisure

athletics (n)
basketball (n)
boxing (n)
(boxing) gloves (n)
court (n)
deep-sea diving (n)
flippers (n)
football (n)
goal (n)
hoop (n)
long jump (n)
net (n)
oxygen tank (n)
pitch (n)
punch (v)
racket (n)
ring (n)
snorkel (n)
tennis (n)
track (n)
track and field (n)
wetsuit (n)

Sport/hobby	Verb	Person
baseball	play baseball	baseball player
chess	play chess	chess player
fishing	go fishing	fisherman
gardening	do gardening	gardener
gymnastics	do gymnastics	gymnast
hockey	play hockey	hockey player
ice-skating	go ice-skating	ice-skater
photography	do photography	photographer
sailing	go sailing	sailor
skateboarding	go skateboarding	skateboarder
swimming	go swimming	swimmer

beat (v)
competitor (n)
defeat (v)
draw (n)
equal (n)
opponent (n)
referee (n)
spectator (n)
umpire (n)
viewer (n)
win (v)
come first / second / last (in a race)
come true (dream)
go mad
go well together (colours/clothes)
go wrong
How did the game go?

Phrasal verbs

hang out
knock out
take up
turn up
work out

Other words

eliminate (v)
exercise (v)
float (v)
fond of (v phr)
obstacle (n)
press (v)
read up on (phr v)
remote (adj)
take up (phr v)
unpredictable (adj)
vertical (adj)

Unit 9
It's a weird, wonderful world

The environment

acid rain (n)
become extinct (v)
behaviour (n)
endangered species (n)
environmentally friendly (adj)
global warming (n)
pollute (v)
protect (v)
sea level (n)
wildlife reserve (n)

The weather

blizzard (n)
drought (n)
flood (n)
heatwave (n)
hurricane (n)
tornado (n)
below zero (n)
degrees (pl n)
freezing temperatures (pl n)
gale-force wind (n)
heavy rain (n)
light breeze (n)
light shower (n)
bang (v)

bend (v)
blow (v)
burn (v)
deep (adj)
electricity (n)
flash (of lightning) (n)
gust (of wind) (n)
pour (with rain) (v)
puddle (n)
scorching (sun) (adj)
shade (n)
slip (v)
soaked (adj)

Weather idioms
(be) a bolt from the blue
(be) a storm in a teacup
(be) on cloud nine
(be/feel) a bit under the weather
(have) a face like thunder
come rain or shine

Other words
alien (n)
ban (v)
beast (n)
bizarre (adj)
distant (adj)
evolve (v)
exceed (v)
fin (n)
prevent (v)
tough (adj)
utterly (adv)
vast (adj)

Unit 10
Food for thought

Health and diet
break a bone (v phr)
cut yourself (v phr)
get a black eye / a bruise (v phr)
graze your knee (v phr)
have your arm / leg in a cast (v phr)
pull a muscle (v phr)
sprain an ankle (v phr)

Phrasal verbs
be/go on
cut down on
get over
go off
put on
take care of

Food and drink
bitter (adj)
bland (adj)
cooked (adj)
crisp (adj)
heavy (meal) (adj)
light (meal) (adj)
mild (adj)
rare (adj)
raw (adj)
ripe (adj)
salty (adj)
soft (adj)
sour (adj)
sparkling (water) (adj)
spicy (adj)
still (water) (adj)
sweet (adj)
tap water (n)
tasty (adj)
well-done (adj)
add (v)
bake (v)
basil (n)
bite-sized (adj)
boil (v)
bowl (n)
chop (v)
crystal (n)
cup (measurement) (n)
cut (v)
dissolve (v)
fresh (adj)
fry (v)
gram (n)
grate (v)
grated (adj)
green salad (n)
ingredients (pl n)
jelly (n)
method (n)
mixture (n)
mushroom (n)
olive oil (n)
onion (n)
oven (n)
packet (n)
pepper (n)
pip (n)
pizza base (n)
pour (v)
recipe (n)
refrigerate (v)
remove (v)
rings (pl n)
serve (v)
set (adj)
slice (v)
spread (v)
sprinkle (v)
stir (v)
tablespoon (n)
tomato paste (n)

Other words
adjustment (n)
antioxidant (n)
be associated with (v phr)
cutlery (n)
damage (n)
essential (adj)
fattening (adj)
grilled (adj)
lose weight (v phr)
nutritious (adj)
point of view (n phr)
roast (adj)
set a limit (v phr)
substance (n)
the set (n)
trigger (v)

Unit 11
Vanished without a trace!

People and crime
accuse (v)
arson (n)
burglary (n)
court (n)
court case (n)
defend (v)
detective (n)
investigate (v)
judge (n)
jury (n)
lawyer (n)
pickpocketing (n)
robbery (n)
shoplifting (n)
suspect (n)
vandalism (n)
victim (n)
witness (n)

Crime and mystery
alibi (n)
clue (n)
commit (v)
cover-up (n)
culprit (n)
evidence (n)
motive (n)
murder (n)
weapon (n)
accuse of (v phr)
blame for (v phr)
charge with (v phr)
get away with (v phr)
sentence to (v phr)

Other words
abandoned (adj)
add up (phr v)
baffle (v)
crew (n)
eerie (adj)
examine (v)
investigator (n)
kidnapper (n)
overboard (adv)
ransom (n)
rule out (phr v)
vanish (v)

Noun	Adjective	Adverb
crime/criminal	criminal	criminally
dishonesty	dishonest	dishonestly
guilt	guilty	guiltily
innocence	innocent	innocently
law	(il)legal	(il)legally
mystery	mysterious	mysteriously

Unit 12
Big spender

Clothes and accessories
belt (n)
bracelet (n)
cardigan (n)
changing rooms (pl n)
denim jacket (n)
do up (phr v)
earrings (pl n)
fit (v)
high heels (pl n)
leggings (pl n)
loose (adj)
necklace (n)
nosering (n)
ring (n)
scarf (n)
size (n)
suit (v)
sweater (n)
take back (phr v)
take in (phr v)
take up (phr v)
tight (adj)
tracksuit (n)
trainers (pl n)
try on (phr v)
waterproof jacket (n)
zip (n)

Shopping and money
brand (n)
buy (v)
cash desk (n)
department store (n)
logo (n)
megastore (n)
newsagent's (n)
product (n)
receipt (n)
supermarket (n)

Money idioms
be broke
be loaded
be made of money
be/get ripped off
have more money than sense

Other words
bank account (n)
bargain (n)
casual (adj)
consumerism (n)
debt (n)
fashion conscious (adj)
find it hard to resist (v phr)
frugal (adj)
haggle (v)
keep up (phr v)
retail therapy (n)
sales are on (phr)
smart (adj)
trendy outfit (n)
window-shopping (n)

Speaking file

Unit 1: Ways to expand

- When you are asked a *yes/no* question, don't simply answer with *yes* or *no*. Expand your reply with a little more information.

Are you good at languages? … No, not really, but I enjoy learning them.

Have you ever flown? … Yes, I have. I flew to Italy last year with my family.

Language chunks

Have you got … ?
Yes, I have. In fact, I've got … / No, I haven't, but …
Do you … ?
Yes, I do. I usually … / No, I don't, because …
Is … ?
Yes, it is, and actually … / No, it isn't. Although …
Does … ?
Yes, she does, and she's … / No, she doesn't, and the reason is that …
Have you ever … ?
Yes, I have. It was … / No, I haven't, but I'd love to because …

Unit 2: Impressions

- When describing pictures, use phrases that make it clear you're talking about your opinions and impressions.

Language chunks

It looks like it could be a farm.
It's a very peaceful place.
I get the impression that the first place is in a wet country.
It makes me think of the Amazon rainforest.
I think it's probably a dangerous place to visit.

Unit 3: Exchanging information and discussing

- A discussion is not a speech. Make sure that you share your ideas and invite your partner to speak too.

Language chunks

Expressing opinions
I think …
I believe …
In my opinion …
I don't know if …
If you ask me …

Agreeing and disagreeing
I think you're right.
I'm not so sure.
Well, yes and no.
I wouldn't say so, no.

Inviting others to speak
What do you think?
What do you reckon about … ?
Wouldn't you agree?
Don't you think?
What's your opinion on … ?
Question tags: *isn't it? / don't you?*, etc

Unit 4: Agreeing and suggesting

- When you have a conversation, be polite. Show you are listening – look at your partner, **nod**, **agree** or **disagree**. Say things like *aha, right, yes*.

Language chunks

Making suggestions

How about … ?
What about … ?
We should …
We could …
Can I suggest … ?
Why don't we … ?

Expressing agreement

I agree.
Alright.
Yeah, OK.
Perfect!
Exactly!
Absolutely!
You're right.
That sounds like a good idea.

Unit 5: Uncertainty

- Use expressions like the ones in Language chunks to show others that you are not sure about something.
- Modals like *might*, *may*, *can* and *could* make opinions and suggestions sound less 'strong'. As a result, you are easier to agree with and more persuasive.

Language chunks

Giving opinions

Yes, I suppose you're right.
I'm not sure …
They might like that …
They may not …
I don't know, I think …
Maybe …
Perhaps …

Making tentative suggestions

I suppose we could …
We could … , couldn't we?
They can …
(Perhaps) we could …
It might be better to …

Unit 6: Asking and answering politely

- Remember that in formal situations you need to ask and answer questions politely. One way to ask politely is to use indirect questions.

Language chunks

Polite questions

I was wondering if …
I'd like to know if …
Could you tell me …
Would you mind telling me …
Do you happen to know if …

Polite ways to say yes

Of course.
Absolutely.
Certainly.

Polite ways to say no

I'm afraid not.
Unfortunately …
I'm sorry, but …

Unit 7: Comparing pictures

- When comparing pictures, you must discuss both the similarities and the differences.

Language chunks

Talking about similarity

similarly …
likewise …
in the same way …

Talking about difference

in contrast …
on the other hand …
whereas …
however …

Unit 8: Interrupting

- When you're having a discussion, it's all right to interrupt as long as you do it politely and don't do it too often!

Language chunks

Interrupting another speaker

Excuse me.
Sorry, … , but …
May I say something?
Sorry for interrupting …

Acknowledging the interruption

Of course.
Please do.
That's all right.
Go ahead.

Unit 9: Supporting opinions

- Whenever you express your opinion, give your reasons for it.
- The discussion is not only about your opinion. Listen and react to your partner's opinion too.

Language chunks

Supporting your opinion

That's because …
The reason I say that is …
For that reason …
So …
Since …
As …

Reacting to opinions

I see what you mean.
I understand what you're getting at.
You've got a point there.
That's a good idea.
Do you think so? I'm not so sure.

Unit 10: Expressing preferences

- When you have to talk about preferences, use expressions like the ones in the Language chunks box to vary the way you express yourself. Remember to invite your partner to express his/her preferences, too.

Language chunks

Asking about preference

Do you prefer X or Y?
What would you rather have, X or Y?
Which do you think is best?
Which do you prefer?
Would(n't) you rather … (than)?

Expressing preference

I'd prefer (not) to …
I prefer X to Y …
I'd rather do X than Y …
I'd rather not have …

Unit 11: Clarification

- It is not a problem if you don't understand what someone says, even in an exam. Just ask politely for clarification.

Language chunks

Asking for clarification

Could you explain what … means?
I'm not sure what you mean.
Would you mind repeating that, please?
Could you say that again, please?

Expressing agreement

Aha …
I think you're right.
Hmm. That's true.
Absolutely.
Exactly.
I see what you mean.

Unit 12: Hesitation and expressing interest

- When you're pausing to think of ideas, don't drag out words or pause for too long. Fill your hesitations with expressions like the ones in the Language chunks box.
- If you're having a conversation, make sure you show you're listening to your partner(s). You can do this by expressing interest, surprise, etc in what your partner says.

Language chunks

Hesitating

Umm …
Let me think …
Just a minute …
Let's see …
How shall I put it, … ?

Expressing interest in what your partner says

Really?
That sounds great/wonderful/nice/good.
I know what you mean …
I see …
I can understand that …
Wow!
Why's that?
That's interesting!

Pairwork

Unit **5**, page **50**, **Dive in!**

1 b, **2** d, **3** a, **4** a, **5** d

Unit **6**, page **65**, **Speaking**, *Exercise* **E**

Student A

You want to book an entertainer for your school Christmas concert. Your partner is the entertainers' manager.

First
Speak to the entertainers' manager and find out this information:
- what they do
- when they are available
- their fee

Then
Choose the best entertainer for your concert. Explain why you made your choice.

Bobbie Bright

The Biz

Unit **7**, page **77**, **Speaking**, *Exercise* **F**

Student B's photos:

Compare the photos and say what feeling the people's facial expressions communicate.

Unit **11**, page **121**, **Say it right!** *Exercise* **G**

Student A:
- The pyramids are in Brazil.
- Tom Cruise is Greek.
- Carrots grow on trees.

Writing bank

Writing: An informal email or letter (transactional)

Example question:
You have received an email from an English-speaking friend, Mark, who is doing a school project about food around the world. Read Mark's email and the notes you have made. Then, write an email to Mark using all your notes.

Write your answer in 120-150 words.

From: Mark Simpson
Sent: 16th March, 2009
Subject: School project

Hope you're well. I'm OK, but busy with school work. Actually, that's why I'm writing. Can you help me with a school project I'm doing? *(say which ones)*

The project is about food around the world. Could you tell me a few things about the local dishes where you live? What's the most famous food in your country? Are there any special dishes which people eat at certain times of the year? *(say what and when)*

What about you? What's your favourite local dish? Drop me a line and let me know. *(give details)*

Take care,
Mark

Model answer

Hi Mark, *(use first names)*

Good to hear from you. I'm not surprised you're busy. You always are! Of course, I'm very happy to help you out with your project. *(be natural and friendly)*

First of all, let me tell you about the most famous Greek dish: mousaka. It's made with minced meat, aubergines and potatoes. As you know, Mark, I'm a vegetarian, so I hate this dish, but it's very popular here. *(use topic sentences)*

You know how we Greeks like our food and fun, so of course there are lots of dishes which we eat on special occasions. At Easter people make a kind of meat soup called magiritsa. At New Year we make a special kind of cake called vasilopita, which I love. *(add some extra information)*

You asked what my favourite Greek food is. That's easy! It's something called dolmathes. They're grapevine leaves stuffed with rice. If you haven't tried them, I'd really recommend them to you. They're delicious.

Is this enough information for you? Let me know if you need more. Good luck with your project. *(refer back to the writing task)*

Bye for now,
Katerina

(sign off in an informal way)

Write successfully ...

- Write in an INFORMAL STYLE – use contractions, abbreviations, phrasal verbs and expressions.
- Write full, GRAMMATICAL sentences.
- ORGANIZE your email logically using the questions and notes.
- Use DIRECT QUESTIONS.
- Begin and end APPROPRIATELY.

Language chunks

Starting an informal email
Hi ... , Thanks for your message.
Dear ... , How are things?
Hello ... , Great to hear from you.

Finishing off an informal email
Hope to hear from you soon,
Take care,
Bye for now,
All the best,
Love,

Writing: An article

Example question:
You see this announcement in your school magazine:
Write your article in 120-180 words.

> **Write about your city, town or village.**
> - Where do you live?
> - What does it have to offer?
> - Why is it a brilliant place to visit?
> - What can you see there?
>
> We will publish the best article here next month.

Model answer

give your article a title →

use questions to get the readers' attention →

separate your ideas into paragraphs →

give your opinion →

← *keep your introduction short, but interesting*

← *develop your ideas with examples or explanations*

← *include a short conclusion*

My City

I live in Rome, which is the capital city of my country, Italy. As a large city, it has all the benefits that large cities have. But what makes my city a special place to visit? Its history and its people.

Rome has a very long history and, as a result, it has many monuments and ancient ruins that are thousands of years old. One of the most famous archaeological sites in the world, the Colosseum, is located in the centre of the city. Millions of people from all over the world come to Rome to see these ruins and to visit all the museums my city has to offer.

Another special thing about my city is its people. People from all over Italy live here and recently it has become a very multicultural city. As a result, throughout the year there are many cultural events and international music festivals to attend.

As far as I'm concerned, Rome is a fabulous place to visit. It has a lot to offer you no matter how old you are or what your interests are.

Write successfully...

- Give your article a TITLE.
- Write four PARAGRAPHS: an introduction, two content paragraphs and a conclusion.
- Develop one topic in each paragraph and give EXAMPLES.
- Write RELEVANT information.
- Use an INFORMAL or NEUTRAL style and be consistent.
- Make it INTERESTING – ask questions, give your opinion or use a personal angle.

Language chunks

Adding/Extending points
moreover
furthermore
and
also
in addition

Contrasting ideas
however
whether
but
although
in spite of
on the one hand / on the other hand

Expressing reason and result
as a result
since
because
because of
as

Giving your opinion
To begin with ...
I think another important benefit ...
As far as I'm concerned ...
What I mean is ...

Talking about a building
It is situated/located in ...
It was built by ...
It was completed in ...
It was designed by ...

167

Writing: An essay

Example question:
Your school magazine has asked students for their opinion on the use of the internet. Write an essay giving your opinion about the advantages and disadvantages of using the internet.
Write your essay in 120-180 words.

Model answer

introduce the topic and make your opinion clear →

Nowadays nearly everyone over the age of 14 has access to the internet. But is this a good thing? In my opinion, it is, but some may disagree.

On the one hand, having access to the internet has made communication between people easier. You can send emails, which are much faster than snail mail, you can communicate via social networking sites, like Facebook, and you can even keep a blog that your friends can read. Furthermore, you have a world of information at your fingertips. This makes it easier to understand what's going on in the world.

← *support your arguments*

divide your essay into separate paragraphs →

link your paragraphs →

On the other hand, the internet can be addictive. Many people spend hours every day surfing it, checking emails and playing online games. Teenagers often neglect their homework and their friends and families because they spend hours playing games on the internet.

make your opinion clear →

In conclusion, because of the advantages of the internet, I think people benefit from having access to it. However, we need to limit the amount of time we use it.

Write successfully ...

- PLAN your essay – think of a few good ideas that are relevant to the topic.
- Write your opinion in the INTRODUCTION or CONCLUSION.
- ORGANIZE your essay into paragraphs (one main idea per paragraph).
- Give EXAMPLES to explain your arguments.
- Use FORMAL LANGUAGE and EXPRESSIONS that link ideas and paragraphs.

Language chunks

Presenting ideas
Most people agree that ...
Some believe that ...
... can often be ...
Because ...

Introducing additional ideas
Furthermore, ...
As a result ...
This means ...
What is more ...

Linking paragraphs
On the one hand, ...
On the other hand, ...
In conclusion, ...

Giving your opinion
I think ...
I believe ...
In my opinion ...

Writing: A story

Example question:
Your school magazine is running a short story competition. For the competition you must write a story which **ends** with the words:
'Oh, it's only you!' I said with relief.
Write your story in 120-180 words.

Model answer

- give your story a title
- start with a short, surprising sentence
- use direct speech for drama
- describe feelings and emotions

A midnight shock

I woke up with a start. My room was very dark, but I managed to see the time on the clock next to my bed. It was four in the morning. What had woken me?

A few moments later I understood. There was a noise coming from downstairs. Someone – or something – was moving around in the living room.

At that moment I remembered the reports in the newspapers a few days earlier. 'Local burglaries increasing!' the headlines had said.

My stomach turned. I was terrified. Nevertheless, I decided to find out who or what was there. I got out of bed and went downstairs. I tried to creep quietly, but the stairs were creaking. 'They must have heard me,' I whispered to myself. I froze on the stairs.

At that moment the living room door began to open slowly. I could feel my heart beating faster and faster. Then a head appeared round the door. My sister's!

'Oh, it's only you!' I said with relief.

- create suspense or add humour with questions
- use a variety of tenses
- use the words from the question

Write successfully ...

- Keep your story SIMPLE. (Describe one event in detail.)
- Include two or three CHARACTERS.
- Use a variety of verb TENSES.
- Use plenty of ADJECTIVES, ADVERBS and colourful expressions.
- Use story writing TECHNIQUES:
  - describe what characters see, hear, feel or smell
  - use direct speech to add drama
  - speak directly to the reader for humour or suspense
  - vary the length of your sentences – use short sentences after long ones

Language chunks

Time phrases
just then
earlier
a moment later
a long time ago
in an instant

Feelings
ashamed
astonished
delighted
furious
heartbroken
terrified
I felt a chill down my back.
My heart sank.
My body froze.
My stomach turned.

Writing: A formal letter/email

Example question:
You are interested in going on a family holiday. Read the newspaper advertisement and the notes you have made. Then write a letter to the travel agent using all your notes. Write your letter in 120-150 words.

Outback Discovery

The ultimate Outback experience.
Enjoy 15 days / 14 nights in the Australian Outback.
Visit beautiful Broome, explore the Bungle Bungle Range and experience an Aboriginal guided cruise through Geike Gorge.
We run 12 tours a year!
Ask about our special family rates!

Contact *Outback Tours* for more information:
TEL: (+61) 9890 4697 • FAX: (+61) 9890 4698
EMAIL: outbackdiscovery@australia.com

Notes:
- Accommodation?
- Ask for more details.
- Ask about dates.
- What are they?

Model answer

begin a formal letter with Dear … ,

Dear Sir or Madam,

say why you are writing

I am writing to enquire about your *Outback Discovery* tour. We are interested in going on this tour, but would like to find out some information first.

divide your letter into separate paragraphs

First, your advertisement states that the tour is two weeks' long. Could you tell me how long we will be spending in each different place? Could you also let me know what type of accommodation we will be staying in? I would rather stay in a hotel than a tent.

Regarding dates, I am interested in travelling over Christmas. Do you offer a tour at that time? If so, what are the exact dates.

Finally, in your advertisement, you mention special family rates. Could you let me know what these are exactly? We are a family of four and we would like to know if we qualify for the special rate.

be polite

Thank you in advance for your help.

end in a formal way

Yours faithfully,
Amanda Bishop

Write successfully ...

- INCLUDE all the information asked for.
- Cover one or similar topics in each PARAGRAPH.
- Use FORMAL language – indirect questions.
- Begin and end in a formal way:
  - If you don't know the name of the person you're writing to, use *Dear Sir,/Madam*, and end with *Yours faithfully*.
  - If you do know the name, begin *Dear Mr/Ms/Mrs …* , and finish with *Yours sincerely*, .

Language chunks

Beginning/Ending a letter
Dear Mr/Ms …
Yours sincerely,
I am / We are writing to enquire about …
Thank you in advance for your help.

Introducing topics/questions
Your advertisement states …
In your advertisement you mention …

Sequencing points
First, …
also
Regarding …
Finally, …

Writing: A review

Example question:
You have seen this notice in a magazine:
Write your review in 120-180 words.

> **Calling all bookworms!** We'd like to hear your opinions about a book you've read recently. Good or bad, it doesn't matter; just tell us what you think. All published reviewers will receive a £10 book token. So ... what are you waiting for?

Model answer

The Silver Sword by Ian Serraillier — *write the title and author*

Danger, excitement, sadness and hope. You can find all these and more in this excellent book. It's about war, but it's also about much more. — *start with an interesting sentence to get the readers' attention*

The Silver Sword is set in Poland during the Second World War. It is about three children whose parents are taken to prison camps. The family home gets blown up and the children have nowhere to stay. The story tells us how the children survive without their parents and how they escape to Switzerland. — *use present simple to talk about plot* / *give a very brief summary of the plot*

Why did I enjoy this book? Well, the plot was really exciting. What's more, Serraillier has created very believable characters who are my age. I think he really understands how my age group think and feel. Also, the writing brings the tragedy of war to life. The book helped me understand how awful war is. — *speak directly to the reader*

All in all, if you like adventure or you're interested in history or you just love a good story, I can thoroughly recommend *The Silver Sword*. — *finish off with a recommendation*

Write successfully ...

- CHOOSE a film, book or play that you have strong opinions about.
- PLAN before you write. How many paragraphs? What is each one for?
- Start with a surprising statement to ATTRACT the reader.
- Give your OPINIONS – **don't** tell a story.
- INCLUDE your views on some of these things:
  - plot
  - characters
  - style of writing (for books)
  - costumes, music and performances (for films and plays)
  - what you learnt from the book, film or play

Language chunks

Positive opinions
... rescued the film / book / play
... was totally believable
... was a pleasant surprise
I'd thoroughly recommend it.

Negative opinions
You're better off avoiding this film / book / play.
I wasn't convinced by ...
... couldn't save the film / book / play
... was a great disappointment

Writing: A formal letter to a newspaper

Example question:
You have read an article in *The Daily Herald* newspaper about problems with graffiti in public places. Write a letter to the editor saying what you think about this problem and what should be done about it.

The Daily Herald

Graffiti Scrawl Over New School Buildings

When pupils and teachers arrived at Waddington High School in Cheshire this Monday morning, they were met by a sad sight. Vandals had covered their brand new gym and events hall in graffiti. Football team slogans and names were scrawled in huge letters across the walls and even on windows. 'This is a sad day for us,' said Headmaster Gillian Parks. 'Graffiti seems to be a problem everywhere these days. Why do people do such things?'

Model answer

- *begin a letter to a newspaper like this*
- *say what you read and how it made you feel*
- *include questions to the reader*
- *remember that you're writing to the newspaper editor*
- *finish off with a strong opinion and a suggestion for action*

Dear Editor,

Yesterday I read your article about the vandalism at Waddington High School. Graffiti is a problem where I live, too, and it makes me feel so angry.

My school walls have been written on by vandals many times. The local parks, all the shops and even people's homes have been covered in graffiti. The problem is everywhere, and it makes everything look so ugly. It is often argued that graffiti is 'art'. On the contrary! What is beautiful about words sprayed all over a wall? Nothing! There is no question that graffiti is simply vandalism.

It goes without saying that it is mostly young people who cause this problem. Why do they do it and how can we stop them? Parents need to teach their young children to respect things that we share with others. Furthermore, schools should talk about the problem with pupils. Many problems can be solved if we just talk about them.

Thank you for reporting this story in your newspaper. It's high time we stopped ignoring the problem of graffiti!

Write successfully ...

- PLAN your letter carefully. How many paragraphs? What will they include?
- Finish with a SUGGESTION about the problem.

Language chunks

Joining similar ideas
likewise
in addition
furthermore

Joining opposing ideas
in contrast
on the other hand
however
on the contrary

Expressing your opinions
It's high time ...
In my opinion ...
I believe that ...

Expressing certainty
Without a doubt ...
It goes without saying ...
There's no question that ...

Introducing other people's opinions
It's often argued that ...
Some people believe that ...
It's thought that ...

Writing: A letter of advice

Example question: I've heard that you are what you eat. I eat a lot of junk food. I wish I could change what I eat, but the problem is I find healthy food really bland. Can anyone suggest a way to make healthy food taste better?
Rebecca

Model answer

Dear Rebecca,

I read your letter in *Teen Magazine* and I'd like to make some suggestions which I think could help.

Firstly, it's true that if you're used to eating fast food or junk food, which are both high in salt but tasty, you'll find healthy food less tasty. But keep trying. After a while you'll get used to the natural flavours of fresh food and not want to go back to eating processed foods. You could try changing your diet slowly rather than changing it overnight. This might help you get used to the new flavours.

Secondly, you might find that adding herbs and spices to salads and food will help with the taste. Also, salt, lemon, vinegar and honey are all healthy alternatives that improve flavour.

It's worth changing to a healthy diet, it'll make you feel better and look good.

Hope this helps and good luck.

Best wishes,

Wendy

- *use an appropriate opening phrase*
- *divide your letter into separate paragraphs*
- *use modals to give opinions and suggestions politely*
- *use an appropriate closing phrase*

Write successfully ...

- ORGANIZE your information in a logical order.
- Lay out your letter in PARAGRAPHS.
- Cover all four points in the NOTES.
- Use an appropriate STYLE.
- CHECK for spelling, grammar and punctuation mistakes.

Language chunks

Openings and closings
Dear Jessica,
Hi/Hello Jessica,
Thanks for your letter/email.
It was great to hear from you.
I hope you are well.

Answering questions
You asked me about …
As for … ,
In answer to your question about …

To advise and suggest
Why don't you …
I suggest …
I think you should …

Reminding and reassuring (informal letters/emails)
Don't forget to …
Don't bother to …
Don't worry about …
Let me know when/how/if …
By the way, …

Writing: A formal letter of application

City Council
Youth Summer Jobs Programme

Are you a teenager looking for a summer job?
We are looking for enthusiastic people to work in our tourist information booths for the summer. If you would like a summer job, we'd like to hear from you. You must be at least 16 years old to apply.
Apply in writing. Please include information about:
- your current situation
- your level of English
- why you would like to work in a tourist booth over the summer

Example question:
You have seen this job advertisement in a newspaper. Write a letter in 120-150 words.

Model answer

use appropriate opening and closing phrases

say why you are writing

give some background information about yourself

say how you will benefit

ask for extra information

say you are available for interview

use set phrases

Dear Sir or Madam,

I am writing in response to your advertisement in *The Moon* newspaper on Friday 11th. I would like to apply to work in a tourist information booth for the summer.

I am a 17-year-old secondary school student in year 11. I have been studying English for five years now and my level of English is good. I will be staying in the city for the summer and I believe this job will give me the opportunity to do something useful with my time. It will also allow me to practise my English, which will benefit me enormously.

I would like to ask for some information which the advertisement does not give. I would appreciate it if you would let me know whether the job is full-time or part-time. I would also be grateful if you could let me know the exact dates the job will be available for.

Please do not hesitate to contact me if you require any further information or to arrange an interview.

I look forward to hearing from you.

Yours faithfully,

Juan Gallego
Juan Gallego

Write successfully ...

- Say WHY you are writing in the first paragraph.
- Say why you WANT the job in the second paragraph.
- Ask POLITE questions about the job in the third paragraph.
- Say you are AVAILABLE for an interview in the fourth paragraph.
- Use indirect questions and FORMAL language.
- Use APPROPRIATE opening and closing phrases.

Language chunks

Opening a letter
Dear Sir or Madam,
Dear Mr/Ms ... ,

Give a reason for writing
I am writing in response to ...

Give information about yourself
I am a 17-year-old student ...
I have been studying English for ...
I believe this job will ...
I will be ...

Asking for further information
I would like to ask for some information ...
I would appreciate it if you would let me know ...

Closing
Please do not hesitate to contact me if you require any further information or to arrange an interview.
I look forward to hearing from you ...
Yours faithfully, or Yours sincerely,

Pairwork

Unit 2, page 21, Speaking, Exercise B

Unit 6, page 65, Speaking, Exercise E

Student B:

You are the manager for these entertainers. Your partner is interested in booking one of them for a school Christmas concert.

First
Answer your partner's questions using the information on this card.

Then
Ask your partner who they want to book and why.

Bobbie Bright
Comedian / available late evening (after 8.00pm) and weekends / £250 per booking

The Biz
Pop band / available weekends only / £300 per booking

Unit 4, page 38, Dive in!

1 b, 2 b, 3 a, 4 a, 5 a

Unit 8, page 82, Dive in!

1 basketball, baseball, bowling, badminton, etc
2 skydiving, bungee jumping, snowboarding, etc
3 a golf, b tennis, c football, d swimming
4 *Blackjack*
5 falling out of a plane with a parachute. It is also known as *parachuting*.

Unit 9, page 94, Dive in!

Bat's don't have two noses.

Unit 10, page 105, Quick chat

1 False. There is no evidence to link wet hair or being cold with catching cold.
2 True. It has been found to have properties that help people feel better faster.
3 False. Experts say there's very little proof that vitamin C actually has any effect on the common cold.

Unit 11, page 121, Say it right! Exercise G

Student B:
- Britney Spears is a plumber.
- Aristotle was English.
- Whales live in the jungle.

Unit 12, page 126, Dive in!

1 a (South China Mall with 1,500 stores in 2005!), 2 c, 3 a, 4 b, 5 c

Macmillan Hellas SA
2 Misaraliotou Street
Athens 11742, Greece

ISBN Student's Book: 978-960-447-293-2

Text © Rosemary Aravanis and Stuart Cochrane 2010
Design and illustration © Macmillan Hellas SA 2010

First published 2010

All rights reserved; no part of this publication may be reproduced, stored in a retrieval system, transmitted in any form, or by any means, electronic, mechanical, photocopying, recording, or otherwise, without the prior written permission of the publishers.

Designed by Eleni Fine 2010
Illustrated by Illias Arahovitis, Tomek Giovannis, Christos Skaltsas
Cover design by Nick Panagiotopoulos
Cover photo by **The Gallery Collection / Corbis / Apeiron Photos**

Authors acknowledgements:
Many thanks to the Macmillan editorial team, and in particular to Erika Stiles and Angela Bandis for all their hard work, support and patience. Special thanks also to Stuart Cochrane, Monica Berlis and Giorgo Aravanis.

The publishers would like to thank:
In Athens: Angeliki Vlassopoulou, Koukaki; Skouras, Neos Kosmos; Polyglosso, Neos Kosmos; Kontopoulos, Ayia Varvara; Vicky Micheloudaki, Neos Kosmos
In Thessaloniki: Maria Votsi, Kordeliou; Mrs Katsioula, Evesmos; Mrs Kallinikidou, Stavroupoli; Jane Mela, Botsari-Egnatia (Lexicon); Roula Kyriakidou, Ano Toumba; Sophia Zervou, Kalamaria; Alexandras Mountzas, Pylaia

The authors and publishers would like to thank the following for permission to reproduce their photographs:

Album / Apeiron Photos pp60 (tl), 80; **Bananastock** pp28 (text), 36 (bl), (br), 38, 39 (tr), 89, 104 (carrots), 105, 112, 115; **BrandX** pp14 (br), 21 (tr), 24 (br), (bl), 43 (tl), (bl), (bc), 56, 58, 76 (television), 98 (tr), (cr), (br), 107 (tr); **Corbis** pp17, 28 (ski resort), 43 (tc), (tr), 45 (bl), 53, 67, 84, 86 (tl), 87 (br), 90, 104 (milk/apple), 127, 175 (tl); **Corbis / Apeiron Photos** pp6 (tl), 7 (tr), 13, 14 (tr), 16, 20, 22, 23, 28 (art gallery/cinema), 36 (tr), 38 (tr), (tl), 39 (bl), 40, 45 (tl), 46, 60 (cm), (cr), (bl), 63, 64 (pB), (pC), (pD), 83 (p4), 86 (bl), 87 (tr), 101 (tc), (tr); **Digital Stock / CORBIS** pp28 (museum), 70, 165 (pC), (pD); **Digital Vision** pp44, 77, (bl), (bm), (br), 98 (tl), (cl), 101 (tl), 175 (bl); **Goodshot** p24 (tl); **Grapheast** p28 (fun fair);

Image Source pp14 (bl), 21 (bl), 24 (tr), 28 (theatre), 30, 35, 43 (br), 64 (pF), 76 (mobile phone/WWW), 104 (headphones), 107 (br), 126 (tr), 131, 133, 134, 175 (br); **Imagestate** pp77 (tr), 82 (p1), 136; **Johnfoxx Images** p28 (zoo); **Macmillan / David Tolley** p76 (newspapers); **Macmillan / Paul Bricknell / Dean Ryan** p76 (magazines/radio); **Macmillan / Raymond Turvey (Turvey Books Ltd.)** p104 (diagram of brain); **Medioimages** p116; **Photoalto** pp102, 104 (chocolate mousse), 126 (tl); **Photodisc** pp21 (tl), 64 (pE), 103, 119; **Photolibrary / Apeiron Photos** p54 (bl); **Pixtal** p50 (tr), (tl); **Reuters /Apeiron Photos** pp6 (tr), 14 (tl), 60 (cl), 64 (pA); **Rex Features / Apeiron Photos** pp54 (tr), 72, 79, 82 (p2), 83 (p3), 87 (cr), 111; **Stockbyte** pp21 (br), 59, 117; **Superstock** pp50 (bl), 175 (tr)

These materials may contain links for third party websites. We have no control over, and are not responsible for, the contents of such third party websites. Please use care when accessing them.

Although we have tried to trace and contact copyright holders before publication, in some cases this has not been possible. If contacted we will be pleased to rectify any errors or omissions at the earliest opportunity.

Printed and bound in Greece

2014		2013		2012		2011		2010	
10	9	8	7	6	5	4	3	2	1